INDEPENDENCE
OR DEATH!

INDEPENDENCE OR DEATH!

British Sailors and

Brazilian Independence

1822–25

by

BRIAN VALE

BLOOMSBURY ACADEMIC
LONDON • NEW YORK • OXFORD • NEW DELHI • SYDNEY

BLOOMSBURY ACADEMIC
Bloomsbury Publishing Plc
50 Bedford Square, London, WC1B 3DP, UK
1385 Broadway, New York, NY 10018, USA
29 Earlsfort Terrace, Dublin 2, Ireland

BLOOMSBURY, BLOOMSBURY ACADEMIC and the Diana logo
are trademarks of Bloomsbury Publishing Plc

First published in 1996 by I.B. Tauris & Co Ltd
This paperback edition published by Bloomsbury Academic in 2022

Copyright © Brian Vale, 1996

All rights reserved. No part of this publication may be reproduced or
transmitted in any form or by any means, electronic or mechanical,
including photocopying, recording, or any information storage or retrieval
system, without prior permission in writing from the publishers.

Bloomsbury Publishing Plc does not have any control over, or responsibility for,
any third-party websites referred to or in this book. All internet addresses given
in this book were correct at the time of going to press. The author and publisher
regret any inconvenience caused if addresses have changed or sites have
ceased to exist, but can accept no responsibility for any such changes.

A catalogue record for this book is available from the British Library.

A catalog record for this book is available from the Library of Congress.

ISBN: HB: 978-1-8606-4060-5
PB: 978-1-3501-8355-1

To find out more about our authors and books visit
www.bloomsbury.com and sign up for our newsletters.

CONTENTS

PREFACE
vii

CHAPTER 1
The Politics of Independence *1*

CHAPTER 2
The Birth of a Navy *13*

CHAPTER 3
General Brant in London *24*

CHAPTER 4
Preparations in Rio *34*

CHAPTER 5
The Blockade of Bahia *45*

CHAPTER 6
The Pursuit *62*

CHAPTER 7
Cochrane in Maranhão *70*

CHAPTER 8
Grenfell in Pará *81*

CHAPTER 9
Victory *90*

CHAPTER 10
Politics and Prize Money *97*

CHAPTER 11
The Gathering Storm *112*

CHAPTER 12
Taylor Blockades Pernambuco *118*

CHAPTER 13
The Confederation of the Equator *127*

CHAPTER 14
Cochrane Sails North *143*

CHAPTER 15
The Parting of the Ways *153*

CHAPTER 16
Recognition and After *160*

CHAPTER 17
Epilogue *172*

APPENDIX
British and Irish Sea Officers
Recruited for the Brazilian Navy *188*

NOTES
199

BIBLIOGRAPHY
209

INDEX
211

PREFACE

The French Revolution and the Napoleonic era had a decisive effect on European nationalism, political philosophy and military organization. But the consequences for Latin America were, if anything, more profound and more immediate. In the Spanish trans-Atlantic Empire nothing could be the same after the disruption of the Napoleonic Wars and the countdown to disintegration had begun. The occupation of peninsular Spain by the armies of Napoleon, the ejection of the Bourbons and the feebleness of the well-meaning Juntas which ruled temporarily in their name both stimulated local nationalism and gave the creole elites and military caudillos the opportunity to overthrow the viceroys and replace them with republican regimes of one hue or another. The monarchs of Europe may have been unwilling to recognize the fact, but by 1820 the independence of Spanish America had become inevitable.

But over the Andes in the great Portuguese dominion of Brazil, things were different. In 1808, the timid Prince Regent – later King – Dom João had voluntarily quit Lisbon for Rio de Janeiro just in time to avoid the advance guard of Junot's invading army. With the Court and the Government safely installed, Brazil became the hub of the Portuguese Empire and boomed as a consequence, both in terms of development and of national self-confidence. And when, seven years later, the country was raised to the status of a kingdom, coequal with Portugal in the Braganza dominions, it appeared that Brazil had comfortably achieved a form of independence which its Spanish-American neighbours were still trying to secure down the barrel of a gun. Neither was there any nonsense about a republic in Brazil. Monarchy was –

the dreams of a few isolated radicals apart – the unquestioned system of government and the acknowledged source of its prosperity.

But by 1822, things had changed. The constitutional revolt in Portugal, the return of the bewildered King to Lisbon and the blatant attempts by the Côrtes to reduce Brazil once more to colonial status caused an outburst of local nationalism. Ill-conceived attempts by Portugal to subdue the defiant Brazilians with military force provoked an explosion, and a simple desire to preserve the status quo rapidly escalated into a demand for outright independence. But, once again, there were no republican trappings to the Brazilian revolt. On the contrary, it was monarchical and therefore legitimate, being led by none other than the heir to the House of Braganza, the youthful, impetuous and charismatic Prince Regent – later Emperor – Dom Pedro.

Legitimate and respectable the Brazilian case may have been, but independence was no foregone conclusion. Indeed, Pedro's chances of pulling it off seemed remote. The Treasury was empty and only half the country recognized his authority, while Portugal was busy raising loans and reinforcing its coastal garrisons. It seemed only a matter of time before the Brazilians were overwhelmed. Only by gaining command of the sea could Pedro and his government cut the Portuguese supply routes, expel the occupying troops and secure the country's independence. But how? Brazil had no navy. It lacked ships, supplies, officers and men who were both experienced and reliable.

This book is about how it was done. How, by careful planning and inspired improvisation, the Brazilian Government created a new national navy; how it solved its manpower problems by secretly recruiting a nucleus of officers and seamen in England; and how, under the leadership of that quirky genius Lord Cochrane, the Brazilian squadrons swept the Portuguese from the seas, ejected their garrisons and then ensured the integrity of the new Empire by suppressing the serious north-eastern revolt which followed.

The dominating figure in this drama is undoubtedly Lord Cochrane. Indeed, his astonishing military exploits, his audacious leadership and his single-minded obsession with pay and prize money provide the backbone of this work. But the book is not just about Lord Cochrane. It also recounts the adventures of the British officers and seamen who followed him and whose skills, application and courage were no less crucial to the Brazilian Navy's success. The records of the time make it possible to piece together their exploits and, in some cases, their ultimate destinies, but fundamentally, they were just ordinary men earning their living. They were not patricians. No one was interested in painting their portraits, recording their dinner-table chitchat or leaving character sketches for the benefit of prosperity. For those few whose achievements were outstanding, or whose propensity for drink got them into trouble, it is possible to gain a brief impression of their personalities. But for the majority, it is only through their deeds and their service records that you can know them.

In unravelling the intricacies of the story I tried not only to look beyond the shadow cast by Lord Cochrane but also to escape from the influence of his own highly publicized and very partial version of events as retold in his 1859 epic *Narrative of Services in the Liberation of ... Brazil*. Establishing the facts of what really happened during this momentous period of Brazilian naval history required detailed research into original documents, journals and records spread over many years. To save the reader from excessive tedium I have kept the number of references to a minimum; but to do justice to the creation and deployment of a complex mechanism like a navy – and to correct or clarify existing misapprehensions – has inevitably required the inclusion of a fair number of facts. I hope that it is not only Mr Gradgrind who finds pleasure in the result.

As with the British armed forces at the time, a substantial number of recruits to the Brazilian service were from Ireland. I hope Irishmen will be content that – in line with contemporary political organization – I have used the term 'British' in this book as shorthand to describe all subjects of King George, whether English, Scottish or Irish. I have at least rejected the Brazilian habit of describing every inhabitant of these islands as *inglês*.

The Portuguese language has changed somewhat in both spelling and diacritical marking over the last 150 years. For simplicity, I have therefore used modern practice in both. Thus *Grão Pará* is used in place of the old *Gran Pará*, *Niterói* in place of *Nictheroi*, and so on. The only exceptions are in regard to the spelling of people's names, where I have used the same form as they themselves used.

I have many people to thank for their help in the production of this book. In Brazil, I am particularly indebted to Captain Max Justo Guedes, Director of the Serviço de Documentação Geral da Marinha, for his encouragement and access to many documents. I am also grateful to the Director and staff of the Arquivo Nacional, the Bibliotéca Nacional and the Instituto Histórico e Geográphico Brasileiro – all in Rio de Janeiro. In Britain, my thanks are due to the Director and staff of the Public Record Office, the National Maritime Museum Greenwich, the Hydrographic Office, Taunton, and, indirectly, the Scottish Record Office. Thanks are also due to the editors of the *Mariner's Mirror* – first Christopher Lloyd and latterly Dr Michael Duffy – for their interest, the opportunity to publish my initial findings and permission to reproduce material originally printed in that journal. I would also like to thank Roderick Cavaliero for useful suggestions and Wendy Stokes, whose phenomenal typing skills with early drafts turned ambition into reality.

Finally, I would like to pay tribute to the support and tolerance of my wife, Margaret, who not only devoted many hours to skilful proofreading but has lived with the gestation of this book for many a long year. Thanks to Dr Lester Crook and his colleagues at I.B. Taurus, we will now have something else to talk about.

Brian Vale
Rio de Janeiro–Madrid–Greenwich 1965–95

Brazil in 1822

Northeastern Brazil

CHAPTER I

THE POLITICS OF INDEPENDENCE

Dom João, by the grace of God, Prince Regent of Portugal and of the Algarves, makes it known by these presents that having in my Royal Spirit the vivid desire to increase the prosperity of those states which Almighty God has entrusted to my sovereign rule; and acknowledging at the same time the vastness of my American dominions and the abundance and riches which lie therein; and also recognizing the advantages of a perfect Union between my Dominions ... it is my pleasure to decree the following: that from the publication of this proclamation, the state of Brazil shall be elevated to the dignity, pre-eminence and denomination of a Kingdom.

Thus, on 16 December 1815, the Prince Regent raised Brazil from colonial status to the rank of a kingdom, coequal with Portugal in the Braganza dominions. The proclamation was a document of historic significance and marked a watershed in Brazil's development. On the one hand, it was a recognition of the country's separate political identity; while on the other, it was a confirmation that in social and economic terms the colony had come of age. It also ensured that when the struggle for freedom from Portugal did come, the legality of the Brazilian position would lead to a situation markedly different from the open rebellions and confused fighting which were to characterize the liberation of Spanish America.

The train of events which was to lead to this historic declaration began eight years earlier, in 1807, when the timid and good-natured Dom João was finally persuaded to escape the rising tide of French conquest in Europe by fleeing to the Portuguese colony of Brazil. With him went the rest of the Royal Family, including his mother the mad Queen Maria, the whole apparatus of government, tons of archives, the entire contents of the Treasury and thousands of courtiers, officials and hangers-on. Packed into leaky, overcrowded transports and escorted by 17 Portuguese warships and a small British squadron under Admiral Sir Sidney Smith, the refugees sailed from the Tagus before dawn on 29 November, and two months later, after a stormy and miserable crossing, sighted the green and welcoming coasts of Brazil. On 7 March 1808 the convoy reached its final destination and, entering between the Fort of Santa Cruz and the Sugar Loaf, beheld for the first time the breathtaking panorama of the Bay of Guanabara with its lofty mountains, rocky crags and luxuriant vegetation. The next day, amid wild rejoicing, the Royal party took up residence in the sleepy colonial town of Rio de Janeiro.

Once secure in his American dominion, Dom João declared war on France and, with the stroke of a pen, reversed the monopolistic policies of centuries by throwing the ports of Brazil open to international trade. The bureaucratic machinery of the Royal Government was then laboriously reassembled in Rio de Janeiro. Public offices and sinecures were soon monopolized by the throng of Portuguese *émigrés*, and the corruption and intrigue which had characterized the Court in Lisbon flourished anew in the tropical atmosphere of Brazil. Few natives of the colony were permitted to attain high office, and the administration kept its European orientation, yet the presence of the monarch was a source of increasing pride to Brazilians, and the centralization of power in Rio served as a stimulus to unification and the emergence of a national identity. The colony thrived as a result of the Royal residence. Cities increased in size and wealth: land was reclaimed, streets were widened, elegant new buildings were constructed. Rio, with its great aqueduct, its filthy streets and its whitewashed convents and houses nestling among the green banks and rocky eminences of the Bay, was transformed from a drowsy, colonial seaport into the capital of an Empire and the seat of a glittering court. Within ten years, it had doubled in size to become a bustling cosmopolitan city, its harbour packed with shipping and its warehouses stuffed with merchandise.

The changes in Brazil's intellectual and cultural life were no less dramatic. Military and naval academies, medical schools, courses for agriculture, chemistry and economics were founded; printing presses and newspapers were introduced; a theatre was opened, and a library with 60,000 volumes; an Academy of Fine Arts and a Botanical Garden were inaugurated. Foreign scientists, artists and naturalists flocked in wonder to the new continent, to capture its exotic panoramas in their writings and watercolours and to help establish the uniqueness and identity of the Brazilian way of life.

The country's trade and commerce were likewise transformed. As a colony, Brazil had existed to supply Portugal with the products of mine and plantation: industry and manufacturing had been forbidden, trade with other nations prohibited. In 1808, all these restrictions were swept away. A Bank of Brazil was established in Rio with branches in São Paulo and Salvador; a Royal Committee for Commerce, Agriculture, Factories and Navigation was created to foster the development of trade and manufactures; and the cancellation of the old Portuguese trading monopolies opened the country to the commerce and experience of the world which, while the Napoleonic Wars lasted, meant the commerce and experience of Britain.

For British merchants, the opening of the Brazilian ports came as a godsend. To them, excluded as they were from the markets of Europe by the enmity of Napoleon, Brazil became the promised land. Within weeks, woollens, glassware, boots, linen, firearms, earthenware, shot, tinplate, utensils, clothing and goods of all kinds that had been stockpiling in British warehouses were pouring into the country, clogging the wharves and overflowing from the customs houses. Rio Bay was packed with British ships disgorging their cargoes or loading with sugar, cotton, rum and hides for the return voyage. The end of the war in 1815 brought African beeswax, French lace, Chinese silk, Dutch gin, Scandinavian tar and other foreign merchandise into the Brazilian market, but British trade remained dominant. In 1822, half of the 434 foreign ships arriving in Rio were British, and the value of Britain's exports seldom fell below £2 million annually. The dockside emporia and pothouses sported a distinctive British air and, as Maria Graham noted in her Journal, there were as many 'Red Lions', 'Jolly Tars' and 'Union Jacks' as there were in Greenwich or Deptford. In political and economic circumstances such as these, Brazil's elevation to the status of a kingdom in 1815 was more than a gesture. It was a confirmation of an irreversible reality.

But meanwhile, as Brazil's prosperity and national pride increased, so those of Portugal diminished. Deprived of the old colonial monopolies, her trade, industry and agriculture began to stagnate. And with the Court now firmly established in Rio, it was Portugal rather than Brazil that was subject to administrative neglect and delay. In 1820, a constitutional revolt in Spain set the spark to Portuguese resentment. In August, a rebellion in Oporto spread like wildfire to the rest of the country. A liberal constitution restricting royal authority was proclaimed, and a democratic Côrtes was summoned to exercise supreme power. Convinced that the root of the nation's troubles lay in the absence of the King – Dom João had reluctantly and emotionally succeeded to the throne following the death of his mother in March 1816 – its first act was to demand his return from Brazil.

Dom João was far from anxious to obey. He liked life in Rio de Janeiro. He liked the food, and he liked the country with its lofty mountains, its lush green hills and its sandy beaches. In Rio, the easy-going and benevolent King found himself loved and respected as never before, and he viewed with gloom the prospect of exchanging the leisurely atmosphere of Brazil for the political intrigues and tensions of Europe. At first he employed his favourite tactic of doing nothing in the hope that the problem would go away. But it did not. Pressure from Britain and from the monarchs of the Holy Alliance, combined with the spread of the constitutional revolt to Bahia, Pernambuco and then to Rio itself, forced his hand. Finally, in April 1821, the nervous King boarded a warship for the return journey to Lisbon accompanied, as he had arrived, by a vast crowd of nobles and capitalists, the state archives, the contents of the Bank of Brazil and the body of his dead mother Queen Maria. Behind him he left his eldest son, Crown Prince Pedro, as ruler of a kingdom which was in the throes of political turmoil and on the brink of economic collapse.

Pedro was then only 23 years old. Inexperienced politically, he was nevertheless a fine figure of a man. Tall, dark, handsome, with magnificent moustaches, he excelled at horsemanship and at every kind of physical and amorous pursuit. He and his brother had had little formal education and had grown up roaming freely around the palace and the grounds, hobnobbing with grooms and servants and indulging every passion. Inheritance, too, had played its part. The younger brother, Miguel, replicated the worst characteristics of his diminutive and malevolent mother – the Infanta of Spain, Queen Carlota – while Pedro inherited from his father his easy-going amiability and his love of music. But that was all he inherited. Whereas Dom João was corpulent and irresolute, Pedro was passionate, impulsive and energetic – a true leader of men. Indeed, his upbringing made him feel at one with the common people. He was impatient with the rules and restrictions of official life and, as time went on, became increasingly suspicious and cynical about those who made them.

At the age of 18 Pedro had been married to the daughter of the Emperor of Austria, the Archduchess Leopoldina. Her sister, Marie-Louise, was the separated second wife of Napoleon so, technically, he was the French Emperor's brother-in-law. Physically Leopoldina was Pedro's opposite, being fair, dumpy and intellectual with a keen interest in natural science. But they got on well enough, and in time provided the necessary offspring for the House of Braganza. It was only later, when Pedro's penchant for cronies and mistresses came to the fore, that things became difficult. But in 1821, Pedro was still young, inexperienced and uncertain.

With the King back in Portugal, the Côrtes enacted a programme of much-needed liberal reform. But when it turned its attention to Brazil, its mood was reactionary. A series of decrees, passed before the Brazilian delegates had even had time to arrive, tried stubbornly to turn the clock back fifteen years. The authority of the Government in Rio de Janeiro was undermined by making the Juntas ruling the Brazilian provinces directly responsible to Lisbon; military commanders were subordinated to the authority of the Côrtes; the government installations which had been established in Brazil since 1808 were abolished; free trade was denounced; and the armies of Portugal and Brazil were merged so – it was thought – that Brazilian units could be replaced by loyal metropolitan troops in time of crisis. Finally, the Crown Prince was ordered to return forthwith to Europe to complete his political education.

As news of these measures trickled across the Atlantic, Brazilians were shocked and angry. They had loyally supported the cause of liberty, and now saw themselves being reduced to colonial status by a reactionary Côrtes intent on restoring the prosperity of Portugal at the expense of Brazil. Opinion in the country was divided. The Portuguese officials and merchants in the towns welcomed a return to colonial status and all the monopolies it would bring. But the native Brazilians, who formed the landed aristocracy and the bulk of the rural population, were determined that Brazil and Portugal should remain equal, and were prepared to resist any move to make their country a colonial appendage once more. The Prince, caught between these two opposites, vacillated between obedience to the Côrtes and open defiance.

The arrival of the *Infante Dom Sebastião* on 9 December 1821, carrying news that the government departments in Brazil were to be closed, caused a dramatic change in the situation. The Portuguese office-holders, now faced with unemployment and ruin, threw their support behind the Brazilian cause. And to Brazilian patriots, news of the Prince's recall to Lisbon came as final proof of the hostility of Portuguese intentions. Stimulated by a network of radical Masonic lodges, resolutions denouncing the Côrtes and begging the Prince to remain flooded in from São Paulo, Minas Gerais, and Rio itself. Pedro deliberated; then on 9 January 1822, he threw his weight behind the Brazilian cause with his historic declaration that: 'If it is for the good of all, and for the general felicity of the Nation, tell the people that I will remain!'

Events moved rapidly. On 11 January, Portuguese General Jorge de Avilez de Souza Tavares, commanding the Rio garrison, tried to force the Prince into obedience by occupying the Castello Hill dominating the city. Pedro immediately mobilized the Brazilian militia and, with a mixture of threats and personality, overawed the unhappy Avilez and made him and his men withdraw harmlessly to Praia Grande across the Bay. Then, blockading them by land and sea, Pedro used his authority as Crown Prince to order the Portuguese troops back to Lisbon. The General protested, but Pedro stood firm, and within days Avilez, with his three battalions of infantry and companies of horse artillery and engineers, had been packed into seven transports. On 15 February, the convoy sailed for Europe escorted by the two Brazilian corvettes *Maria da Glória* and *Liberal*. Off Bahia, two transports managed to elude their escorts and made for the Portuguese garrison in Salvador,

THE POLITICS OF INDEPENDENCE   7

but the rest were firmly shepherded out of Brazilian waters. Thus were Rio and the southern parts of Brazil freed from Portuguese troops and military interference.

A month later, on 5 March 1822, a new crisis loomed when a Portuguese squadron commanded by Commodore Francisco Maximiliano de Souza in the *Dom João VI* appeared off Rio after a seven-week voyage from Lisbon convoying a dozen transports carrying a replacement garrison of 1200 men. Pedro's government once more stood firm. The ships were allowed to enter the Bay, but were made to anchor harmlessly under the guns of the fortifications. No troops were allowed to disembark, and the officers were permitted to communicate with the shore only after they had sworn obedience to the Prince. The convoy was quickly re-provisioned, and the men were paid. Then, on 23 March, the whole force was ignominiously despatched on the return voyage to Portugal, leaving behind them a useful addition to the Brazilian Navy in the shape of the 44-gun 18-pounder frigate *Real Carolina*.

On 16 January 1822, one week after Pedro's decision to remain in Brazil, a new government had been formed under the leadership of the Paulista patriot José Bonifácio de Andrada e Silva. José Bonifácio was then 58 years old, short in stature but with a dominating personality and a sharp intellect. Although he had spent more than half his life in Portugal – as professor of mineralogy, as a combatant in the Peninsular War, and then as a scientific civil servant – he was totally committed to the Brazilian cause. He was also a conservative and a monarchist, and was hostile to the republican elements in the Masonic lodges on the fringes of the independence movement. Transformed overnight from civil servant as Intendant-General of Mines to politician as Secretary of the Junta of São Paulo, it was José Bonifácio who dominated the politics of the period, and it was his influence which finally fixed the resolve of the young Prince and set Brazil firmly on the road to independence.

José Bonifácio and his ministerial colleagues quickly restored the situation. In a series of decrees they reunited the Brazilian provinces under the control of Rio, prohibited the landing of Portuguese troops, made the application of acts of the Côrtes illegal without the consent of the Prince, and summoned a Brazilian Constituent Assembly to articulate the national will. In

May, Pedro accepted the title 'Perpetual Defender and Protector of Brazil', and in August he issued a Manifesto which expressed his desire for amicable union with Portugal, but called on Brazilians to be prepared to fight for their independence if necessary. The Côrtes reacted with equal vigour. Arms shipments to Brazil were banned. Orders were sent to Pedro demanding that he dismiss his government, arrest the Junta of São Paulo and cancel the convocation of the Brazilian Constituent Assembly. It was the delivery of these insolent orders on 7 September 1822 which precipitated the most famous event in Brazilian history, now immortalized in story, paintings and banknotes. The courier caught up with the Prince as he paused at the Ypiranga stream during a flying visit to São Paulo. Pedro took the despatch case, read the papers, and threw them angrily to the dust. Then, pale with fury and defiance, he drew his sword and, to the cheers of the escorting Brazilian dragoons cried: 'The time has come. It is Independence or Death! We are separated from Portugal!'

On the Prince's return to the capital, independence was carried to its logical conclusion. On 12 October 1822 – his 24th birthday – Pedro was proclaimed 'Constitutional Emperor', a title chosen to symbolize the happy union between liberty and legitimacy which the Brazilian monarchy represented. His first act was to design a patriotic green-and-yellow armband emblazoned with the words *Independência ou Morte!* – Independence or Death! – and his second was to compose the national anthem of the new state. A fortnight later, José Bonifácio feigned resignation when Pedro intervened to prevent a purge of the radicals and democrats in the patriot camp, and was swept back to power at the head of a government of native Brazilians. On 10 November, the new national flag – green with a yellow lozenge bearing the Imperial arms – was raised and saluted for the first time by the forts and the warships in the harbour: the British first, followed by the French. There could be no going back.

The inhabitants of the Empire which Pedro and José Bonifácio were about to lead to independence comprised four and a half million people scattered along a seaboard which stretched from the tropical rainforests of the Amazon to the temperate grasslands of the River Plate. Only one-third of this number were white. The rest were made up of a million black slaves, a quarter of a million Indians, and a huge semi-free population of *mulatos* and *caboclos* spreading deeply but thinly into the interior – the result of centuries of interbreeding between Europeans and, respectively, Negroes and Indians. The distribution of this racial kaleidoscope was uneven, and the areas of settlement were separated by formidable natural barriers, but there were three areas of concentration and importance. In the north-east, along a flat and fertile coast protected from the Atlantic swell by a parallel reef, lay the sugar states of Pernambuco, Paraíba and Rio Grande do Norte, bordered on the west by the dusty cattle lands of Ceará and Piauí. To the south lay the state of Bahia, itself producing an abundance of sugar, molasses and tobacco, but also the centre of a thriving trade in goods and slaves through the filthy, baroque city of Salvador. Lastly, further south still, lay the Brazilian heartland, the area around Rio which stretched from the lagoons and bays of the coast to the fertile uplands of São Paulo and the diamond- and gold-bearing hills of Minas Gerais. There were also two areas of lesser importance: the northern coastline which stretched from Pará at the mouth of the Amazon to the rice and cotton lands of Maranhão and, in the deep south, Montevideo and the thinly populated pampas on the eastern bank – the Banda Oriental – of the River Plate, seized from Spain during the confusion following the Napoleonic Wars.

When Pedro made his dramatic bid for independence, only the Rio–Minas Gerais–São Paulo area was unequivocally loyal to the Brazilian cause. In the south, the army had divided on the independence issue. The Portuguese regiments commanded by Dom Álvaro da Costa had remained loyal to the Côrtes and had shut themselves up in Montevideo, where they were promptly besieged by the Brazilian units under Frederic Lecor, Barão da Laguna. In the north, Pará and Maranhão too had ignored the call. Both provinces were dominated by Portuguese Juntas which had eagerly thrown off the authority of distant Rio and were quick to suppress any Brazilian patriotic feeling. The north-eastern states were divided: Piauí and Alagoas were obedient to the Côrtes; Rio Grande do Norte and Ceará were in confusion; Pernambuco wavered, but finally sided with the cause of independence.

But the strategic situation was dominated by Bahia, with its great naval arsenal and populous hinterland. The struggle for control began there in February 1822, when Brazilian patriots had resisted the replacement of the Brazilian-born military commander by the Portuguese Brigadier Ignacio Madeira de Melo. After severe street fighting, in which there was widespread looting and over 100 casualties – including the Abbess of Lapa, who died defending her nuns – the Portuguese regulars captured the Brazilian headquarters in the Fort of S. Pedro, and seized control of the city. With the timely aid of troops from two transports which had evaded the warships escorting Avilez's regiments back to Europe, Madeira de Melo consolidated his grip on Salvador. Brazilian troops and officials abandoned the city and began to organize resistance in the countryside until, one by one, the towns of the interior all declared for the Brazilian cause. Arms were manufactured or improvised, and volunteers enlisted. Patriot control of the province was soon complete and a motley Brazilian army of 10,000 men, though lacking officers and artillery, began to advance on the capital. Madeira de Melo fortified the city and waited confidently for reinforcements.

The Brazilian government did all it could to help its adherents. Emissaries were sent to spread the word; Pedro himself paid flying visits to Minas Gerais and São Paulo; and in May, in an attempt to win over the Pernambucanos, the frigate *Real Carolina* and a transport were sent to Recife with troops. In Bahia, Pedro tried to overawe Madeira de Melo as he had Avilez, and ordered him back to Portugal with all his men. But Madeira de Melo remained defiant, and Pedro's government determined to launch the first naval expedition of the campaign to force him out. On 14 July 1822 the frigate *União*, under the command of Commodore Rodrigo Delamare, with the corvettes *Maria da Glória* and *Liberal* and the brig *Reino Unido*, sailed from Rio for Bahia flying Portuguese colours and carrying muskets, powder, cannon, 300 officers and a new commander for the patriot army, French General Pierre Labatut. Delamare's orders were to deliver his cargo to the Brazilian land forces and then, if the Portuguese were still in occupation, to blockade Salvador by sea to prevent the arrival of munitions or reinforcements from Lisbon.

As the Brazilian squadron approached Bahian waters, six Portuguese warships were sent to intercept them. Contact was made at dawn on 4 August 1822, and all day long the two squadrons sailed in sight of each other. The brig *Audaz*, flying a flag of truce, desperately tried to close with the Brazilians, but without success – Delamare was keeping well to windward to prevent the Portuguese coming within hail. He was taking no chances. The shaky loyalty of the Portuguese sailors manning the Brazilian ships had already become apparent, and by this time their mood was openly mutinous. The situation was so bad that Delamare avoided all contact with the Portuguese, although they remained in sight for three days. Finally, he gave up and sailed away to look for the Brazilian army. As he did so, the *Calypso*, with three transports carrying 700 troops from Lisbon, sailed unmolested into Salvador.

On 18 August Delamare's squadron reached Alagoas, where General Labatut, his troops and his military stores were disembarked. Then it headed for Pernambuco, where the officers held a Council of War. Gloomily, they concluded that a blockade of Salvador was out of the question. The unreliability of the sailors, the strength of the Portuguese in Bahia, the impossibility of finding reinforcements and the reluctance of the ambivalent Pernambuco Junta to supply provisions meant that there was no option but to return to Rio. On 16 September the squadron set sail once more. It was a perilous voyage. Some of the crews openly demonstrated in favour of Portugal, and a mutiny was suppressed only by the greatest of good fortune. At last, after twelve tense days, Delamare's ships reached the safety of the Bay of Guanabara, to a wave of courts martial and recriminations. The voyage had been a humiliating experience which boded ill for Brazil's future.

The situation in Bahia, as in Montevideo, was a stalemate: the Portuguese could not break out, and the Brazilians could not break in. But time was on the side of the Portuguese. Brazil was close to bankruptcy and lacked the resources to maintain an indefinite war effort, while Portugal was vigorously raising loans and sending troops. Every packet brought news of military preparations or the sailing of further reinforcements. On 30 October, eight more transports reached Bahia with 1,200 men escorted by the 74-gun *Dom João VI*, which carried a new naval commander, Commodore João Félix Pereira de Campos. His instructions were clear and carefully drafted to prevent any further conflict of loyalty. The maintenance of the Portuguese bridgehead in Bahia was to be his primary concern, and he was to obey no orders except those emanating from the Côrtes in Lisbon.

The Brazilians watched the growing Portuguese strength with alarm. Then in November, a report from General Brant in London told of a third expedition of 2,000 men and a second 74-gun ship. According to him, new instructions were also on their way to Félix de Campos which would order him to arrange the transfer of Dom Álvaro da Costa's troops from Montevideo, to complete the re-conquest of Bahia and Pernambuco, and then to destroy the nerve centre of the Brazilian revolt once and for all by blockading Rio de Janeiro. The threat to the new Empire was very real.

CHAPTER 2

THE BIRTH OF A NAVY

As José Bonifácio's government attempted to impose its authority over a country scattered along a coastline 4700 miles long, the most crucial element in the situation was obviously sea power. Only by gaining command of the sea could it blockade and expel the Portuguese garrisons, coerce the north into submission and subordinate Brazil's diverse and turbulent provinces to the Imperial authority. The situation was critical. It was also dangerous, for in Salvador da Bahia was a powerful Portuguese naval squadron which already consisted of one 74-gun ship, one newly launched frigate, four corvettes, two brigs-of-war, six armed ships and various schooners. This force was quite large enough to impose a crippling blockade on Rio de Janeiro unless the Brazilians could first challenge it at sea.[1] The organization of a reliable navy to neutralize this threat was clearly the new government's most urgent priority.

The responsibility for this vital task fell to the new Minister of Marine, Captain Luis da Cunha Moreira. One of the few Brazilians in the Portuguese Navy, Cunha Moreira was a convinced patriot, a man of great integrity and an experienced sailor. He had served throughout the Napoleonic Wars, and had taken a leading part in the Anglo-Portuguese capture of French Cayenne by Sir James Yeo in 1808, in the suppression of the Pernambuco rebellion of 1817, and in the seizure of Montevideo the same year. As captain of the *Maria da Glória* during Delamare's humiliating sortie against Bahia in 1822, he had also had first-hand experience of the feebleness and unreliability of the naval forces which Brazil had at its disposal.

But as he set about his task, Cunha Moreira had one great advantage, for the naval installations which had been established in Rio in 1808 remained intact. These comprised the Ministry of Marine, staffed by a Chief Secretary and seven clerks; the Intendência, with its departments for accounting, pay and stores; the Naval Hospital, the Naval Academy, the arsenal and the dockyard. The Bay of Guanaraba, on which Rio was built, also offered the most magnificent and defensible harbour on the coast – one in which, according to observers, whole fleets could shelter and manoeuvre in perfect safety. On the debit side, most of these assets had been neglected during the years of the Royal residence. The fortifications were derelict, the dockyard was sunk in idleness, the stores of the Intendência, following years of corruption and neglect, were filled with inferior and deteriorating material, and ships rotted at their moorings for want of attention. The raw material from which Cunha Moreira had to forge his navy was both weak and wanting.

A number of Portuguese warships on the Brazilian station had, however, fallen under Imperial control, and it was these which formed the nucleus of the new navy. Based on Rio de Janeiro were 15 fighting vessels large and small, and a dozen transports and gunboats. These were the frigates *União* (62 guns) and *Real Carolina* (44), the corvettes *Maria da Glória* (26) and *Liberal* (20), the brig *Real Pedro* (14), the brigantines *Real* (10), *Independência ou Morte* (14) and *Leopoldina* (10), and the schooners *Cossaka, Carolina, Seis de Fevereiro, Maria da Glória, Catarina, Maria Francisca,* and *Maria Zeferina* – the last operating a mail service between Rio and the northeast. In the south, patrolling the River Plate, were two more: the 44-gun frigate *Thesis*, flying the flag of Vice Admiral Rodrigo Lobo, and the schooner *Maria Teresa*. There were also five schooners which formed the Flotilla of the Uruguay. Whether the Imperial Government could rely on their forces in the south was uncertain. At first there were divided allegiances, with some commanders secretly supporting the Côrtes. It was only after they had been removed that Admiral Lobo was able to assure José Bonifácio on 9 November 1822 that the squadron was loyal to the Brazilian cause. But almost immediately the *Thesis* was lost when Álvaro da Costa managed to seize the frigate, eject a humiliated Lobo, and order it to be prepared for a voyage to Lisbon. In the event, neither a return to Portugal nor its recapture by Brazil was possible, and the *Thesis* spent the rest of the war immobilized under the guns of Montevideo.

Drawing on all its resources, the Imperial Government could therefore muster only eight sizeable vessels carrying around 200 guns with which to confront a continually reinforced Portuguese squadron of 14 warships mounting twice as much artillery: to lessen this disparity was clearly Cunha Moreira's most urgent task. Fortunately, three ships were in the Naval Arsenal in Rio undergoing repair and refit: the 64-gun *Martim de Freitas* – nicknamed 'the dog' after its figurehead which showed a lion gripping a key between its teeth – the frigate *Sucesso* and the brig *Reino Unido*. All three were taken into service, and repair work speeded up while the dozen disarmed vessels in the harbour, which included five old two-deckers, were surveyed to see if they could be salvaged. But climate, neglect and the worm had done for them, and only two – the *Vasco da Gama* and the *Principe Real*, which in happier times had actually carried Dom João's Royal person to Brazil in 1808 – were found to be usable, and then only as receiving ships or floating batteries.

The Government also looked elsewhere for suitable vessels. In September 1822 a despatch from the Brazilian Agent in London, Caldeira Brant, reported that a certain Captain James Thompson had offered to supply Brazil with two frigates, fully manned and fully armed, for between £12,000 and £16,000 each.[2] On 4 October, José Bonifácio ordered him to hire or purchase both. In November, as news of further Portuguese reinforcements began to reach Rio, Brant was sent additional instructions to buy four more warships and to pay for them by raising loans or issuing letters of credit payable by the Treasury.[3]

The Brazilian Government was acting decisively, but the financial situation was rapidly deteriorating. In 1821, expenditure stood at 5600 contos of reis (£1.1 million), while revenue from the provinces which recognized the Prince's authority totalled only half that amount.[4] In July, the Bank of Brazil went bankrupt and, by December, the National Debt had reached 9800 contos of reis (£1.9 million). A year later, still denied the revenues of a number of important provinces, the Imperial Government was forced to resort to internal loans to ease its desperate plight. On 24 January 1823 it launched a National Subscription to pay for vessels for the Navy. Subscribers were invited to buy monthly shares payable for three years, and agents were appointed in every locality to encourage participation. Contributions were to be sent quarterly to the cental coffers of the fund in Rio, and a special commission was appointed to supervise the purchase and equipment of suitable vessels. The scheme was immediately popular, and with the Emperor and Empress taking the lead with 350 shares, patriots all over the country were soon flocking to subscribe.

With this promise of financial support, the expansion of Brazil's naval forces continued. On 23 January 1823 the Emperor himself purchased the 18-gun brig *Maipú*, and on 12 February he presented it to the nation as the *Caboclo*. The British brig *Nightingale* was surveyed and bought from its owners, Brown-Watson & Co., complete with its sails, gear and cargo of coal, and on 11 March its name was changed to *Guarani*. That same month the 10-gun brigantines *Atlanta* and *Rio da Plata*, purchased respectively by Labatut in Bahia and Laguna in the Banda Oriental, arrived in Rio to be added to the Imperial Squadron. Orders were sent to Caldeira Brant in London for the purchase of tons of naval stores, including cables, cordage, gunpowder, cannon, shot and firearms, and for their speedy despatch to Brazil. In early 1823, the work of refit and repair reached an intensity hitherto unknown in the Imperial Dockyard. A regular visitor was the Emperor himself, who frequently arrived at dawn to spend the day clambering over the ships in dock, urging on the carpenters, riggers, caulkers and sailmakers to even greater efforts.[5]

There seemed at first to be no shortage of officers for the Imperial Navy. Some 160 were either serving in the ships in commission or had settled permanently in Brazil since 1808. But it had long been Portuguese colonial policy to discourage the employment of Brazilians in the senior ranks of the armed forces, and the majority were inevitably Portuguese by birth. The Brazilian Government clearly had to determine their allegiance, and on 5 December 1822 Cunha Moreira appointed a seven-member Commission to demand of every officer from the rank of sublieutenant to captain a statement as to whether he wished to serve Brazil or return to Portugal. Within weeks it was clear that the majority of officers adhered to the Brazilian cause. Only 27 opted for Portugal, and they were sent home with their families and goods on the hired Danish brig *Aurora*. When the names of the aged and the sick had been removed from the list of those loyal to Brazil, a total of 96 remained – 8 flag officers, 8 captains, 13 captains-of-frigate, 19 commanders, 10 lieutenants and 38 sublieutenants. There were clearly sufficient senior officers available, but the number in junior grades was sufficient only to bring the vessels already in commission up to their war establishments. To man the additional ships being prepared in Rio would call for at least 25 to 30 more lieutenants.[6]

The final rupture between Brazil and Portugal took place at the end of 1822. The Côrtes declared Pedro and his ministers rebels, and stepped up its military preparations. In Rio in December the final scenes of the drama were enacted. On the first of the month, amid great pomp and popular enthusiasm, Pedro, with Leopoldina at his side, was crowned Emperor, wearing – as if to symbolize the Napoleonic and American traditions of the Brazilian revolution – a green gold-laced uniform, a red feathered cloak, and cavalry boots. On the eleventh, a decree was issued confiscating Portuguese goods and property. And finally, on the thirtieth, in a gesture which amounted to a declaration of war, privateering was authorized against the flag of Portugal. With fighting now inevitable on sea as well as land, Brazilian patriots wondered at the wisdom of leaving their navy under the direction of Portuguese-born officers. All had declared their allegiance to Brazil, but the strength of that loyalty when they were faced with the necessity of firing on their countrymen could not be foreseen. The allegiance of the Plate squadron was particularly in doubt, and foreboding deepened on 31 January 1823, when the first officer and crew of the schooner *Maria Teresa*, escorting three transports loaded with artillery for Colônia on the Banda Oriental, arrested their commander and delivered the ship and its valuable convoy to the delighted Portuguese garrison in Montevideo. Caldeira Brant echoed the thoughts of many when he urged the recruitment of British or Americans to form the nucleus of the new navy, and stressed his lack of confidence in a force officered and manned by Portuguese nationals.

José Bonifácio's Government was already considering this method of filling the key post of commander-in-chief. None of the admirals available had a reputation which would strike fear into the hearts of an enemy. All were Portuguese, and the most likely candidate, Vice Admiral Rodrigo Lobo, commanding in the River Plate, had a reputation for incompetence and cowardice, and was hated by Brazilians for his brutal suppression of the Pernambuco revolt of 1817. Caldeira Brant in London was horrified to hear that he was even under consideration, and it was he, in a long memorandum written as early as May 1822, who recommended the obvious candidate, Thomas Lord Cochrane. José Bonifácio had come to the same conclusion, and on 13 September – one week after the Prince's declaration of 'Independence or Death' which made open war now inevitable – he sent his instructions to the Brazilian Agent in Buenos Aires, Antônio Corrêa da Camara:

> In order to repel unexpected attacks on any point of his extensive coasts, HRH the Prince Regent, Perpetual Defender of his peoples, has resolved to invite into his Royal Service Lord Cochrane, whose proven military skill and adherence to the American System may make him wish to profit from yet another opportunity to co-operate in the defence of the Sacred Cause of this Hemisphere. You are therefore authorized to communicate with the said Lord Cochrane, acquainting him with the hope of HRH that such an able officer will join him, assuring him ... that HRH with his customary beneficence will not allow Lord Cochrane to enjoy fewer advantages here than he has enjoyed in other parts of America.[7]

Corrêa da Camara hastened to obey the order. On 4 November 1822, he passed the invitation on to Cochrane in Chile in stirring rhetoric. 'Come, my Lord', he began:

> Honour invites you. Glory is calling to you. A Generous Prince and a whole Nation await you. Come, reborn Hercules, and with your honourable efforts help to tame the Hundred-Headed Hydra of a frightful Despotism. The west of America is saved by virtue of your Arm ... the Sacred Standard of Independence is unfurled from the Galápagos as far as the Cedar Isles of California! Come now and furnish our Naval Arms with the wonderful order and incomparable Discipline of Mighty Albion...![8]

At this time, Lord Cochrane was at the height of his powers and reputation. As an officer in the British Navy during the Napoleonic Wars, he had had a brilliant career as a frigate commander. In 1800, at the age of 25, as captain of the brig *Speedy* – a tiny inappropriately named vessel with 14 small guns and only 84 men – he had first demonstrated his ingenuity and daring by capturing the Spanish warship *El Gamo*, with 32 heavy guns and a crew of 300. Promoted and in command of the frigate *Pallas* between 1804 and 1806, he was so successful in raiding enemy commerce and winning prize money that his ship was nicknamed the 'Golden *Pallas*', and his recruiting posters were able to state jauntily that no man should apply unless he could run three miles with a hundredweight of silver on his back! Cochrane was given command of the frigate *Impérieuse* in 1808, and in the years that followed he kept the coasts of Spain and France in such a state of alarm that he became known as the 'Terror of the Mediterranean'. The following year he organized an attack by fireships against a French fleet sheltering in the Aix Roads, and it was only the caution shown by the British commander, Admiral Lord Gambier, that enabled the enemy ships to escape without significant loss.

But the single-minded energy which made Cochrane a genius in war made him a menace in peace. Mistrustful of anyone in authority, he quarrelled frequently and rashly with his superiors, and as a radical Member of the British Parliament he was a thorn in the side of the Government, delighting in exposing corruption in the Prize Courts and abuses in the naval establishment. His attitudes and personal qualities made him admired by his subordinates and popular with the underdog, but within the establishment his activities were viewed with displeasure. Lord St Vincent, one of the greatest admirals of his age and himself a scourge of naval corruption, described Cochrane and his family as 'romantic, money-getting and not truth-telling'.

There was certainly a romantic streak to his personality. Indeed, at 38 he had contracted a runaway marriage in Scotland with Kitty Barnes, a petite, raven-haired, half-Spanish beauty of 16 who, to the dismay of Cochrane's relations, was not an heiress. But in other aspects of his personality, he was entirely practical. His father, the 9th Earl of Dundonald, had spent the family fortune on failed scientific experiments, and Cochrane had inherited his keen interest in technical matters. As for money, his obsession with pecuniary reward was notorious. This was perhaps understandable in an impoverished eldest son with rank and social position but no fortune to back them up, but it was hardly admirable.

In 1814, Cochrane was implicated in a Stock Exchange swindle engineered by some of his shadier relations. A fake colonel appeared at Dover, proclaimed that Napoleon was dead, and took post-chaise to London, spreading the good news noisily on the journey. Share prices soared, and the conspirators made a handsome profit. Unfortunately for Cochrane, the 'colonel' went to his house in Green Street and borrowed clothes to cover his uniform. Largely on the basis of this fact, and despite protestations of innocence and politically motivated persecution, Lord Cochrane was found guilty, fined and briefly imprisoned. He continued to enjoy the vociferous support of the electors of Westminster, but his public career was over. His Knighthood of the Bath was stripped from him, and he was dismissed from the Navy. Officially disgraced, he was therefore only too pleased to receive an invitation to leave Britain in order to command the naval forces of Chile in its struggle for independence against Spain. So, in 1817, he took his military genius, his personality and his young wife and son to the Pacific. In South America he was received with enthusiasm and, starting with the slenderest resources, he proceeded to sweep the Spanish Navy from the seas – seizing the frigate *Esmeralda* from under the guns of Callao, capturing the royalist stronghold of Valdivia, and blockading the enemy's fortresses and towns.

By 1822 the naval war in the Pacific had been victoriously concluded, and Cochrane, who had almost inevitably begun to quarrel with his employers over pay and prize money, was looking for other outlets for his talents. The Brazilian offer was therefore opportune, and Cochrane's reaction was favourable. On 30 November 1822, he sent his reply to Corrêa da Camera and prepared to leave. 'I have this day tendered my resignation to the Government of Chile,' he wrote, 'and am not aware that any material delay will be necessary previous to my setting off for Rio de Janeiro ... it being understood that I hold myself free to decline as well as to accept the offer made through you by His Majesty.'[9]

While Cochrane was considering his invitation, the Imperial Government began to recruit other foreign officers into its service in Brazil. The first was an American, David Jewitt – owner of the *Maipú* – who had had long experience both as a privateer and as an officer in the service of the Government of Buenos Aires. He was commissioned as a captain on 6 October 1822. The second and third were two young Englishmen, William Eyre and George

Manson, who were appointed sublieutenants in November. The fourth, whose recruitment was carried out in more dramatic circumstances, was Lieutenant John Taylor, an officer serving with HMS *Blossom* in the British South America Squadron. Taylor was in Rio during December 1822 awaiting transport to Salvador, where he was to become second-in-command of the *Doris*, then flying the broad pennant of the commander-in-chief, Sir Thomas Hardy. While he was in the capital, Taylor had a series of secret meetings with José Bonifácio in which he was offered a senior post in the Brazilian Navy. The temptation was enormous. Up to that time, John Taylor's career had been typical of an officer caught in the slump which followed the Napoleonic Wars. He had served in frigates as a midshipman throughout the conflict, but had been unemployed for six years after being promoted to lieutenant in 1812, and his appointment to the *Blossom* in 1820 was likely to be his last. It may also have been difficult for him to make his mark when he had to be described in the Navy List as 'John Taylor (C)' to distinguish him from two other lieutenants with the same name. Now he was being offered the chance of promotion and distinction in Brazil.

John Taylor was persuaded, and on 9 January 1823 a decree was published appointing him as a captain-of-frigate in the Imperial Navy. The following day he wrote to Sir Thomas Hardy to resign his British commission. Hardy refused to accept his resignation, marked Taylor as a deserter in the ship's books, and reported the matter to the Admiralty, advising that it be treated with moderation to avoid problems with the Brazilian authorities. London, however, took the matter seriously, and an Admiralty minute of 1 April noted: 'my Lords desire that Sir Thomas Hardy should avail himself of any occasion that may offer, without violating Brazilian territory or flag, of seeking the deserter and ... bringing him to trial before a court martial'.[10] The Admiralty was clearly alarmed by the possibility of further desertions by officers or men to the Imperial service, and in spite of Hardy's advice felt impelled to take a strong line.

The matter was then passed to the British Foreign Office, which protested strongly against the recruitment of a serving officer and demanded Taylor's dismissal from the Brazilian Navy. Month after month through 1823 and 1824, Consul-General Henry Chamberlain in Rio kept up the pressure, while the Foreign Office attempted to overawe Brant and Gameiro in the Brazilian Legation in London. The Imperial Government replied with courteous evasion and polite misunderstanding, and it was eighteen months before remorseless British diplomatic pressure secured Taylor's discharge, but by that time he was a national hero.[11]

In addition to the warships and officers, the Imperial Navy had inherited a corpus of seamen and marines. Unfortunately, the great majority of these men were Portuguese by birth, and their unreliability had been amply demonstrated during Delamare's ill-fated sortie against Bahia. Nevertheless, they were vitally necessary to the new navy, and the Government hoped that they would remain loyal if they were given officers faithful to Brazil and if their numbers were augmented by a stiffening of reliable sailors. The war complement of a 74-gun ship was 650 officers and men; a frigate such as *Real Carolina* required 350; a corvette around 200; and a brig-of-war 120. Thus, in order to man the ships already in commission, the ship-of-the-line, the refitted frigate and the four new brigs and brigantines the government needed 2100 seamen and 590 marines. The vessels based in Rio could provide no more than 1200 sailors and 340 troops: a quick and successful recruiting exercise was therefore a prime necessity.

Early in the new year the work on the two-decker was completed, and on 14 January 1823 the ship was renamed *Pedro I*. Two weeks later the frigate *Successo*, which had been refitted at private expense by a group of patriots, was renamed *Niterói*, and John Taylor was appointed as her commander. Recruiting for both vessels began promptly. The monthly pay offered by the administration was 8 milreis (£1.60) for Able Seamen, 6 milreis .500 (£1.30) for Ordinary Seamen and 4 milreis 800 (96p) and 3 milreis (60p) respectively for 1st- and 2nd-class Boys. As an inducement, the recruiting posters offered volunteers a tempting bounty of one month's pay. The recruiting campaign began in a mood of patriotic enthusiasm and optimism. Indeed, back in September 1822 the Chief Secretary of the Ministry of Marine had even proposed a far-sighted scheme for the creation of a professional naval corps consisting of volunteers serving on ten-year enlistments to replace the old haphazard system of manning. But the recruiting campaign quickly fizzled out. In spite of its extensive coastline,

Brazil remained a continental country with little maritime tradition and no reserve of seamen on which to draw in time of war. Its fishermen were mostly *mulatos* going to sea in primitive wooden rafts, and its coastal trade, though extensive, was largely made up of vessels of small tonnage manned by Portuguese and slaves. Few men offered themselves for the naval service, and the Brazilian Government soon found itself faced with a serious manpower shortage.

CHAPTER 3

GENERAL BRANT IN LONDON

The Brazilian Government was fortunate to have as its agent in London during this critical period a far-sighted and courageous Bahian landowner, Felisberto Caldeira Brant Pontes. Brant was a native of Minas Gerais, where he had been born on 19 September 1772. Like other children of the colonial aristocracy he had received his education at the Colégio dos Nobres in Lisbon, moving on to the Royal Naval Academy, from which he had graduated loaded with prizes. He had then transferred to the Army and, after a useful if uneventful career, had become a Major General in 1818.

A prominent figure in Bahian society, Brant was both politically well connected and a firm adherent of the patriot party. Like José Bonifácio de Andrada e Silva, he was also a conservative and a monarchist. In 1821, he had travelled to England on a private visit aimed at purchasing steam packets to carry mails between Rio and the north. Under sail the voyage could take as long as two months. Brant calculated that a steamer of 100 horsepower making a steady 10 knots even against the wind could cut the time to a fortnight, and in the interests of national unity he was keen to establish such a service. As a result, he was in England in April 1822 when news arrived of Pedro's defiance of the Côrtes and the appointment of José Bonifácio as head of the Government. Brant's first instinct was to hurry back to Brazil, but – seeing clearly the value to the new administration of a reliable agent in London able to influence opinion, raise loans and give instant warning of developments in Portugal – he decided that his duty was to remain.

Brant's first thoughts were contained in a series of letters dated 1 May 1822, and for the next twelve months he provided José

Bonifácio with a steady stream of information, military analysis and political commentary, keeping him fully informed of actual and rumoured events in Portugal, and invariably adding his own views and advice.[1] An indispensable source of support during this anxious period was Hipólito José da Costa, publisher of the influential London-based *Correio Brasiliense*, which rapidly became the mouthpiece of the Brazilian cause. For the most part, there was little in the way of support or guidance from the Government, months away in Rio. At first, information on happenings in Brazil came as much from private as from official sources, and at times Brant had to meet his expenses from his own pocket or borrow from his friends. But fortunately for the Brazilian cause, he was a man of initiative who was ready to act on his own judgement if specific instructions were lacking.

Brant's arrival in London coincided with a watershed in British social and political life. The coronation of George IV in 1821, with its quasi-mediaeval pomp and gargantuan banquets, marked the end of the Regency and the beginning of a more purposeful and prosperous era. Bucks and blades, prizefighters, horseflesh and the sabres of the cavalry ceased to be the dominant social images of the time, and were giving way to evangelicals, economists, the steam engine and a civilian police force; while in politics, the spying and repression which had marked the regime of Sidmouth and Eldon were slowly being replaced by the more enlightened and rational Toryism of Peel, Canning and Huskisson. Foreign policy, however, was still the private province of the cold and distant Lord Castlereagh, who saw it not as an area of public concern but as something to be settled behind closed doors by statesmen and kings meeting in periodic Congresses. When Brant began his work, foreign affairs were dominated by two issues. One was the determination of the monarchs of Europe, now combined in a reactionary league called the Holy Alliance, to crush the rising tide of liberalism on the continent. The second was the status of the ex-Spanish colonies in Latin America which, in the confusion and aftermath of the Napoleonic Wars, had declared themselves independent.

Castlereagh was convinced that recognition of South American independence was inevitable, and his principal aim was to protect the huge and vital trade which Britain now carried on in the region. True to his principles, however, he was also convinced that independence would be acceptable to the governments of Europe only if the principle of 'legitimacy' was observed – in other words, if the South American states became independent as monarchies ruled by Bourbon princes. It was this bizarre solution which he was determined to press on the next Congress, scheduled for autumn 1822 in Verona.

Brazil had not so far featured in Castlereagh's thinking. He was poorly informed on the situation there, and had little desire to become involved. It was obvious, however, that Brazil played a major part in the slave trade, which Britain was determined to see abolished. Brant's initial feelers therefore produced little. But the rules of the game were clear enough, and in May 1822 he wrote to José Bonifácio to warn him that Dom Pedro's actions in Brazil had to be presented as those of the 'legitimate' representative of the House of Braganza defying the machinations of a 'democratic' Côrtes, and to stress that recognition would have to be linked to the abolition of the slave trade.[2] Castlereagh's desire to obtain a 'European' solution to the knotty problem of recognizing South American independence had also come over loud and clear, and in the summer of 1822 Brant moved to Paris to be nearer the action. In a letter to José Bonifácio dated 20 August, he described the probable agenda of the Congress of Verona, dominated now by French concern at the situation in Spain. Almost as an afterthought, he noted the absence of Castlereagh. A week before, the British Minister had taken his razor and committed suicide.[3] A month later, back in London, Brant reported the sequel: George Canning was to be the new Foreign Secretary, an appointment forced on a reluctant King George by Lords Liverpool and Wellington, who needed to strengthen the Government's voice in the House of Commons. Canning was, as Brant wrote with satisfaction, a well-known supporter of South American independence.[4]

In 1822, however, the Brazilian drama was still unfolding. Independence was a long way off, and Brant's despatches were preoccupied with the political and military struggle, and with news of Portuguese preparations and countermeasures. He had strong views on questions of strategy, and his early training had made him aware of the importance of sea power. The need for a reliable Brazilian Navy was a constant theme, and as early as 6 May 1822 he produced a memorandum on 'Extreme Measures to repel Portuguese Attacks' in which he urged the Government to recruit Lord Cochrane and the foreign seamen who had fought with him in Spanish America. Brant's views were prophetic:

> Now that Chile has declared its independence, would it not be to the purpose to send someone of rank ... to negotiate with Cochrane to come with his ships to serve HRH? When the time comes to confront the Portuguese expeditionary force in Bahia and blockade the port, his name alone would strike terror into our enemies. To speak the truth, I would never have faith in Portuguese sailors, but if they are mixed with British and North Americans all should go well.[5]

On 5 July he reported that a former officer of the Royal Navy, Captain James Thompson, had offered to supply two fully manned frigates for between £12,000 and £16,000 each. Brant was convinced that this force, supported by the warships already in Rio, would secure the safety of the Brazilian coast. He passed on the offer and waited for a reply.

Through the summer of 1822, Brant faithfully reported increasing Portuguese military preparations and hostility to both Brazil and the Prince Regent. On 17 June he relayed news that an expedition of 600 men and four ships had sailed for Bahia. On 20 August he reported the departure from Lisbon of 1500 more troops with a powerful naval escort, including the 74-gun ship *Dom João VI*. On 18 September, he gloomily informed José Bonifácio that another 2000 men were preparing for a third expedition. There was a rumour that the garrison of Montevideo would be transferred to complete the conquest of Bahia, after which the Portuguese forces would attack Rio de Janeiro.

For months Brant received nothing by way of reply or guidance, and with a round trip of four months between London and Rio, this was not surprising. Then at last, on 24 October 1822, a bulky official package arrived from the Brazilian Government. In it were his credentials as *chargé d'affaires*, and his instructions. Article 1 ordered him to establish contact with the British authorities to explain the justice of the Brazilian position; Article 14, to see to the publication of material favourable to the patriot cause; and Article 11, to recruit officers and men for the Imperial Army and Navy if he felt it necessary. A low stipend was provided for ordinary expenditure but, as Brant bitterly complained, there was no financial authority for the translation or recruiting work.

Addressing the political issue, Brant cautiously made contact with the Foreign Office, and in November and December he had four separate interviews with George Canning, one of which was attended by the Prime Minister, Lord Liverpool. Unfortunately little progress was possible. Canning was still finding his feet, neither the King nor the Government was ready for a radical change of policy, and Castlereagh's views on South American independence still prevailed. The only difference was that without him, no 'European' solution had emerged from the Congress of Verona. The issue had been shelved and attention focused on the Spanish problem and the possibility of French and Russian intervention. Brant repeated his version of events: that the Brazilian problem was no anti-monarchical struggle but justified resistance by the Prince Regent of Brazil to the impositions of a radical Côrtes which had seized power from the hands of its rightful King. Canning was cautious, and predictably raised the slave trade issue. The meetings were amicable, but Canning sensed that Brant's views were his own rather than those of his government, and events in Brazil began to move so fast that it became obvious that Brant was being taken as much by surprise as anyone else. In these circumstances there was little Brant could do at the political level to help his country's cause, but on the military side his contribution was momentous.

Brant's instructions gave him the widest discretion to raise officers and men if preparations in Portugal seemed to warrant it. The order was vague, but he had been able to discuss it with the Chief Minister's brother, Antônio Carlos, who was returning hastily to Rio via London, having been the principal exponent of the Brazilian case at the increasingly polemic and menacing sessions of the Côrtes. Antônio Carlos had agreed that Brazil's most vital need in time of crisis would be 600 British seamen and a dozen officers to remove her dependence on Portuguese sailors and prevent a repetition of the Delamare fiasco. But Brant hesitated before committing himself to an expensive recruiting exercise. Then came alarming news of further Portuguese mobilization. On 28 November 1822, he reported that the Côrtes was raising loans and preparing to send 4000 men against Pará,

Maranhão and Bahia. On 4 December he wrote: 'already three expeditions have been launched and now a fourth is being prepared on an enormous scale. A ship-of-the-line is making ready, frigates are being launched and armaments are being purchased. For our part what can we do?'[6]

The arrival of mails from Rio in December brought despatches written in October. From these Brant learnt of Pedro's Acclamation as Emperor. Fresh orders also instructed him to send arms and naval stores with all haste, and to buy the two ships offered by Thompson. To Brant's anguish, this last task proved impossible, but the Government's anxiety to strengthen its naval forces was now clear, and after 'suffering a thousand torments in [my] imagination to discover the means of sending at least officers and sailors to man the vessels of our navy', he decided to take the bull by the horns and begin recruiting – although he lacked the confidence to raise 600, he aimed initially at half that number. On Boxing Day 1822 Brant appointed a compatriot, Antônio Meirelles Sobrinho, as Vice-Consul in Liverpool where he hoped to find the bulk of the men. Meirelles was told to offer £2.60 (13 milreis) a month, a figure which compared favourably with the £1.60 paid to Able Seamen in the Royal Navy, and ordered to raise 150 sailors as speedily and secretly as possible. In London, Brant used his old contact James Thompson. Thompson was appointed as captain-of-frigate, and authorized to find 50 men and five junior officers. Orders for the recruitment of another 100 men were also sent to an agent in Le Havre.

Recruitment in France was a non-starter, but in Liverpool there was no problem, and within a fortnight Meirelles was reporting success to a well-pleased Brant. Thompson, too, had no difficulty in finding men. There were enough hardy souls ready to exchange the chilling fogs of the Pool of London in winter for service in the sun, good pay, and the prospects of prize money. Neither was it difficult to engage a group of officers. The Royal Navy was in the depths of the depression which had followed the Napoleonic Wars, and had only 134 ships at sea compared with the 713 which had been in commission in 1813. Thus, when Brant began his recruiting efforts, 88 per cent of the 5450 officers in the Navy List were without employment. There were more than 3000 lieutenants on halfpay, and many more midshipmen and master's mates without even this compensation. Among these thousands it was not difficult to find half a dozen eager for the prospects of action and promotion offered by a foreign war.

The pay scales of the Brazilian Navy were not generous: £8 a month for lieutenants and £5 for sublieutenants were only two-thirds of the rates paid in the Royal Navy, but the comparison meant little to men who had long since abandoned hope of serving again under the British flag. And the contracts offered by the Brazilian Agent were attractive. Each officer was to sign on for five years; if at the end of that time he remained in the service he would receive an extra 50 per cent on top of his normal salary; if he returned to Britain he would receive Brazilian halfpay for the rest of his life. Free passages were provided, and pay was to begin from the date of embarkation.[7] By 12 January 1823, Thompson's officers had been formally engaged. All had served in the Royal Navy. Brant reported that James Thompson had been promoted lieutenant as long ago as 1804, and had received the thanks of the Admiralty for his capture of the *Mathilde* when he was in command of the *Lion* in 1813. Of the others, Vincent Crofton, Samuel Chester, Francis Clare and Richard Phibbs had been midshipmen and became lieutenants. The last, Benjamin Kelmare, had been a lieutenant and had later served with Cochrane in Chile, where he had been wounded in the attack on the *Esmeralda*. He was commissioned as a commander.

The recruiting exercise was a complete success, and was conducted with all the secrecy needed to escape the attentions of the British authorities and the hostile scrutiny of the Portuguese consuls. To avoid detection under the Foreign Enlistment Act of 1819, Brant maintained the fiction that the recruits were free settlers emigrating to Brazil to follow honest occupations on the land. In official documents the seamen were described as 'labourers' and the officers as 'overseers'. Within two weeks the men were ready and the ships chartered. On 27 January 1823, the merchantman *Lindsays* sailed from Liverpool with the first party of 125 men and six officers. Three days later the *Lapwing* left the Pool of London with the second group of 45 salty migrants. Brant reported his efforts with satisfaction. The cost of the recruitment in London had been reasonable, and the men had accepted monthly pay of only £2. But in Liverpool, the 'perfidious' Meirelles had ignored his instructions and had not only offered minimum pay of £5.50 a month but, disregarding the need for secrecy, had 'criminally and unnecessarily' signed a contract to that effect! Brant reported hotly that on being reprimanded on the excessive pay offer, the Vice-Consul had merely retorted that when the men were in Rio, the Government could pay what it liked. On the matter of the contract, Brant could only 'hope to God that the Portuguese do not discover it lest they prosecute us!'[8] In the procurement of arms and naval stores, he was just as successful. It was not easy to persuade suppliers to accept the risks involved in shipping illegal munitions to an area officially in rebellion against the Portuguese crown, but with moral and financial support from the friendly firm of 'Freitas & Costa', he succeeded. By the end of December, supplies of cannon, muskets, powder and naval stores were being loaded into two ships. The first, the *Nancy*, sailed on 23 January 1823 bound for Gibraltar, where she was to wait for her consort before continuing the voyage to Brazil. The second sailed a fortnight later.

The news which began to arrive from the continent during the winter of 1822–23 was disturbing. The Holy Alliance was now determined to act against Spanish liberalism. In January 1823 the ambassadors of Russia, France and Prussia were withdrawn from Madrid, and Louis XVIII announced that a French army of 100,000 men was poised to invade in support of King Ferdinand. With absolutist rule restored in Spain, constitutional Portugal was the next obvious target; but the Côrtes seemed oblivious to the threat and continued its single-minded efforts to crush Brazil. On 16 February 1823, a third expedition of 11 transports escorted by the frigate *Pérola* sailed from the Tagus for Bahia carrying 1200 men and orders for a renewed offensive.

The packet from Rio which arrived on 3 February brought letters for Brant dating from November. One, from the Minister of Marine, ordered him to buy substantial quantities of much-needed cables and cordage. This presented little difficulty and Brant, rising from the sickbed to which he had been confined by his second London winter, completed the transaction quickly and sent the supplies to Rio in three ships: the *Elrick*, which sailed with the first consignment of 100 tons in April; the *Leghorn*, with the second in May; and the *George IV*, with the last in June. He also received orders to purchase four armed ships, but this time, although financial authority was given, it was impossible to find any finance house willing to advance funds. The implications of the order, however, were clear, and when Brant heard from an officer of HMS *Conway*, recently returned from Brazil, that the frigates in Rio were unable to sail due to a shortage of junior officers and men, he decided it was time to recruit a second contingent of sailors.

Through March and into April, Brant and Meirelles conducted a recruiting campaign as quick and as secret as before. Within six weeks they had found 265 seamen and 12 officers, all of whom had served in the Royal Navy. This time the officers were engaged through the agency of Captain James Norton, a 34-year-old officer of aristocratic connections who had fought in the Napoleonic Wars in the Royal Navy, and then served with the East India Company. In India he had married the widow of Colonel Esme Erskine, a Waterloo veteran who was heir to Lord Erskine. Norton was commissioned as a captain-of-frigate while five of his companions – John Rogers Gleddon, George Clarence, Charles Mosselyn, Samuel Gillett and Raphael Wright – became lieutenants. The rest – Duncan Macreights, George Broom, George Cowan, Ambrose Challes, Charles Watson and William George Inglis – were appointed as sublieutenants. As well as officers and seamen, the recruits included master's mates, petty officers, boatswains, and 25 young men who signed on as volunteers in the hope of eventually gaining promotion to the quarterdeck. One of them, appointed as a midshipman, was José Fitzcosten, the young illegitimate son of General Brant's confidant, the editor of the *Correio Brasiliense*. These hopefuls were not disappointed. Within six months, 12 of their number had been appointed sublieutenants.[9] The rest were promoted within a year.

On 12 April 1823 the first party of 102 seamen and two officers, under the command of Lieutenant Wright, sailed from Liverpool in the *Alice*. Eight officers followed, two in the packet *Montague* and six in the *Alexander*, which left from London with a cargo of spars on 20 April. The last group, comprising 145 men under the command of Norton, Lieutenant Gleddon and Naval Surgeon John Little, sailed from Liverpool for Brazil on 4 May in the *Mary*. Four months later Brant, too, was on his way to Rio de Janeiro in the August packet from Falmouth. In many ways his mission to London had been an outstanding success, notably in providing the military stores and the naval flesh and blood which his country needed to make its declaration of independence a reality. But his political discussions had been inconclusive. He was not party to the Government's current thinking and, indeed, had no plenary powers to negotiate. It was to remedy both defects that General Brant had been summoned to return.

CHAPTER 4

PREPARATIONS IN RIO

Back in Brazil, the strategic situation had hardly changed. In the south, the Portuguese remained firmly entrenched in Montevideo awaiting reinforcements. In October 1822 there had been a glimmer of hope when Dom Álvaro da Costa, depressed by his defiance of the Prince Regent and by the province's total adherence to the Imperial cause, had wearily indicated that he was prepared to follow in Avilez's footsteps and return with his men to Lisbon. But by the time David Jewitt arrived a month later in the *União* with eight warships and transports to take him there, the Portuguese commander had changed his mind. Urgent messages from Madeira de Melo had stiffened his sinews and strengthened his resolve. The Brazilian tactic of tempting him out was therefore replaced by a strict blockade to keep him in. It was on this occasion that the *Thesis* was lost to the Brazilians. As soon as Vice Admiral Rodrigo Lobo left his flagship to collect fresh orders from the *União*, Portuguese partisans promptly seized the frigate and handed it over to Dom Álvaro. It was small wonder that Lobo was quickly replaced by Captain Pedro Antônio Nunes.

In Bahia, the situation was swinging inexorably in the direction of Brazil. Under General Labatut, the Imperial Army had advanced on Salvador, established a strong point at Pirajá and taken a secure grip on the peninsula on which the city was built, thus cutting it off from supplies and provisions from the interior. By September 1822 the whole of the province was in Brazilian hands, including the rich and fertile island of Itaparica across the bay from Salvador. In October, Madeira de Melo launched a seaborne attack on the island to regain this vital supply route, but he was beaten off by the Imperial forces led by a flotilla of small boats under the command of Sublieutenant João de Oliveira Bottas. In November the Portuguese attacked Pirajá, the key to the Brazilian's besieging position, but were repulsed with heavy losses. In January 1823 they launched a massive amphibious attack on Itaparica once more. The Portuguese gained the beach, but in a mighty counterattack in which the whole population took up arms in the Brazilian cause, the invaders were steadily forced back and finally ejected. The island was illuminated for nights afterwards in celebration of the victory.

The position of the Portuguese in Salvador became daily more difficult. Brazilian military pressure and this succession of rebuffs sapped the morale of both troops and the seamen. Trade was at a standstill, the Custom House yielded no revenue, and despite substantial loans from resident Portuguese merchants, the financial resources of the city were strained to breaking point. Troops, sailors and dockyard workers went unpaid, confidence fell, and desertions to the enemy increased. Even senior members of the Government began to quit Salvador for the Brazilian lines.[1] One was the Intendant of Marine, Captain Tristão Pio dos Santos, who escaped just in time to avoid arrest for his Brazilian sympathies.

By this time the Imperial forces numbered over 10,000 men, and in appearance presented a microcosm of Brazilian society and military organization. At the core were 1500 regular troops of the line comprising a battalion of white Caçadores light infantry and the crack 'Henrique Dias' regiment of free blacks. They were supplemented by a host of local Bahian militia units, by contingents from Paraíba, Rio and – most significantly – Pernambuco, and by a fringe of more exotic formations which included Indians armed with bows and arrows and irregular horsemen clad in the leather gear of the vaqueiro. On the Portuguese side, Madeira de Melo commanded fewer than 5000 troops and militia, even with the reinforcements that had arrived from Lisbon in August and October. He was able to man the defences and launch the occasional sally against the besiegers only by using the seamen from the naval squadron which, as a result, was left almost idle at its anchorage. Madeira de Melo was a man of limited strategic vision, and without direct orders he did not dare to withdraw the sailors from their defensive role in order to strike a possibly decisive blow against Rio de Janeiro. Foreign observers, including Sir Thomas Hardy, the British commander, noted with surprise that despite the presence of a considerable naval squadron under Commodore Félix de Campos, Portuguese maritime strategy seemed to be entirely defensive, directed at carrying reinforcements or seeking supplies.[2] The position of the Portuguese forces was difficult, but while the sea routes remained open, they posed a considerable threat. The Brazilian Army was large in numbers, but it lacked the equipment to conduct a formal siege and could never have reduced Salvador by regular assault. On the other hand, Madeira de Melo's army was being continually reinforced from Lisbon, and it was clearly only a matter of time before the Portuguese naval squadron went on the offensive and attacked Rio de Janeiro.

The Brazilian Government was all too aware of the danger, and desperately deployed its slender forces so as to contain the Portuguese in Montevideo while increasing the pressure on Salvador. On 28 January 1823, reinforcements had been rushed from Rio to Bahia in the form of military stores and 700 picked troops of the 'Emperor' battalion of the Brazilian Army under Colonel José Joaquim de Lima e Silva. The naval escort was commanded by David Jewitt in the *Piranga*, and consisted of every major warship in commission and every available seaman in the Brazilian service. To preserve total secrecy an embargo had been placed on all sailings from Rio a week before Jewitt's departure, and when the British corvette *Beaver*, assuming that the ban applied only to merchant ships, attempted to leave, she was promptly fired on by the forts guarding the harbour. After diplomatic intervention the ship was permitted to sail, but angry protests from the British Government over the insult to its flag continued for eighteen months.[3]

By the time Jewitt's force was safely back in Rio de Janeiro in the middle of March, the pieces making up the new Brazilian Navy were beginning to fall into place. Under Cunha Moreira's firm direction, the administrative departments were working as effectively as their leisurely traditions and cumbrous structures would allow. The inefficient and the idle were swiftly dealt with. Every Saturday, the Chief Secretary was required to furnish the names of any clerk or employee who had absented himself without due cause, or had failed to work the specified number of hours. From the Ministry of Marine flowed a steady succession of orders covering all the minutiae of naval administration. Decrees were issued dealing with the survey, the purchase and the victualling of ships; and with medals, pensions and promises of half pay for the dependants of those killed fighting in their country's defence. Pay scales for seamen and boys were advertised, and a recruiting campaign was launched, backed by promise of generous bounties. The rates of pay for petty officers, boatswains, carpenters and sailmakers were increased. The first register of officers in the Imperial Navy was established, and those who were inactive or over-age were officially retired. At the same time, Brazilians all over the country were rushing loyally to contribute to the National Subscription for the Navy. As an extra incentive, the organizers carefully listed the names of subscribers and the size of their donations in the *Diário do Governo* so that the extent of their patriotism would be known. Soon seven contos of reis (£1400) were flowing into the coffers of the fund regularly every month. The merchants of Rio provided 100 contos (£20,000); those of Porto Alegre, 7343 milreis (£1446); and the citizens of Villa de Campos undertook to build a brig-of-war for the Imperial Service. Those who could not give cash contributed in kind: some gave dried meat, some casks of vinegar or wine, others offered their slaves for service as seamen.

Throughout the crushing heat of the Brazilian summer the dockyard toiled to refit, repair and provision the ships that would give the Navy its teeth. Within six months of Pedro's dramatic declaration at the Ypiranga stream, the number of guns and warships at the disposal of Brazil had more than doubled. By March 1823, 28 vessels were ready or being commissioned:

Ship	Guns	Details
Pedro I	74	Former Portuguese *Martim de Freitas*. Built Bahia 1762 as a 64-gun ship. Refitted in Rio and renamed 14 January 1823: 28 × 32-pounders on the lower gun deck, 28 × 18-pdrs on the main deck. 1600 tons.
Frigates		
Piranga	62	Built Bahia 1817. Ex-*União*. 1500 tons, 28 × 24-pdr main-deck guns.

Real Carolina	44	Built Damão, East Indies, of teak 1819. 1108 tons: 24 × 18-pdr main-deck guns. Renamed *Paraguassú* 17 May 1823.
Niterói	38	Built Lisbon as the *Sucesso*. 1818. Refitted and renamed 25 January 1823. 22 × 12-pdr main-deck guns.
Thesis	44	Immobilized in Montevideo.

CORVETTES

Maria da Glória	26	Originally the *Horatii*, built for Chile in the USA. Bought in August 1819 for 64 contos of reis (£12,800). 540 tons. 24-pdr carronades.
Liberal	20	Built Lisbon 1791 as the *Gaivota*. Refitted Rio 1822. 450 tons.
Maceió	20	Building in Alagoas. Completed October 1823.

BRIGS-OF-WAR

Cacique	16	Ex-Portuguese *Reino Unido*. Repairing in Rio.
Real Pedro	14	Ex-Portuguese. Stationed off Montevideo.
Caboclo	18	Ex-*Maipú*, purchased by the Emperor for 22 contos of reis (£4400) on 12 February 1823 and presented to the nation.
Guarani	14	Ex-British merchantman *Nightingale*. Purchased in March 1823 for 13 contos of reis (£2600).

BRIGANTINES

Real	10	Ex-Portuguese. In Rio.
Atlanta	10	Purchased by Labutut in Bahia for 5.5 contos of reis (£1100).
Rio da Plata	10	Purchased by Laguna in Montevideo.
Independência ou Morte	10	Ex-Portuguese. At Pernambuco.

Leopoldina	10	Ex-Portuguese.

SCHOONERS

Stationed at the Plate and the Uruguay:
Dom Álvaro da Costa, Luis de Camões, Cossaka, Seis de Fevereiro, Isabela Maria, Maria Isabela, Oriental

Stationed at Rio and the North:
Carolina, Catarina, Maria da Glória, Maria Zeferina, Maria Francisca

GUNBOATS, FIRESHIPS, TRANSPORTS   20

The Brazilian Government had reason to feel satisfied with what had been achieved so far, but even at the eleventh hour, the success of its efforts was threatened by a looming manpower crisis. By stripping the smaller vessels it could supply the major ones with minimal crews; but the spectre of Delamare's voyage was a continual reminder of the unreliability and mutinous disposition of the Portuguese seamen on which Brazil was still dependent. And in spite of all the government's efforts, recruiting was going badly. Few Brazilians had any knowledge of the sea, and those who volunteered were the riffraff of the waterfront.

The authorities began to resort to desperate measures. Fifty convicts on the prison ship were pardoned and sent to the warships as seamen or marines, a special order permitted slaves to serve as sailors,[4] and the press gangs began to haunt the dockside taverns, snapping up seamen of any nationality. Prompt action by the foreign consuls in Rio secured the release of most of their nationals, but a few were unlucky and a number even succumbed to the inducements offered by the Brazilians to desert their ships for the Imperial service.[5] In early March, the Government raised the pay of Able and Ordinary Seamen to 10 milreis (£2) and 8 milreis (£1.60) respectively, but volunteers continued to be few. And where was Lord Cochrane? His favourable reply to the Brazilian offer was known, but with further Portuguese reinforcements on the way, his arrival could not come too soon for the Imperial Government.

At last, early in March, a ship from the Plate brought the

long-awaited news that Cochrane had left Valparaiso on 12 January and was on his way. The Government received the news with relief and satisfaction, and excitement began to mount. In the British Consulate-General, Henry Chamberlain reported the development to Canning, adding: 'there is no doubt that his Lordship's Talents and Enterprise will be of incalculable Advantage to the Brazilian Navy at this critical juncture; his name alone is a tower of strength', and asking (in code) how he should behave towards the admiral when he arrived.[6] At last, on 13 March 1823, on a cloudy morning amid pouring rain, the brig *Colonel Allen*, carrying Cochrane, his secretary William Jackson, and four officers who had served with him in Chile, sailed into the Bay of Guanabara. The Port Captain's representative came over the side, but on learning the identity of the passengers he became so excited that he leapt back into his boat, shouted to Captain Hayden that he could anchor where he liked, and was rowed ashore to spread the good news. Captains Taylor and Garção of the *Niterói* and *Liberal* went aboard immediately to greet Lord Cochrane and give him details of the Navy's state of preparedness. That same afternoon, Cochrane and his flag captain, Thomas Sackville Crosbie, were taken ashore to the residence of the Chief Minister to see José Bonifácio and the Emperor himself, who had leapt into the saddle and sped over from the Palace of São Cristovão on hearing the news. The discussion was cordial, and Cochrane returned to the ship later that evening much pleased with his reception.

On 15 March, Cochrane rose early to accompany the Emperor on an inspection of the ships-of-war in the harbour. At first sight, he was well satisfied with the condition and readiness of the squadron. The *Pedro I* particularly caught his eye: it had received a thorough refit and contained all the requirements of a flagship, including a handsome panelled stern cabin upholstered in green morocco leather. The next-largest ship, the *Piranga*, was a modern frigate of the largest size, with 24-pounder guns on her main deck; while the American-built *Maria da Glória* was clearly designed for speed, and could deliver a devastating punch at short range with its 24-pounder carronades. These and other vessels were ready for sea, with three months' supply of stores loaded on board. Cochrane was impressed with the physical condition of the ships, but he was also forcibly struck by the poor quality of the sailors and the general lack of discipline. All the captains complained of the difficulty of finding men for their ships and, as Cochrane noted with surprise, the great majority were Portuguese – nationals of the enemy! He was also puzzled to hear that in the Emperor's speeches to the men, the enemy were described as the 'Portuguese parliamentary forces', as if to imply that it was the Côrtes, not the King or the nation, against which Brazil was fighting.

The following day, 17 March, Cochrane visited the Minister of Marine to settle the details of his appointment as commander-in-chief. The interview began with an exchange of compliments and congratulations and remained amicable until Cunha Moreira, turning to the matter in hand, offered Cochrane the highest rank in the Brazilian service – that of Admiral. To the Minister's consternation, the offer was flatly refused. As soon became evident, the objection was based solely on financial considerations for, as Cochrane was fully aware, the 'embarked' pay of a Portuguese Admiral was only 400 milreis (£80) a month. This figure compared poorly with the £140 paid to a British Admiral, and was less than half of Cochrane's pay in the Chilean service. Cochrane pointed out bluntly that the invitation that had brought him to Brazil had guaranteed at least the same 'advantages' as he had received in Chile, and made it clear that he would serve for no lower salary. Cunha Moreira protested that the Empire would naturally live up to its obligations and, after some haggling over the exchange rate, agreed to Cochrane's condition that his pay should be the same as he had received in Chile. It was also agreed that the officers who had accompanied the Admiral from Valparaiso should be commissioned into the Brazilian service and appointed to the *Pedro I*, Crosbie in command as Captain-of-Frigate, the others – John Pascoe Grenfell, James Shepherd and Steven Clewley – as lieutenants.

With all the urgency demanded by the situation, Cochrane's letter of appointment was hastily prepared, and delivered on 19 March. As requested, the salary and command pay were spelt out precisely, but unfortunately the clerk who had drawn up the document had assumed that the full salary would be paid only during periods at sea, and that half pay would otherwise be the norm.

The letter was indignantly returned for correction. Even then the difficulties were not over. Cochrane suddenly realized that his appointment would naturally place him at the bottom of the list of Admirals, and would not give him the supreme authority he had expected. Cunha Moreira tried to overcome the new problem by pointing out that although Cochrane would in theory be third in seniority, he would have untrammelled tactical command, since one of his seniors, Pinto Guedes, held an important administrative post as Head of the Supreme Military Council, while the other, the Barão de Bagé, was over 80 and had been in effective retirement for years. But Cochrane was adamant: his experience of politics and his naturally suspicious nature had made him wary of verbal undertakings, and he declared that he would serve only if he was given clear overall authority.

Things were now beyond the competence of the Minister of Marine, and a Cabinet meeting was required to solve the problem. But Brazil's need was great. The Government quickly agreed to Cochrane's demands, and decided to create the new and unique rank (and pay) of First Admiral. The news of the concession was conveyed in person by José Bonifácio, who urged him to accept the appointment and to take command without delay.[7] His terms now satisfied, Cochrane concurred, and at 4 p.m. on 21 March 1823, amid the thunder of gun salutes, he hoisted his flag in the *Pedro I*, taking command of the *Piranga, Real Carolina, Niterói, Guarani, Maria da Glória, Liberal, Leopoldina* and *Real*. The same day his commission was issued:

> Being well known the valour, intelligence, activity and other qualities that are to be found in Admiral Lord Cochrane, which have been demonstrated in the different services with which he has been charged, each of which has provided proofs of the greatest bravery and daring. And acknowledging that it is to the advantage of the Empire to profit from the recognized worth of such a distinguished officer: it is judged well to confer upon him the patent of First Admiral of the National and Imperial Navy receiving an annual salary of 11,520 milreis [£2304] whether on land or sea, and in addition receiving a subsistence allowance of 5770 milreis [£1154] when embarked, being the same emoluments as he received when in Chile; no other Admiral in the Navy having the right to occupy the post ... which is created uniquely on this occasion from the particular consideration of the above mentioned Admiral Lord Cochrane.[8]

In other words, he was to be paid three times as much as any other Brazilian flag officer and almost £500 a year more than even a British Admiral commanding-in-chief!

While Cochrane was negotiating these highly favourable terms of service, the final stroke of good fortune needed to solve the manpower problem was dealt. On 18 March, in the nick of time, a sea-stained *Lapwing* sailed into harbour after a fast 45-day passage from London, followed a week later by the *Lindsays*. Between them the two ships carried 170 vitally needed British sailors. The crews of the warships were immediately reshuffled, and the British seamen allocated to the more powerful vessels of the squadron. The *Pedro I* received 80, the *Piranga* 33, the *Niterói* 24; the rest went to the *Real Carolina* and the smaller ships. The men were read-in, paid their rum money, and then allowed ashore for the first time in six weeks. In the manner of British seamen, within a few hours amid all the pleasures of a foreign port, the majority were gloriously drunk. When some officers complained to the Empress, it is said that she laughed and said 'Oh, 'tis the custom of the north where brave men come from. The sailors are under my protection; I spread my mantle over them!'[9]

Grateful as it was for the men, the Government was surprised by the arrival of the officers, who had been expected only if the negotiations over Thompson's warships had been successful. But now that they had arrived, the Brazilians were only too pleased to put their ships into hands which were both experienced and reliable. James Thompson was given command of the *Real Carolina*, with Benjamin Kelmare as his first officer. Lieutenants Chester and Clare were posted to the *Niterói* under John Taylor, and Lieutenant Crofton was appointed first to the fireship *Luiza*, then to the *Guarani*. Richard Phibbs was found medically unfit but was replaced by one of the mates of the *Lapwing*, James Nichol, who went to the *Piranga* as a lieutenant. William Parker, one of the mates of the *Lindsays*, also volunteered, and was posted to the *Pedro I* as a midshipman.[10]

By this time the harbour was crammed with shipping unable to leave because of the embargo which had been imposed to suppress news of Cochrane's arrival, and the dockyard was abustle with last-minute preparations for putting to sea. With the last of the stores and water now being loaded on board, the Brazilian Navy was at last ready to take the offensive, and on 29 March 1823 the coast of Bahia was declared to be in a state of blockade.

The same day, HMS *Tartar* arrived from England bearing news, none of it good. Captain Brown reported that at sea he had met a powerful Portuguese squadron taking reinforcements to Bahia. He also had to tell the hapless Lord Cochrane that his wife, unaware of the Brazilian turn to the Admiral's career, had sailed from England for Chile in the merchantman *Sesostris* accompanied by their little daughter Elizabeth and a bevy of servants. It looked as if they would have to endure two stormy passages round Cape Horn before the family could be reunited.

But there was no time to brood. Next morning, Cochrane received his orders. He was to make sail for Salvador the following day and 'put that port under rigorous blockade, destroying or taking all Portuguese forces he may fall in with, and doing all possible damage to the enemies of the Empire'. The order concluded: 'It remains at the discretion of the First Admiral to work by all convenient means against the forces of the enemy in order to save that city from those who are foes of the Brazilian cause, co-operating in this aim with the forces of General Labatut, commander of the Army of the Reconcavo, in the successful achievement of this end to the glory of our National and Imperial Arms.'[11]

On 1 April, the squadron set forth on an adventure which was to decide the Independence of Brazil. The race for the command of the seas had been won – but only just in time, for on the same day on which Cochrane was given his instructions, the Portuguese commanders in Salvador received orders to take the offensive and attack Rio de Janeiro. But the Portuguese move had come too late. The Brazilian Navy was at sea, and ready to seize the initiative.

CHAPTER 5

THE BLOCKADE OF BAHIA

The first day of April 1823 dawned grey and cloudy. The crews of the Brazilian squadron had been working since 4 a.m. so that the expedition could sail on the morning tide. At 5.30 Lord Cochrane boarded the flagship, to be joined an hour later by the Emperor and the Empress. At 7.30 the signal for departure was hoisted, the squadron weighed anchor, and one by one the ships gathered way for the mouth of the bay. In the lead went the 74-gun *Pedro I*, commanded by Captain Thomas Sackville Crosbie, flying Cochrane's flag and the Imperial Standard, followed closely by the frigate *Piranga* (Captain David Jewitt), the corvettes *Maria da Glória* under the command of a French officer, Teodoro de Beaurepaire, the *Liberal* (Commander Antônio Salema Freire Garção), and the brig-of-war *Guarani* (Commander Antônio Joaquim de Couto). Following in the rear came the smallest vessel, Sublieutenant Justino de Castro's brigantine *Real*.

As the flagship approached the mouth of the bay and began to exchange a 21-gun salute with the Fort of Santa Cruz guarding the entrance, the weather suddenly broke and the clouds lifted. To the crowd of patriots and onlookers who had risen early to witness the squadron's departure, the scene became dramatic as well as historic. Maria Graham, widow of one of the captains of the British South America Squadron who had met Cochrane and his companions in Chile and travelled with them to Rio de Janeiro *en route* for England, was inspired by the sight and thrilled by the percussions of the guns rolling among the hills. She confided in her Journal: 'as the fort began to salute, the sun broke from behind a cloud and a bright yellow flood of light descended behind the ships to the sea where they seemed to swim in a sea of glory'.[1] By

45

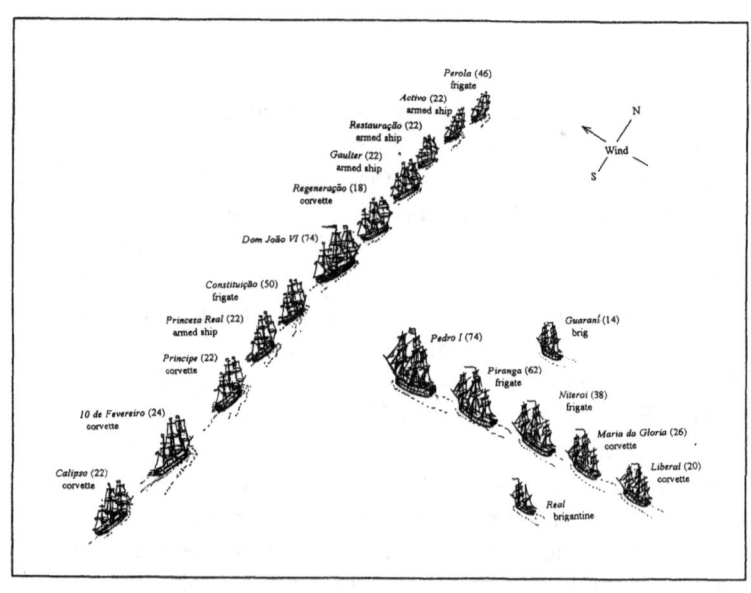

THE BATTLE OF 4 MAY 1823

The position at noon, 30 miles south-east of Salvador: the Portuguese sailing north on the starboard tack; the Brazilians, led by Cochrane in the *Pedro I*, heading west with the intention of breaking their line and isolating the last four ships.

9 a.m., the *Pedro I* had reached Round Island through the entrance to the bay. There, amid more salutes, the Imperial Party boarded the State Barge to return to Rio, the Emperor standing in the sternsheets to acknowledge the cheers of each ship's company as it passed. An hour later, the ceremonial concluded, Cochrane rallied his ships and sailed eastward to their first rendezvous.

The following day, the squadron anchored off the Maricá Islands to wait for the *Guarani*, which had remained off the Fort of Santa Cruz waiting for Lieutenants Shepherd and Grenfell, who had experienced last-minute bureaucratic difficulties with their commissions. But the time was not wasted. The last frenzied week in Rio dockyard had left most of the ships dirty and disorganized – decks and cabins were strewn with gear and stores, the landsmen were bewildered with shipboard life and the seamen weak after the excesses of their last night in port. The stay off the Maricás provided a welcome opportunity to sort out the muddle. As Cochrane explained in his first letter, dated 2 April, the delay was unfortunate, but his ships were approaching the state of efficiency expected of men-of-war, 'the indispensable duty of stationing and quartering the men had been effected, the English seamen have got sober and things on board are going well'.[2] The following day, the *Real* was sent back with messages of impatience, and that afternoon the *Guarani* appeared with the missing lieutenants. Now complete, the squadron weighed anchor and began the first leg of its sortie against Portuguese-occupied Bahia.

With Cochrane safely on his way, the Brazilian Government relaxed its embargo on departures. On 4 April, HMS *Tartar* continued its voyage to Salvador with despatches for the British commander-in-chief, Sir Thomas Hardy, and two days later all restrictions on the departure of merchantmen were lifted. Vessels of all kinds poured out of the bay – coastal smacks, deep-sea merchantmen, convict ships, transports and packets – all carrying goods, passengers and news of the Brazilian offensive to the four corners of the globe. Work in the dockyard redoubled. On 12 April Taylor's frigate *Niterói* was ready, and sailed to join Cochrane's squadron carrying munitions, rockets and mortars. On board as a passenger was Captain Pio dos Santos, on his way back to Bahia to resume his old post as Intendant of Marine following the liberation of Salvador. A week later the 10-gun brigantine *Leopoldina* left Rio de Janeiro for Cochrane's northern rendezvous convoying the fireships *Luiza* and *Catarina*.

For the first week the squadron made a broad sweep into the Atlantic to avoid adverse winds and the hazards of the Abrolhos Shoal before steering north for the coast of Bahia. As the voyage progressed, Cochrane; at his most affable, used the social life of the flagship as a means of discreetly assessing the merits and personalities of his officers. He was a regular visitor to the wardroom, and frequently invited his subordinates to dine with him in pairs in the great cabin of the *Pedro I*. The same invitation was extended to the captains of the other vessels of the squadron. One by one, each was rowed over to the flagship so that Cochrane could size him up and convey his ideas on tactics – the idea being that in action his intentions would be understood with the minimum of signals and the least chance of misunderstanding. Life was also becoming more congenial for the officers. Their cabins were at last cleared of the stores which had littered them since the beginning of the voyage, and it was agreed that the Brazilian and British officers should share a common mess – an arrangement which was not only economical but helped to create an atmosphere of harmony and comradeship.

At the same time, the captains, by regular drill, slowly welded their motley crews into a semblance of unity. The task was not easy: most ships' companies consisted of Englishmen who spoke no Portuguese, Brazilian landsmen who were ignorant of the sea, and sullen Portuguese. The Brazilian marines were no better. Most were freed slaves who were now too proud to clean their quarters and were ignorant of both small arms and the workings of the ships' guns. On the twelfth day of the voyage, the slings of the flagship's lower yards were reinforced with iron chains and Cochrane introduced the first gun drill. For the next three weeks the crews were turned out daily to go through the motions of running out, firing, sponging and reloading until they became instinctive – only automatic drill could keep the ordnance in action amid the din and confusion of battle. The guns themselves were without flintlocks and had to be fired by the old-fashioned method of igniting the touchholes with a linstock. This was less efficient, but it seemed unlikely that the enemy were any better off. While the gun crews toiled, the boatswains and sailmakers refurbished the squadron's stores, most of which were of inferior quality and had lain neglected in the arsenal for years. Little could be done for spars and rigging, but the sails were patched and repaired, and new cartridges were manufactured from spare flags to replace the dangerous canvas ones supplied.

In manoeuvring the squadron, speed was Cochrane's greatest problem. The American-built *Maria da Glória* and the *Pedro I* both proved to be fast vessels, the latter remarkably so for a ship of her size. But the *Piranga* and *Liberal* were slow and heavy sailors, and the sturdy build which had made the *Guarani* suitable for carrying artillery also made her slow and cumbersome. As soon as the voyage began, the differences in speed revealed themselves, and by the third day out the *Liberal* and *Guarani* had fallen so far behind that the squadron had to heave-to and wait. Separation under these circumstances was inevitable, and dawn broke on 22 April to reveal no sign of the *Liberal, Guarani* or *Real*. The corvette and the brigantine caught up later, but it was three days before the *Guarani* finally reappeared, sailing in company with the frigate *Niterói*. The brig had lost her main topmast in her frantic efforts to catch up, but fortunately the *Niterói* in search of the squadron, had discovered the *Guarani* and assisted in repairs at sea.

The squadron was now within striking distance of Bahia. Cochrane spent 25 April exercising his ships by signal, then made his final dispositions: cutlasses, pistols and pikes were issued to the crews, the extra munitions carried by the *Niterói* were transferred, and the *Real* was converted into a fireship. He also took his first prize, a smack carrying flour and beans to the Portuguese garrison in Salvador. On 3 May the coast of Bahia at last came into sight as a purple smear on the distant horizon. The squadron immediately stood out to sea again, and maintained course until nightfall under easy sail and in order of battle. Cochrane's movement was designed to ensure that daybreak would find his ships approaching land with the prevailing easterly winds behind them. If any hostile force were encountered, he would have the weather gauge and all that went with it: he would be able to select the time and place of any engagement, and attack whatever point in his opponent's line he chose. For a numerically inferior squadron, determined to force a result and confident of victory, Cochrane's tactics were classic.

For the Portuguese besieged in Salvador, the month of March ended on a refreshing note of hope. On the 29th the frigate *Pérola*, with a convoy of 10 transports carrying 1800 troops from Lisbon, had dropped anchor in the Bay of Bahia. This addition to Brigadier Madeira de Melo's strength was too small to make a profound difference to the stalemate which existed between the two sides, but it did mean that the sailors manning the defences could now be replaced, and the fleet which had lain in semi-idleness for months used for offensive action. Indeed, the *Pérola* carried despatches ordering Madeira de Melo to send an expedition to Montevideo in order to transfer the Portuguese forces blockaded there to Salvador, while at the same time putting a stop to the Brazilian rebellion once and for all by clamping a blockade on Rio de Janeiro.

The new instructions were at variance with the original orders given to Commodore Félix de Campos, so on 4 April the naval commanders held a Council of War to reconcile the two and prepare a plan of action. As a result, Félix de Campos wrote to Madeira de Melo later the same day proposing an immediate attack on Rio de Janeiro and asking that the necessary pay, stores and rations should be gathered. The plan was for a blockade of the Brazilian capital by the *Dom João VI* and a flotilla of smaller vessels, while the brig-of-war *Audaz* and a corvette proceeded to Montevideo to embark the troops. On 5 April Félix de Campos, whose relations with the military commander were becoming increasingly strained, wrote again. He had changed his mind and now doubted whether it was wise to leave Salvador undefended against a Brazilian seaborne attack by removing the fleet in this way. Madeira de Melo, however, stood firm, stressed the imperative nature of the new orders, and began to assemble transports, stores and munitions. Félix de Campos was promptly stricken with a fever, and his second-in-command, Captain Vasconcellos of the *Pérola*, assumed responsibility for preparing the expedition. But the Portuguese offensive had come too late. On 19 April, HMS *Tartar* sailed into the bay with despatches for Commodore Hardy and news of events in Rio. The news spread rapidly – the arrival of Cochrane and the British sailors, the order to blockade Bahia, the size and strength of the Brazilian squadron. Thoughts of a Portuguese offensive disappeared and Félix de Campos, now recovered, resumed command.

Morale in Salvador nevertheless remained high, and the *Gazeta da Bahia*, remembering perhaps the fate of the Delamare expedition, exuded confidence. In no. 65, it derided and belittled Cochrane's reputation, and concluded complacently: 'our squadron is superior in physical force, at its head are brave officers and an abundance of troops and it is commanded by an admiral with victory within his grasp. We are confident of a happy outcome.' As an extra incentive the merchants promised medals and bonuses for the victorious fleet on its return. There seemed to be good reason for this optimism: the Portuguese squadron now consisted of one ship-of-the-line, two frigates, four corvettes, six armed-ships and two scouting vessels mounting between them 380 cannon. Against them, the Brazilians had sent five ships, poorly fitted, poorly manned and mounting only 234 guns. But even if Madeira de Melo shared the general optimism, he believed in making victory doubly sure in the face of an opponent of Cochrane's legendary reputation. On 22 April, through Vice-Consul Follett, he wrote to Sir Thomas Hardy requesting, in terms of the Anglo–Portuguese Defensive Alliance, the help of the British South America Squadron against the Brazilian force. At this time there were four ships of the Royal Navy in Salvador harbour: HM Ships *Doris*, *Tartar*, *Fly* and *Beaver*. Hardy considered the request, but politely declined to intervene.[3]

The Portuguese sailed on 29 April. Two days later, in the open sea, they began a north-to-south patrol as they awaited the appearance of the Brazilians. Dawn on 4 May found the Portuguese 30 miles south-east of Salvador sailing north in two columns, the windward led by the *Dom João VI*, the leeward by the *Pérola*. At 6 a.m., the Portuguese lookouts sighted suspicious vessels to the north-east. By 8 a.m., identification of the Brazilian squadron was certain, and Félix de Campos cleared for action and began to marshal his ships to receive the attack – the leeward column advanced, while the windward fell in behind to form one line sailing north on the starboard tack. At twelve o'clock the distance between the Portuguese ships was reduced to one-third of a cable.

As the two squadrons drew closer, excitement mounted in the Brazilian ships. Officers delivered patriotic speeches to their men, amid wild cheering. In his diary the flagship's chaplain, Father Manoel da Paixão e Dores, noted: 'I cannot omit to mention the enthusiasm of the crews at seeing his Lordship's determination to fall upon an enemy so superior ...; the officers could not have appeared more content if they had been going to a ball ... and the repeated cheers to victory were convincing proof of the valiant spirits with which all entered the battle.'[4]

By noon the squadrons were two miles apart – the Portuguese steering north, the Brazilians sailing west to intercept them. Cochrane, signalling 'Attack the centre and the rearguard,' bore down on the Portuguese with the intention of cutting their line at the eighth ship and overwhelming the four vessels in the rear before the van could intervene. As the squadrons converged, Captain Pereira de Sá of the *Princeza Real* saw that it was his ship which was the object of Cochrane's attack, and fired his starboard battery at the approaching two-decker. The *Pedro I* responded with a straggling broadside, and for a brisk ten minutes the ships exchanged fire, leaving two dozen casualties. Then, having unsuccessfully called on her opponent to surrender, the Brazilian flagship swept through the Portuguese line and disappeared in the smoke to leeward. The *Princeza Real* and the corvettes following her now came under the fire of the *Piranga* and *Niterói* which, lacking the speed to cut through the tight-knit enemy line, engaged the Portuguese from windward: only the *Pedro I* had managed to break through their formation.[5]

But something was seriously wrong with the Brazilian flagship. A well-drilled two-decker would have left the *Princeza Real* a shattered wreck: apart from cutting up her rigging and lesser masts, the *Pedro I* left her scarcely damaged. After the action, the Portuguese captain reported that his casualties after being engaged by both the *Pedro I* and the *Piranga* were 'two dead and fifteen wounded of which three are likely to die'. His report on the *Pedro I*'s movements was equally telling:

> Seeing that the two-decker at the head of their column continued to advance with the intention of crossing my stern, I called for cheers for the Constitution and gave the order to open fire. Seeing my determination she increased her speed to remain in company with me and then, less than a pistol shot away, directed a terrible fire of artillery at us, using ball, grapeshot and musketry, to which we replied with alacrity. The enemy ship, wanting then to free itself from our attentions began to forge ahead with the intention of passing in front of me – which I attempted to prevent, firing into her with the starboard battery

until, due to superior speed, she gained sufficient distance to cross my bows.... Immediately I fired into her with the port battery, to which there was no reply, perhaps because her guns were not loaded. Judging by the many voices that could be heard, I should think that great confusion was reigning on board.[6]

Captain Pereira de Sá was right. Under the strain of action, not only had the newly acquired proficiency with the guns crumbled, but Portuguese elements in the *Pedro I*'s crew were deliberately hampering the flagship's efforts. At one stage in the battle, two Portuguese seamen prevented the supply of powder from the magazine until they were seized and dragged on deck by Lieutenant Grenfell. The same sentiment manifested itself in other ships. The crews of the *Liberal* and *Guarani* were so openly disaffected that their captains feared to take part in the action, and the captain of the *Real* reported that only luck had prevented his crew from turning his ship over to the enemy.

By nightfall, the position of the Brazilian squadron was critical. The *Pedro I*, *Piranga* and *Niterói* were still engaged with the enemy's rear, but the ships in the Portuguese van had now tacked and joined the action, outnumbering their opponents by three to one. An angry and disappointed Lord Cochrane decided on retreat and, giving the signal for withdrawal, retired in haste to the south. Félix de Campos, complacent and pleased with his victory, made a half-hearted attempt at pursuit. 'The squadron promptly gave chase,' he reported to Madeira de Melo, 'but it was with great disgust that I noticed that all of their ships were faster than ours, and because of this I was obliged to abandon the pursuit.'[7] Thus, a great opportunity was lost to the Portuguese. Lumbering in Cochrane's wake, the *Guarani*, *Real* and *Liberal* must surely have been captured if the chase had been prosecuted with vigour. But Félix de Campos did not have the vision to see the devastating effect such a reverse would have had on the retreating Brazilians, and allowed them to escape to fight another day.

The night which followed the battle was stormy, with heavy rain which prevented the counterattack which Cochrane was already planning. In view of the fighting efficiency of his ships and the unreliability of his crews, it was just as well that it did. And so, unmolested, the Brazilian squadron made for its rendezvous at the Morro de S. Paulo, a small and neglected harbour some thirty miles south of Salvador, while Cochrane wrote his despatches. In a long private letter to the Chief Minister, José Bonifácio, he gave vent to his feelings and listed at length the deficiencies of the force he commanded:

> From the defective sailing and manning of the squadron, it seems to me that the *Pedro I* is the only one that can assail the enemy's ships-of war, or act in the face of a superior force so as not to compromise the interest of the Empire and the character of the officers commanding. Even this ship is so ill-equipped as to be much less efficient than she could be ... our cartridges are all unfit for service ... the guns are without locks ... the sails of this ship are all rotten ... the head of the mortar I received on board was crushed on the first fire, being entirely rotten ... and the Portuguese sailors on board have been so prejudicial to the success of the expedition ... that to tell Your Excellency the truth, one half of the squadron is needed to watch the other half!

It was a devastating account, but Cochrane was not indulging in recriminations. He continued:

> I am aware of the difficulties under which a new government labours and am ready to do all in my power under the circumstances. What I would request of you, is that you will do me the justice to feel that the predicament in which I am now placed is somewhat analogous to your own and that if I cannot accomplish all I would wish the deficiency arises from causes beyond my control. [8]

Cochrane's official report was formal and factual, giving the bare outline of the action and his plans for immediate reorganization. The battle had been a disappointment, but Cochrane was not beaten and, with typical resilience, was already planning his next move. If the squadron could not meet the Portuguese at sea, then he would blockade Salvador with his two fastest vessels manned by the pick of his crews, and rely on fireships to attack the enemy fleet.

On 8 May, the squadron anchored off the Morro, joining the brigantine *Leopoldina* and the fireships which had already arrived from Rio de Janeiro. Immediately Cochrane's reorganization was put into effect. All 180 British officers and men were embarked on the *Pedro I*, and the unreliable men in both the flagship and the *Maria da Glória* were replaced by sailors from the other vessels. The *Piranga*'s 24-pounder guns and 32-pounder carronades were then ferried over to the *Pedro I* and exchanged for the flagship's main-deck 18-pounders – an exercise involving the transfer of over 200 tons of artillery. At the same time, Cochrane made arrangements for a permanent water supply for the squadron, reinforced the three diminutive forts defending the harbour with a detachment of marines, and sent messengers to make contact with General Labatut and the Brazilian Army.

At dawn on 13 May, the *Pedro I* and *Maria da Glória* sailed to blockade Salvador, leaving the *Piranga*, *Niterói* and *Liberal* at anchor in the harbour and the *Guarani* on patrol outside. Appearing off the Bay of Bahia, Cochrane's two ships, ignoring the powerful Portuguese cruising to the eastward, began to snap up prizes. Within a fortnight, five vessels had been taken: the smack *Nova Constituição*, the slaver *Vigilante Guerreiro*, the brig *Amazonas* and two schooners, *John Thomas* and *Conceição*, carrying rice and flour to the Portuguese garrison. At the same time, the *Guarani* captured the schooner *União*, laden with honey and tobacco. On 24 May, the *Pedro I* reinforced the *Maria da Glória* with an extra 40 men and returned to the Morro for water and supplies. It had been a good start.

While Cochrane slowly tightened his grip on the sea routes to Salvador, the atmosphere in Rio de Janeiro was one of increasing confidence and expectation. News from Europe told of French troops poised to invade Spain in order to stamp out the dangerous contagion of liberalism, and rumours from Portugal talked of rising hostility to the Côrtes and the possibility of a royalist counter-revolution. Brazilians received the news with satisfaction – the absolutists welcoming the resurrection of Royal power, the patriots seeing the downfall of the Côrtes as removing the primary obstacle to Brazilian independence. Both hoped that the King's restoration to real power would lead to a settlement of the present conflict, with Brazil's separate status confirmed. There was cheering news, too, from the north, where the provinces of Piauí and Ceará had joined Pernambuco in declaring for the Empire.

On 3 May 1823, the long-awaited Brazilian Constituent Assembly was opened in Rio by the Emperor. In a great cavalcade headed by the regiments and bands of the Army, and made up of the high officers of state and the nobility, the Imperial couple processed through the city in a state coach drawn by eight mules. The streets through which they passed were lined with troops, strewn with evergreens and packed with enthusiastic crowds. Witnessing the spectacle from the balcony of a house belonging to a new Brazilian friend, Dona Ana Carvalho e Melo – wife of a Deputy for Bahia and future Foreign Minister – Maria Graham recorded the event in her Journal, noting that 'the houses were hung with all the damask and satin that they could supply, and the balconies stored with ladies whose bright eyes rain influence, dressed in gala dresses, with feathers and diamonds in profusion; and as the royal carriages passed, we waved our handkerchiefs and scattered flowers on their heads!' On arrival at the Assembly, the Emperor, wearing a great cape of yellow feathers over his gold-laced uniform, the Imperial crown before him and the Empress at his side, inaugurated proceedings with a defiant and triumphant speech from the throne.

In the evening the city was illuminated while the Emperor, together with members of the Assembly and the privileged public, attended a performance at the theatre. Maria Graham was present again, this time sitting modestly in mourning attire in the box of the Viscondessa de Rio Seco, whose own flamboyant outfit and jewels were said to be worth £150,000. The principal piece had little merit, but an additional item, entitled 'The Discovery of Brazil' and showing the arrival of the Portuguese and their first encounter with the native Indians, was rapturously received. And when, in a surprise climax, a 'genius' was cranked down from the ceiling carrying the Brazilian flag, the audience went wild with excitement. For his part, the Emperor was seen to turn pale, lean soulfully on the chair before him, then cover his face with his hand to conceal the depth of his emotion.

Meanwhile, under Cunha Moreira's firm direction, the Ministry of Marine concentrated its resources on supporting Cochrane's efforts at sea. On 12 May, the frigate *Real Carolina* sailed with two supply ships loaded with biscuit, rice, flour, vegetables and rum. Three weeks later the Dutch merchantman *Camillus* left for the Morro de S. Paulo with more supplies, to be followed in early June by the brigantine *Rio da Plata* and a storeship carrying firewood and water. At the same time, the National Subscription for the Navy continued to grow, reaching 33 contos of reis (£6600) by the beginning of June. The number of ships available for service also increased. In June, the brigantine *Atlanta* was ready for sea. In July work on the brig-of-war *Cacique* was completed, and the vessel was ordered south to reinforce the small Brazilian squadron watching Montevideo. The desperate shortage of munitions and cordage had also been relieved by the arrival on 22 April of the *Nancy* from London carrying the warlike stores purchased secretly by General Brant.

As May passed without news of Cochrane, the capital began to buzz with speculation. Correspondence in the *Diário do Governo* sought to interpret the contradictory stories of Portuguese manoeuvres and reinforcements brought by vessels arriving across the Atlantic. On 30 May, the *Diário* published a list of the United States Navy at the time of its independence, drawing the conclusion that if such a tiny force could defeat the might of Britain, then the Brazilian Navy could not fail to triumph. At last, on 13 June, the prize *Amazonas* sailed into the harbour with Cochrane's despatches. Their tone was one of disappointment. He had attacked the enemy but had been denied victory by poor ships, worse gunnery, disaffected Portuguese and clumsy landsmen. He had withdrawn to regroup and reorganize his forces before returning to the attack. To Cochrane the action had been a failure, because he was accustomed to so much more. To the Brazilians it seemed a success, because they were used to so much less. To them, five poorly equipped and manned vessels had attacked without flinching a Portuguese squadron of twice their strength, and had withdrawn only in the face of a superior concentration of force. Under Cochrane's audacious leadership, the Brazilian squadron – purged of disaffected elements, and reinforced – was seen clearly in Rio as being within sight of victory.

Cunha Moreira replied in cordial terms. Cochrane's proceedings were applauded; disaffected personnel were ordered to Rio de Janeiro under arrest; men and supplies were promised without delay. The Minister was as good as his word. On 13 June, the *Alice* reached Rio after a 62-day voyage from Liverpool carrying 102 British sailors and two officers. Lieutenant Wright and his men were promptly transferred to the *Colonel Allen* – after some slight hesitation by the Government, now purchased and commissioned as the brig-of-war *Bahia* – and sent off to the Morro de S. Paulo with letters authorizing Cochrane to distribute the seamen among the ships of the squadron, and to take Captain Hayden under his orders. A fortnight later, on 29 June, there was another windfall. The *Mary* sailed into the Bay of Guanabara with 148 more British sailors commanded by Captain James Norton and Lieutenants Gleddon, Sewell and Blakely. Forty men were retained in Rio to man the *Atlanta* and *Cacique*, but the others stayed aboard the *Mary*, which was turned round and sent off to reinforce Cochrane off Bahia. In the weeks which followed, the other eight officers arrived: three (Charles Watson, Ambrose Challes and George Cowan) followed their comrades northwards as passengers on the *Atlanta*, which sailed on 17 July under the command of Lieutenant Samuel Gillett.[9]

Cochrane's unexpected reappearance off the coast of Bahia reduced the Portuguese to despair. Salvador had been under siege by land for a year, and was now dependent on seaborne supplies. Disputes within the Brazilian land forces – which had eventually resulted in the ousting of General Labatut and the elevation of Colonel José de Lima e Silva as commander-in-chief – had in no way weakened their stranglehold on Portuguese land communications. Now, the naval blockade brought disaster. Trade was at a standstill, refugees were leaving in increasing numbers, and slaves were left to starve to death in the streets. Foodstuffs were in critically short supply – a chicken cost 4 milreis 800 (£1), a loaf of bread 240 reis, (5p). an egg 160 reis (3p). As the situation continued to deteriorate, the Portuguese squadron cruising before the port proved incapable of preventing Cochrane's seizure of vital supply ships. On 9 May, Madeira de Melo declared martial law and took over the civil government of Salvador. Ten days later he wrote to Commodore Félix de Campos in the strongest terms demanding action:

> We are now in the disgraceful situation of being blockaded when our own squadron is bigger than that of our enemies! And the worst thing is that if the enemy finds a favourable opportunity I am convinced that he will try to enter the port and burn some of our ships.... Your Excellency must therefore take measures to ensure that the poor situation in which we find ourselves does not become completely untenable.[10]

Among the merchants in the city, feeling against Félix de Campos rose to fever pitch, and he returned to harbour on 21 May to be met by a storm of abuse and a petition demanding his dismissal. Madeira de Melo was not sorry to oblige, but the squadron refused to put to sea without him in command, and the move to oust him failed. On 25 May, Félix de Campos sailed once more: this time with orders to attack the Morro de S. Paulo and destroy the fireships which Cochrane was known to be preparing.

The sight of the Portuguese advancing against their base caused the Brazilians considerable alarm. Its flimsy defences could never repel a force of such size, the *Pedro I* was busy watering and the frigates had been moved up river to a safe but harmless anchorage. Cochrane made what preparations he could, and waited for the worst. Fortunately, it never came. Félix de Campos cruised for two days before the harbour, then, deciding – inaccurately – that it was too strongly defended, returned to base. For a second time, the Brazilian squadron had been saved by Félix de Campos's caution. Astonished at his luck, Cochrane completed the watering of the *Pedro I*, then sailed to rejoin the *Maria da Glória* and the recently arrived *Real Carolina*, still blockading Salvador.

For the Portuguese, it was the beginning of the end. The Treasury was now exhausted, and unable to meet the demands on it for pay and provisions. A survey of foodstuffs in the city showed that there were enough provisions for only 50 days, and no hope of relief. On 10 June, Madeira de Melo reported on the situation to Lisbon in gloomy tones:

> The enemy squadron has paralysed all our plans for blockading Rio, bringing our forces from Montevideo and commencing a campaign in the Reconcavo. Only by carrying out such projects could we gain any advantage, and today it is impossible for us to undertake any useful offensive action.... The enemy squadron is cruising along the coast as far as the Morro de S. Paulo, a well-defended and naturally strong position..... In Rio de Janeiro they are repairing another ship-of-the-line, and the government there is convinced that the future of Brazil will be decided by naval power.... If they gain maritime supremacy over us, all is lost.[11]

Finally on 12 June, came the last straw. Just after dusk, the *Pedro I*, *Real Carolina* and *Maria da Glória* slipped silently into the Bay of Bahia on the last of the sea breeze. Cochrane's plan was a bold one. Posing, if challenged, as a British force from Rio, he intended to sail calmly down the line of anchored Portuguese warships, launch a surprise attack, then sail out again on the land breeze which blew regularly at night. At first all went well, but as the Brazilian ships came within striking distance, the sea breeze dropped and no land breeze arose to replace it. Windless in the middle of a hostile harbour, the Brazilians abandoned their objective, and with impeccable discipline, drifted out to sea with the tide. Fortunately, the darkness, the confusion and the absence of many Portuguese officers ashore, attending a ball, enabled the intruders to escape unscathed. But this additional proof of Cochrane's daring destroyed the last threads of Portuguese confidence. On 20 June, the commanders finally accepted the inevitability of evacuation: the civil authorities were warned, every available ship was requisitioned, and the removal of all munitions and stores began.

The abortive attack of 12 June reinforced Cochrane's conviction that fireships were his most effective weapon. Returning to the Morro, he wrote for detailed charts of the Bay of Bahia, ordered the *Piranga* to Rio for repairs, completed his conversion of the fireships, and narrowly escaped disaster when a fire discovered in the spirit room of the *Pedro I* was extinguished only just in time by a party led by Cochrane himself! Then, on 25 June, the *Maria da Glória* appeared over the horizon under full sail with messengers from the Brazilian Army carrying momentous news: the Portuguese were preparing to leave! Sending the corvette ahead, Cochrane immediately weighed anchor and sailed to join the *Real Carolina* on its blockading station. Arriving within sight of Salvador, he sent in messages warning civilians of the consequences of leaving under armed escort, and threatened the military commanders with reprisals should they attempt to land on any other part of Brazil. Then, having taken the fifteenth and final prize of the blockade – the brig *Visconde de S. Lourenço* – he settled down to wait and watch as the Portuguese warships slowly prepared themselves for sea.

Cochrane's problem in ensuring that the Portuguese were shepherded out of Brazilian waters and prevented from making a descent elsewhere on the coast lay in his shortage of crews and the poor condition of his ships. On 30 June, almost on the eve of the evacuation, his strength was reduced by one-third when the

Real Carolina lost its fore-topmast. James Thompson was ordered back to base, to return as soon as he had completed the necessary repairs. On board as he limped back to the Morro were Captain Taylor and the 80 British officers and men who had been transferred to the *Pedro I* from the *Niterói*. Taylor was to prepare his frigate for sea and rejoin Cochrane off Bahia so that the First Admiral could confront the Portuguese with at least four minimally manned warships.

But Lord Cochrane was in luck. In the nick of time, on 28 June, Bartholomew Hayden had anchored the *Bahia* at the Morro de S. Paulo after a lightning eight-day voyage from Rio. On board was Cochrane's erstwhile prize agent in Chile, Henry Dean, but also – more significantly – the 100 vitally needed British sailors whom Lieutenant Wright had brought from Liverpool in the *Alice*. The crews were immediately reshuffled, allowing the *Niterói*, the *Real Carolina* and the *Bahia* itself to be fully and reliably manned. On 1 July, repairs and reorganization completed, the three ships sailed to join Cochrane as he waited and watched.

He did not have to wait long. On 2 July 1823, the Portuguese finally evacuated Salvador in a massive convoy of 17 warships and over 75 merchantmen loaded with the contents of the dockyard, the arsenal and the warehouses. At noon the green-and-yellow flag of Brazil was hoisted on the forts by an advance guard of Imperial troops, and by nightfall the whole city had been peacefully occupied by the Brazilian Army. The war in Bahia was over.

CHAPTER 6

THE PURSUIT

While the Portuguese convoy laboriously assembled outside the Bay of Bahia, watched at a respectful distance by the *Pedro I*, Lord Cochrane attended to his correspondence. First he dictated his official report to the Minister of Marine: 'I have the satisfaction to acquaint Your Excellency, that the enemy have this day evacuated Bahia, their resources by sea being no longer available...'[1] Then he wrote to his wife, for HMS *Creole*, encountered at sea the day before, had delivered letters reporting that the *Sesostris* had put into Rio de Janeiro on 13 June. Lady Cochrane had been immediately incapacitated by an insect bite to her right hand, but British merchants Young and May, and Captain Robson himself, had all written to tell Cochrane the happy news. Rather than battling round Cape Horn on a false trail to Chile, Lady Cochrane and Elizabeth were sampling, with slight bewilderment, the social life of the Brazilian Court!

There were also letters to be written to friends and acquaintances. One was to Maria Graham, who had met Cochrane and his British officers in Chile, and got to know them well. She had even been one of their fellow passengers on the *Colonel Allen* on the voyage from Valparaiso. In addition to being the future author of *Little Arthur's History of England*, Mrs Graham was the daughter of a Royal Navy Dockyard Commissioner, and widow of the captain of HMS *Doris*, who had died in Chile. As such, her naval knowledge was impeccable, and Cochrane and the others had written her long letters describing the campaign in Bahia. All this information had been included in her daily Journal, although without attribution and with few direct quotations.

The despatches and letters were sent off to Rio with all haste in the *Liberal*, while Secretary Jackson copied out Cochrane's orders to the squadron. Captains were reminded that the object of the chase was to prevent any landing in Maranhão and the northern provinces of Brazil, and to seize as many troopships and as much military equipment as possible. The registers and logs of all prizes were to be retained, but to avoid weakening the ships' complements, prize crews were to be kept to a minimum; instead, water casks were to be staved so that only enough remained for the vessel to reach port and, as an extra precaution, the rigging of the troopships was to be so dismembered that they could only sail before the wind. Captain Thompson of the *Real Carolina* was ordered to maintain the chase for some days, and then to return to Salvador to take command of the naval station. Hayden in the *Bahia* was to accompany the *Pedro I* to the latitude of Recife, and then to cruise before the port seizing all vessels flying the flag of Portugal. Taylor in the *Niterói* was given the duty of harassing the convoy as far as Portugal itself.

On 3 July, the *Real Carolina*, *Niterói* and *Bahia* joined the *Pedro I* and *Maria da Glória*, and together the squadron sailed north in pursuit of the Portuguese. The night was rough, wet and stormy, precluding any action, but the weather cleared the next afternoon to reveal the convoy spread over some 20 miles of sea. A line of Portuguese warships sailed to windward in a position to frustrate any attack on the transports and merchantmen which were crowded between them and the land. Rapidly the Brazilians overhauled their prey and fell on the scattered convoy. The *Pedro I* was the first to swoop into the attack, seizing the *Bizarria* with 174 troops of the Lusitanian Legion before the Portuguese squadron could bear down to ward off the blow. But as soon as the men-of-war were off station, the *Real Carolina* attacked the ships to leeward, snapping up the *Leal Portuguêz* and the brig *Promptidão* with 300 infantrymen and their families. Each day the haul increased as the Brazilians pounced on the stragglers which the escorts were powerless to protect. The *Maria da Glória* took the *Conde de Peniche* with 135 men of the 3rd Infantry Battalion, while the *Niterói* seized the merchantman *S. José Triunfo*. The *Bahia* added the troopship *Ulysses*, while the *Pedro I* captured the hired Russian vessel *Meteor*, with 223 men of the 2nd Caçadores, and the troopship *Grão Pará* on which were discovered despatches showing that the Portuguese had indeed intended a descent on Maranhâo.

On 7 July, the *Bahia* parted company and steered for Recife escorting the captured transports *Harmonia*, *Principe Real*, *Caridade* and *Fragatinha de Macao*. Commander Hayden carried letters from Lord Cochrane to the Junta of Pernambuco informing it of the Portuguese evacuation and the liberation of Bahia, and requesting the recruitment of seamen. 'We must have sailors to end the war', he had written, 'and if Your Excellencies will give a bounty of 24 milreis as in Rio de Janeiro you will render a great service to the country. I do not mean Portuguese seamen who are enemies; but those of any other nation, and I need scarcely say that ... I should prefer British seamen to all others.'[2] The appearance of this letter in the *Gazeta* caused a flurry of concern among British merchants throughout Brazil, who feared that the steady trickle of men from their ships would turn into wholesale desertions. Consul-General Henry Chamberlain in Rio was annoyed and indignant at the 'efforts to entice British seamen to enter the Brazilian service', and even Sir Thomas Hardy felt it wise to order the captains of the South America squadron to be extra vigilant in the face of such temptations.[3]

The Portuguese convoy straggled northwards, with the *Pedro I* and *Maria da Glória* in pursuit. On 9 July the transports *Triunfo da Inveja* and *Diana* were taken and escorted to Recife, where Commander Beaurepaire was ordered to assemble the rest of the prizes and convey them to Rio for adjudication. The *Pedro I* was left alone following the remnants of the convoy past the rocky peaks which mark the island of Fernando Noronha, and then northwards to the Equator. With the capture of 16 ships[4] and 2000 troops, the threat of a large-scale landing in the north of Brazil was over, but Cochrane was not content merely to shadow the convoy out of Brazilian waters. Employing his legendary ingenuity, he succeeded in keeping the Portuguese in a state of constant alarm. He launched surprise night attacks from windward in the *Pedro I* and, using empty casks filled with gunpowder, constructed primitive mines which drifted down on the unsuspecting enemy and exploded amid a gratifying amount of panic. Later a more sophisticated design was produced consisting of a sail and a lantern, but bad weather prevented its use.[5]

By 17 July, the *Pedro I* and the convoy had crossed the equator and had reached latitude 5 degrees north. The Portuguese were clearly bound for home and Cochrane, abandoning the chase, turned his attention to the next task before him. When he had left Rio, the important northern provinces of Maranhão and Pará had remained firm in their allegiance to Portugal, and were openly hostile to the Brazilian Empire. Although his orders did not require it, Cochrane's strategic instinct told him that the blockade of these provinces and the evacuation of their Portuguese garrisons was clearly his next duty.

While the other ships of the squadron pursued the transports, the *Niterói* had spent the first week of the chase doggedly shadowing the enemy warships. Dawn each day had revealed the Portuguese ploughing resolutely northwards, with the Brazilian frigate following in their wake like a sheepdog after its flock. As an additional piece of bravado, during the night of 7 July Taylor had overhauled the squadron and coolly sailed down the length of the Portuguese line next morning before firing a broadside into the last vessel, the armed-ship *Gaulter*. On 10 July they passed the latitude of Recife, and Taylor steered westwards in search of any transports which might have been detached to reinforce Maranhão. Hugging the coastline, the *Niterói* saw nothing except a prize of the *Maria da Glória* off course and sailing into dangerous waters. The young officer in charge was redirected, and the frigate continued northwards. The following day, 12 July, they sighted a cutter bound for Fortaleza, and sent in a proclamation giving the authorities in Ceará news of the Portuguese evacuation of Salvador. 'Valiant inhabitants of the north of Brazil', it began, 'free from tyranny, unhappy Bahia already rejoices, happy to be in the embrace of the best of sovereigns....'[6] Two days later, off Maranhão, Taylor decided that any Portuguese reinforcements had either landed or been diverted and, taking advantage of a favourable wind, stood northwards in accordance with his orders to search for the convoy.

The *Niterói*'s refit had left the frigate with a sound hull and a fair turn of speed but, like the rest of the squadron, her spars and rigging were weak and the condition of her masts had already aroused concern. Taylor's decision to cross the Atlantic in pursuit of the Portuguese was therefore a courageous one, but he clearly felt that his vessel had sufficient speed to elude larger warships and a good enough crew to manoeuvre in stress of weather or in action. The *Niterói* was a 38-gun 12-pounder frigate with a complement of 300, comprising 180 sailors, 57 marines and 7 commissioned officers. Because of the voyage facing the frigate, Taylor had received his fair share of reinforcements, and 80 of his seamen were British. The majority of the rest were Brazilians – an unusually high proportion which resulted from the fact that the *Niterói* was one of the first ships to be manned. The officers also reflected this Anglo-Brazilian flavour, with three of each nationality. They comprised Commander Luis Barroso Pereira, Lieutenants Justino de Castro and Samuel Chester, and Sublieutenants Antônio Wenceslau da Silva Lisboa, Francis Drummond and James Wallace. Also on board, serving as a volunteer before attending the Naval Academy, was Joaquim Marques Lisboa – later, as Admiral Marquis Tamandaré, to be Brazil's greatest naval hero.[7]

For three weeks the *Niterói* maintained course across the equator and into the North Atlantic without sight of an enemy flag. On 21 July she met a merchantman bound for Gibraltar from Recife, and from those on board heard of the triumphant arrival of Cochrane's prizes. Three days later another vessel gave cheering news of the overthrow of the Portuguese Côrtes by the Royalists. On 7 August, 39 degrees west of Greenwich and in the latitude of Madeira, the frigate sighted and gave chase to a large ship flying the flag of Portugal. After three warning shots, the vessel surrendered and proved to be the *Grão Pará* filled with troops and on her way to Lisbon, having repaired the damage done by the *Pedro I*'s boarding party. A return to Brazil was out of the question, so Taylor took the parole of the 270 men aboard and allowed the ship to proceed.[8]

The *Niterói* had now been at sea for over six weeks, and Taylor was anxious to fill his water casks and obtain the latest news before reaching European seas. Accordingly, on 19 August, with the Brazilian crew members hidden below and only the English sailors and officers on deck, the frigate hoisted the British flag and sailed boldly into the Portuguese island of Flores in the Azores. Maintaining the perfectly legitimate *ruse de guerre* that she was an English ship ('to avoid disagreeable embarrassments', as the *Relação* tactfully phrases it), the *Niterói* took on water, indulged in some reciprocal hospitality, and received confirmation of the news of the overthrow of the Côrtes and the restoration of King João VI to full power. That done, the frigate continued its voyage, heading eastward and against contrary winds for Europe. On 26 August, the yacht *Alegre* was taken and sent to Rio de Janeiro with Taylor's despatches. Unfortunately, they never arrived. Four days out, the crew recaptured the vessel, arrested the prize-master, Sublieutenant Wenceslau da Silva Lisboa, and delivered the yacht to the Portuguese port of Viana.

The *Niterói* was now approaching European waters. It was a time of peril and maximum alert for all on board. The first alarm came on 29 August, when dawn broke to reveal the frigate sailing in company with two ship-rigged vessels, one astern and one ahead. As the mists lifted further, one proved to be the *Dom João VI* and the other a Portuguese corvette. The Brazilian frigate once more hoisted British colours and coolly sailed on in their company all day before changing course and slipping away at nightfall. Next morning, far to windward, the *Niterói* revealed her true identity and seized another yacht, the *Correio de S. Miguel*, under the noses of the powerless Portuguese. For the next fortnight, the *Niterói* cheekily patrolled the sea lanes off the Tagus, registering every sail and snapping up prizes. The yachts *Esperança*, *Vigilante* and *São José* were caught and sent to Rio. The brig *União* and the yacht *Bon Sucesso* were captured and destroyed. The *Prazeres e Alegria*, bound for Lisbon from Pará, was taken within sight of five more of the convoy's escort and sent to Rio after its cargo had been used to supplement the *Niterói*'s depleted stores. The supply problem was further alleviated when a passing English brig, the *Elizabeth*, was persuaded to take 25 prisoners to Gibraltar at a cost of 40 pesos per head.

Operating within striking distance of Lisbon required vigilance as well as daring: the frigate's crew slept by their guns, and Taylor was on deck twenty-four hours a day to guard against being surprised by a superior force. But in spite of these precautions, one night the vessel inadvertently sailed once more into the midst of the returning Portuguese escort and extricated herself only by posing as a British vessel. On 10 September the *Niterói* captured two merchantmen leaving the Tagus, the *Providência* and the *Nova Amazona*, and learnt that Félix de Campos's squadron was now at anchor in Lisbon. Cochrane's orders had now been obeyed to the letter, and Taylor felt able to return to Brazil. The remaining prisoners were transferred to yet another prize, the *Paquete de Setubal*, with jaunty letters addressed to the Portuguese Minister for Foreign Affairs justifying the case for Brazilian Independence and listing the troops who had given their parole. Alas, their receipt won neither hearts nor minds: they merely inspired the Portuguese authorities to detach two frigates and a number of corvettes on 3 October to search for, and capture, the insolent Brazilian warship.[9] But by then it was too late. Taylor and his men were on their way home.

With favourable winds, the *Niterói* ran down to the latitude of Madeira, capturing three small prizes – the *S. Antônio Triunfo*, *Emilia* and *Harmonia* – and the brig *S. Manuel Augusto*, and then, taking the north-east trade winds on her quarter, sped southwards past the Canaries. Taylor intended to fill his casks before recrossing the Atlantic, and 5 October found the frigate anchored off the lonely island of São Nicolau in the Cape Verde Islands loading 12 tons of water. As she prepared to leave, the weather suddenly deteriorated and the roadstead was struck by a furious gale. The *Niterói* cut her cable and ran before the storm. The seas grew mountainous and the wind increased until a violent gust tore the headsails to shreds, causing the frigate's bows to yaw uncontrollably from side to side. Already riding light, with most of her stores consumed, the *Niterói* began to roll dangerously. Masses of water were taken over the bulwarks, and the frigate began to list as the wild movement shifted some of the cargo. The crew worked madly to avert disaster. To compensate for the headsails, the mizzen shrouds were cut with axes and the wind obligingly snapped off the mast, which restored enough balance to make the frigate respond once more to the helm. Then some of the starboard guns were heaved over the side to restore equilibrium.

All day long the *Niterói* ran before howling winds and crashing seas. Then, after 12 hours, the tempest subsided in a violent rainstorm, and calm was restored. Taylor rigged a jury mizzenmast, sorted out the mess left by the storm, then steered southwards once more away from the Cape Verde Islands. On 28 October the frigate crossed the equator, worked her way across the calms and squalls of the doldrums then, taking the south-east trade winds on the port quarter, made her way to the coasts of Brazil.

On 9 November 1823 a weatherbeaten *Niterói*, her stores exhausted and with only two days' water remaining in her casks, sailed into the Bay of Bahia to a hero's welcome after an epic voyage of four months in which 17 prizes had been taken and the Imperial flag flaunted within sight of Portugal itself.

CHAPTER 7
COCHRANE IN MARANHÃO

The northern provinces of Brazil had eagerly thrown off the authority of Rio de Janeiro when the Portuguese Côrtes had decreed the political dismemberment of the country in September 1821. It was not surprising. Maranhão had been a separate region until 1779, and the wind system in the Atlantic ensured that the rich crops of rice and cotton which were the main products of its lush tropical coast were traded with Europe and not with the rest of Brazil. Whatever the Brazilian planters and the huge population of slaves in the countryside thought about things, it was the views of the Portuguese merchants and officials in the towns which counted, and they remained fiercely loyal to Lisbon. The six members of the Junta which had taken office in February 1822 – including its President – Bishop Dom Joaquim Nazareth, were all Portuguese by birth, and would tolerate no talk of Brazilian independence. Pedro's despatches were sent back unopened, and the people were exhorted to ignore the blandishments of the youthful usurper in Rio.

It was in the neighbouring cattle state of Piauí that the first spark of rebellion was struck on 19 October 1822, when the port of Paraíba declared for the Empire. The Maranhão Junta acted quickly to help stifle the outbreak. The brig-of-war *Infante Dom Miguel* was sent to blockade the town, and the Portuguese garrisons which policed the ranches and hamlets of the interior were reinforced as a precaution. On 11 November, the Junta issued a proclamation designed to whip up enthusiasm. It urged loyalty to Portugal, and stressed the deep ties which linked the two peoples. The south of Brazil, it argued, was further away than Europe in travelling time due to winds and currents, provided no market for local produce, and had no common ties of blood or interest. Geography, interest and sentiment all dictated solidarity with Portugal and the rejection of Brazil. It was a compelling argument to the Portuguese trading communities in the towns. It was less so to the rural Brazilians – particularly to the ranchers and half-breed cattle drovers of the interior, whose activities were largely unconnected with the export trade but had opened up extensive lines of communication which served to knit Brazil from north to south.

On hearing news of the rebellion in Paraíba, the Portuguese military commander of Piauí, Major João da Cunha Fidié, left his inland capital of Oeiras and marched his men northwards to restore order. The Brazilian patriots in Paraíba immediately fled eastward to Ceará, which had already declared for Brazil, and Portuguese rule was reimposed. But as soon as Fidié's back was turned the cattlemen of the interior promptly rose in favour of the Empire. Fidié marched back again at the head of a disciplined force of 1600 men with 11 field pieces. On 13 March 1823, he met a motley force of 2000 Brazilian irregulars on the banks of the river Jenipapo and routed it in a brisk two-hour battle, capturing or killing a third of their number. The defeat blunted the spearhead of the Brazilian attack, but did nothing to halt the wave of patriot enthusiasm. On the contrary, the whole of the interior rose in support, and the towns one by one declared for Brazil. Fidié, powerless, short of supplies and cut off in the inhospitable scrub, gave up the struggle and retreated into Maranhão, where he accepted an invitation from the city fathers of Caxias to defend their city. No sooner had he left Piauí, than the adherence of the province to the Brazilian Empire was triumphantly proclaimed.

A month later, in May 1823, the crisis deepened. A Brazilian Expeditionary Force from Ceará and Piauí crossed the border with an Imperial charge to rid Maranhão of Portuguese troops. At its head was the military commander of Ceará, José Pereira Filgueiras. The interior of the province needed little encouragement and rose enthusiastically in support as the tough half-breed vaqueiros flocked to the banner in search of loot and excitement. In spite of reinforcements rushed to their aid by the Junta in S. Luis, the Portuguese cliques in the towns of Maranhão were overwhelmed one by one until by July only S. Luis and Caxias – held by Major Fidié's men against an army ten times their number – remained under Portuguese control. The patriot grip on the province was so firm that the local strong man, military commander José Félix Pereira Burgos, set up a thirteen-man Provisional Junta at Itipicurú-mirim, 50 miles south of S. Luis. Nine seats were filled from the 'liberated' areas of the province, while the other four – including the presidency – were left vacant pending the fall of the capital.

The Portuguese Junta in S. Luis had at first reacted firmly to the news of the Brazilian revolt. But patriot successes, the almost total loss of Maranhão and the invasion of the southern areas by troops of the Expeditionary Force reduced determination to apprehension; and when, in July, news arrived of the overthrow of the Côrtes and the restoration of King João to full power, the will to fight disappeared. Reluctantly, the Municipal Council of S. Luis agreed to meet on the morning of 14 July 1823 to decide whether the city should declare for Brazil or continue a seemingly hopeless resistance.

On the appointed day, the councillors met in an atmosphere of gloom and resignation. Adherence to Brazil seemed to be the only sensible course of action, although the commander of the garrison, General Agostinho de Faria, insisted on continued loyalty to the Portuguese crown. But before any vote could be taken, the meeting was disrupted by the arrival of the schooner-of-war *Emilia* escorting six troop transports from the convoy taking the Bahia garrison back to Europe. Somewhere they had given Cochrane the slip. On board were 275 men from the 1st Light Infantry Battalion and 50 from the 6th Infantry Regiment with news that four more battalions were on the way. With additional troops at his disposal, Agostinho de Faria broke up the meeting and announced that the army would tolerate no change in the city's allegiance. The civil authorities tried to make the most of the situation by sending emissaries to the Brazilian Junta giving news of the counter-revolution in Portugal and proposing an armistice until news was received from Lisbon and Rio of the compromise which would doubtless be reached between the Royal father and Imperial son. But the Brazilians, within sight of total victory, flatly refused to consider any such plan. On 23 July, Pereira Burgos and his colleagues sent a despatch to the Emperor in Rio describing their successes in Maranhão, confirming that the province was now almost entirely under Brazilian control, and looking forward to the speedy surrender of S. Luis.[1]

In S. Luis, the Portuguese Junta, too, was writing to its sovereign, graphically describing its desperate situation. In a personal letter dated 22 July the President, Bishop Dom Joaquim de Nazareth, reported in similar terms to King João VI, adding ominously and prophetically: 'it is not obedience to the Emperor or respect for his person that moves these people to proclaim independence. They do not love the Emperor and obey his orders only in order to satisfy their hatred of the Europeans.'[2] With Caxias under siege, the bulk of the province in Brazilian hands and their peace overtures rejected, the citizens of S. Luis faced the future without hope. The city continued its resistance only because of military coercion and Agostinho de Faria's assurances that more Portuguese troops from Bahia would soon arrive. Then, on 26 July, a large warship appeared sounding its way carefully up the estuary towards the city. A schooner which had overhauled the vessel in the Bay of São José and had been visited by a very English boarding party, revealed that it was a British ship arriving to aid the Portuguese cause. The brig *Infante Dom Miguel*, commanded by Commander Francisco Freire Garção, sailed out with messages of gratitude and welcome: but the illusion was abruptly shattered – the vessel was the *Pedro I*.

Cochrane's plan for the capture of S. Luis was a typical piece of ingenuity and daring. When the *Infante Dom Miguel* was within hail, the British colours were replaced by the green and yellow of Brazil and the brig found herself trapped under the guns of a powerful enemy. Cochrane accepted Captain Garção's surrender on the *Pedro I*'s quarterdeck, then, explaining casually that over the horizon was a Brazilian fleet and army fresh from victory in Bahia and eager to liberate Maranhão, released him on parole to carry despatches and the formal notification of a blockade to the civil and military authorities in S. Luis. In these letters Cochrane elaborated his *ruse de guerre*. He stressed the enormous naval and military forces at his disposal, his reluctance to unleash the Imperial troops on Maranhão, and the unpleasant consequences of an ineffectual resistance. 'The forces of HIM the Emperor of

Brazil, having delivered the city and province of Bahia from the enemies of their independence,' he wrote to the Junta:

> I, in conformity with the wishes of HIM, am desirous that the fruitful province of Maranhão should enjoy a like freedom. I am come to offer to the unfortunate inhabitants the protection and assistance necessary against the oppression of foreigners ... and to salute them as brethren and friends.... But should there be any who ... oppose the liberation of this country, such persons may be assured that the naval and military force which expelled the Portuguese from the south are ready to draw the sword in the same just cause.

In his letter to the military authorities, the threatening tone was more pronounced: 'The naval and military forces under my command leave me no room to doubt the success of the enterprise in which I am about to engage,' he wrote, 'namely, to liberate Maranhão from foreign oppression and to allow the people to choose their system of government. I am anxious not to let loose the Imperial troops of Bahia upon Maranhão,' he continued casually, 'exasperated as they are by the injuries and cruelties exercised towards themselves and their countrymen.... It is for you to decide whether the inhabitants of these countries shall be further exasperated by a resistance which appears to me to be unavailing.'[3]

A meeting of the civil and military authorities was hastily assembled. In the face of a threat of overwhelming force, and under the guns of the biggest warship ever seen off S. Luis, it was unanimously decided to accept the inevitable and embrace the cause of Independence. Letters confirming the same were immediately sent to Lord Cochrane. General Agostinho de Faria wrote separately, declaring that his troops would not obstruct any decision for Maranhão to adhere to Empire, but protesting that they had in no way acted as 'foreign oppressors', and had throughout enjoyed the support of the majority of the people. His decision on 14 July to prevent any vote in favour of Brazil, he argued, had been made to prevent any outbreak of anarchy in S. Luis until news of a settlement had been received from Lisbon and Rio. He concluded by asking Cochrane to take measures to ensure public order after Independence, and to permit his troops and staff to embark for Portugal with full military honours, together with as many citizens as chose to accompany them.

These terms were acceptable to the First Admiral, but to maintain the appearance of negotiating from strength he stood firm, and insisted on unconditional surrender. Accordingly, on 27 July 1823, the Bishop, the Junta and a representative of the military commander went on board the *Pedro I* to greet Cochrane and confirm the formal adherence of Maranhão to the Empire. At 10 a.m. the following day, Independence was solemnly proclaimed at the Palácio do Governo, and to the thunder of salutes and the ringing of church bells, Brazilian colours were hoisted on the city, the forts and the ships-of-war in the harbour. It was a historic occasion, the rejoicing marred only by the absence of both the First Admiral and General de Faria, who were prevented from attending by ill health. The first of August was selected as the day on which oaths would be sworn by all citizens, whether Brazilian or Portuguese, who wished to declare loyalty to the Empire. The official ceremonies safely concluded, Cochrane sent letters to the commanders of all military forces in the province telling them of Maranhão's adhesion to the Empire, urging an immediate suspension of hostilities, and ordering all troops to remain in their positions until further instructions were received. Other letters looked forward to a speedy resumption of commercial activity.

Independence now secured, Cochrane's next task was to get rid of the Portuguese troops before their suspicions were aroused by the non-appearance of the imaginary Brazilian fleet and army. Transports were assembled, outlying detachments were withdrawn to S. Luis, and the garrisons in the forts and the city were prepared for embarkation. Under pressure from Cochrane on the grounds that a military withdrawal was essential if the forthcoming provincial elections were to be free from outside interference, arrangements were soon concluded. There was some hesitation by Agostinho de Faria, who still feared a breakdown of public order, but on 1 August, with Crosbie and a heavily armed shore party from the *Pedro I* in attendance to ensure no last-minute change of mind, the General and his men were embarked with their flags, arms and families on the transports *Conde de Caveleiros* and *Constitutional* for the return voyage to Lisbon.[4] The Portuguese militia units were then disarmed and replaced by Brazilians, and the city prepared for civilian rule. On 7 August, after an unavoidable delay, the capital filled its four vacant seats and the new Provincial Junta took up office with a local lawyer of Scottish descent, Miguel Freire Bruce, as President.

The Junta's actions soon showed that for many Brazilians independence meant more than a new flag and a surface change of allegiance. As Bishop Nazareth had predicted, the lower orders saw it as an opportunity to seize property and settle old scores with the unpopular and prosperous Portuguese, while the middle classes used it to acquire power and the spoils of office. Portuguese officials were dismissed from their posts; Portuguese merchants were harassed and insulted in the streets. Cochrane used his influence in favour of moderation, but his efforts were unavailing and he began to complain bitterly to Rio of the selfish and oppressive actions of the Junta.

Cochrane's political attitudes may have been generous, but when it came to other aspects of the capture of S. Luis, his views were just as uncompromising. As far as he was concerned, the city and the province had been captured by force of arms from the Portuguese, and its wealth was now rightly at the disposal of the conquerors. He took possession of the brig-of-war *Infante Dom Miguel* (renamed *Maranhão* and sent off on 6 August under John Pascoe Grenfell to negotiate the surrender of Pará), the schooner *Emilia*, eight gunboats together with the slaves who manned them, and the 16 merchant vessels in the harbour, together with their cargoes, on the grounds that the prize legislation in force awarded the value of all enemy ships to their captors. He laid claim to the contents of the provincial Treasury, together with all debts owing to it, the property belonging to the previous administration, the munitions and gunpowder in the forts, the stores in the arsenal and the government warehouses, and the monies in the customs houses. He also claimed all private property belonging to Portuguese non-residents on the grounds that the Imperial Decree of 11 December 1822 – which had permitted the confiscation of enemy property – had also awarded it to the captors in order 'to attract foreign seamen into the Brazilian service'.[5] As Cochrane was aware, the prize laws of Portugal, which formed the basis of Brazilian rules on the subject, accepted the principle that legitimate prizes seized by naval ships in time of war remained the property of the takers. In his view, therefore, all the money and goods taken in

Maranhão, both public and private, belonged by right to the officers and men of the *Pedro I*. Cochrane also knew that the regulations in force laid down clear rules for the distribution of prize money among those involved in its capture, and allocated one-eighth of the value of all legitimate seizures to the commander-in-chief.

At first, the Junta and citizens of Maranhão were unaware of the extent of Cochrane's claims, or the seriousness of his intentions. On 28 July, only a few hours after the adhesion of S. Luis to the Brazilian Empire had been officially proclaimed, he wrote to the Junta asking for a full inventory of public property, debts and assets, together with a statement showing the amounts held in cash in the customs house and the military chest.[6] Henry Dean, who had travelled from Chile as the First Admiral's financial agent to deal with situations such as this, was sent ashore to scrutinize the information. The Junta gave the necessary orders, and by 4 August most of the details were in Dean's possession. The next day, 5 August, Cochrane turned his attention to private property, and issuing a proclamation demanding full details of all goods and merchandise owned by non-resident Portuguese, and decreeing the confiscation of two-thirds of its value.

To the merchants of Maranhão the proclamation came as a bombshell. Four days later they had recovered sufficiently to address a petition to the First Admiral. If the proclamation were enforced, they explained, the commerce of the province would be destroyed. Any confiscation of Portuguese goods in Brazil would inevitably mean the confiscation of Brazilian goods in Portugal, and such a reprisal would mean ruin. Similarly, the ports of Portugal were the main markets for the rice and cotton on which Maranhão's prosperity depended, and the province could not afford to antagonize its most important customer. They asked Cochrane to reconsider his decision, and to allow the agents and consignees of Portuguese goods to retain them in their custody until a final settlement was reached between the Emperor and King João VI. But Cochrane remained unmoved, his only reaction being anger against the new Brazilian Junta for having sent on the petition and, by implication, supporting it. On 11 August President Miguel Freire Bruce, anxious not to antagonize the First Admiral further, replied on behalf of the Junta by apologizing for sending on the petition and disclaiming any sympathy with its contents. On 14 August, Cochrane issued two more proclamations. One pointed out that his decree of 5 August had not been observed, and threatened dire consequences unless it was complied with within one week. The other announced that all debts owing to the previous administration were legitimate prize of war, but that one-third of their value would be remitted if the remaining two-thirds were paid over by 20 August. Alarmed by his tone, the Junta intervened and, to avoid any further difficulty, appointed a commission of three members to compile the information demanded by Cochrane on both Portuguese property and unpaid debts.[7]

By the time the commission submitted its report on 23 August, the Junta was horrified at the enormity of Cochrane's claims. On 27 August, it tried to reason with the truculent First Admiral. His understanding of the position, it argued, was faulty. He had not captured a foreign town but had merely expelled the Portuguese troops whose arrival on 14 July had prevented the city from declaring for the Empire. In addition, at the time of Cochrane's arrival almost the whole of the province was in Brazilian hands, so that although he had expelled the Portuguese from S. Luis, there was no question of any right of conquest or grounds for seizure of the provincial Treasury. Furthermore, they argued, the legal ownership of all public funds and property in the city had been automatically transferred from one Junta to the next – it remained the property of the province and there was no question of capture or prize.[8] But Cochrane had made up his mind and, in a matter so advantageous, could not be shaken. The seizures continued, the money was collected, and tons of merchandise were shipped to Rio de Janeiro in the prize brig *Pombinha* for adjudication by the Prize Courts. According to the information provided to Henry Dean, the total value of the goods and monies which had fallen into the squadron's hands was over 479 contos of reis, or £100,000 sterling. This sum comprised 62,560 milreis and 54,167 milreis in cash from the Treasury and the customs house; 147,316 milreis in letters of credit; 45,000 milreis' worth of captured warships, gunboats, gunpowder and military stores; and private Portuguese property to the value of 170,196 milreis.[9]

Meanwhile, the last spark of Portuguese resistance in northern Brazil was being extinguished. The siege of Caxias had already lasted for over two months, with Major Fidié's 700 men surrounded by more than 8000 Brazilian militia and irregulars. On 23 July the commander of the Expeditionary Force, José Pereira Filgueiras, treated the defenders to a triumphant proclamation which told them of the evacuation of Bahia and the almost total adhesion of Maranhão to the Imperial cause: he urged them to abandon their futile and isolated resistance. A Council of War in the city glumly reviewed the situation and inevitably decided on capitulation. After some haggling over terms, Caxias finally surrendered on 31 July 1823. Major Fidié and his men became prisoners of war, and the Brazilian army took possession of 20 cannon, five regimental flags, and quantities of munitions and stores. Its first act was to impose a fine of 150 contos of reis on the town to pay the Brazilian troops who had captured it.

In August, Cochrane's letters giving news of the adhesion of S. Luis to the Empire and ordering a suspension of hostilities were received by the victorious patriots in Caxias. Emissaries were immediately sent from the Expeditionary Force to the capital demanding new provincial elections, pay for the troops, the persecution of all who had opposed independence, and the right of the captors to enemy property and goods they had taken. The new Maranhão Junta managed to resist the demands for new elections and political persecutions, but it was forced to agree to the others, including a commitment to pay the patriot army occupying the interior. Without Cochrane's help this was, of course, impossible, but fortunately the First Admiral recognized the serious threat presented by the irregular troops unless they were paid off and sent home. Stressing verbally and in writing that any sums paid over should be regarded as loans from prize money, and that recompense was expected in full, he advanced 116,727 milreis (£23,345) in cash and 147,316 milreis (£29,423) in letters of credit from the Treasury and the customs house.[10] Supplemented with quantities of cloth and merchandise, these amounts were sent to the troops of the Expeditionary Force in Caxias who, now that the excitement was over and they had money in their pockets, promptly disbanded and returned to their home provinces.

That problem solved, the political situation in S. Luis became the next source of concern as the rival factions began to struggle for power. Freire Bruce filled the public offices with supporters from the city, and brought in loyal troops to enforce his will in the streets. On 12 September Cochrane tried to calm the situation by proclaiming that there should be a new Provincial Junta, and that elections would take place in ten days' time. The following day, in a pre-emptive strike, the leader of the 'Itipicurú-mirim' faction, military commander Pereira Burgos, seized and imprisoned Bruce's allies on the city council. Next day, he and his adherents were arrested in their turn by troops loyal to the President, and packed off to Rio de Janeiro for trial. The victors then turned on the hapless Portuguese, who were rumoured to have been behind the attempted *coup*. There was widespread violence and looting, and leading Portuguese citizens and their families were forced to take refuge on the ships-of-war under Cochrane's protection.

On 15 September, the civil and military authorities met to review the situation. Under strong pressure from the Brazilian garrison, they agreed to the expulsion of Portuguese residents and the convocation of fresh elections. It was also decided that in view of their alleged responsibility for the uprising, each Portuguese national should be fined 6400 reis to provide a bonus for the Brazilian troops who had restored order. Cochrane attempted to modify the harshness of these reprisals against the Portuguese, but had little success against the wave of patriot enthusiasm.

Lord Cochrane's task in the north had now been completed. S. Luis had been liberated, the Portuguese troops were on their way home, and the Province of Maranhão had declared its adherence to the Empire. News from Grenfell indicated that Pará had followed suit. Only the continual political infighting in the capital continued to cause problems, and this seemed likely to be settled by the forthcoming elections. With a strong sense of relief, Lord Cochrane prepared to sail, leaving George Manson to keep an eye on Maranhão in the captured schooner *Emilia* (now renamed *Pará*). His orders were to sell the six prizes which remained in the port, to apprehend the merchant ships still expected from Portugal, and to rejoin the squadron if they did not arrive within a month. And so, on 20 September 1823, apparently satisfied with the state of affairs in Maranhão, Cochrane said his farewells and sailed over the horizon in the *Pedro I*, bound for the open sea and a hero's welcome in Rio de Janeiro.

CHAPTER 8

GRENFELL IN PARÁ

On the western borders of Maranhão lay the vast equatorial province of Pará, stretching from the maze of river channels and green islands which mark the mouth of the Amazon deep into the tropical rainforests of the interior. As in Maranhão, there was a division between the Brazilians scattered thinly in the rural areas and the prosperous Portuguese who congregated in the capital, Belém, and the larger settlements. But the politics of the area were dominated by the military commander, Brigadier José Maria de Moura. Completely loyal to the Côrtes, he ruthlessly suppressed any murmur of independence, ordered mass deportations of political suspects, and ensured that the civil Junta ignored the regime in Rio de Janeiro and remained aloof from developments in the rest of the country.

But as news of events in the south began to trickle into Belém, the courage and confidence of the Brazilian patriots began to increase. Clandestine pamphlets appeared criticizing the Côrtes and the authorities. Tensions began to develop between the military and the civil government, and the columns of the newspaper *O Paraense* began to feature inflammatory articles in favour of Brazilian Independence written by a fanatical Brazilian priest, João Baptista Campos. By 1 March 1823 the Portuguese rulers had had enough, and the inevitable happened. The military commander dismissed the Provincial Junta for being lukewarm in its zeal, placed its members under house arrest, suppressed *O Paraense* and confiscated its printing press. A new Junta was appointed, with members specially selected for their loyalty to Portugal. Brazilian resistance went underground until, on 14 April, troops and citizens who favoured the cause of Independence staged an uprising.

Hand-to-hand fighting and artillery duels went on all day, but by nightfall Brigadier Maria de Moura's men had emerged victorious. Retribution was severe. Over 270 people were arrested, tried and deported to Lisbon in irons.

During July, disturbing news began to reach Pará of the overthrow of the Côrtes in Portugal and the unexpected adherence of the previously loyal province of Maranhão to the Brazilian cause. On 5 August, the civil and military authorities in Belém called a council to examine their situation in the light of these events. The resolution of the ruling Portuguese clique was shaken, but it nevertheless decided to maintain the *status quo* until further instructions were received from Lisbon. Thus, Pará remained firmly in the grip of the Portuguese, but was seething with Brazilian resentment. It was at this point that the *Maranhão* arrived in the estuary.

Commander John Pascoe Grenfell had sailed from S. Luis on 6 August in the 18-gun brig-of-war *Maranhão* with two officers – Sublieutenants Victor Santiago Subrá and James Watson – and a picked crew of 90 men, 60 of whom were British. His orders were dramatically simple. He was to secure the adherence of Pará to the Brazilian Empire by employing the same *ruse de guerre* which Cochrane had used so successfully in S. Luis. Grenfell's instructions were drafted with the First Admiral's usual attention to detail:

> 1st After taking the pilot, you will proceed to the River Salinas. 2nd You will take all precautions to ensure that there is no communication with the land nor any delivery of letters with the exception of those which I have given you. 3rd The orders with which you have been provided in Portuguese are those which you should show.... It is necessary to make the Government of Pará believe that you are not alone but that I and the squadron are close at hand and ready to give assistance: it is therefore important that you complete the letter by filling in the date on which you reach the mouth of the river. You will carry three letters addressed to the Junta de Pará: two of these contain printed matter, the third is a notification of blockade. On the same day as your arrival off the bar of Pará you should therefore date the said letters and notification of blockade irrespective of the time which you may have to spend going further up river. You will understand that it is my intention to attain in this manner the same objective which would otherwise require an expedition: both skill and care are therefore necessary.... The other objective which you must achieve after the liberation of Pará is the seizure of the new frigate.[1]

With favourable winds, the *Maranhão* and its 23-year-old commander sailed north-north-west to Pará, keeping land just in sight on the horizon. On 9 August, the brig reached the mouth of the Amazon and edged closer to the shore to pick up a pilot. Next day, Grenfell made his way carefully up river until the houses and churches of Belém came into sight, standing white and dazzling against the deep shades of the tropical vegetation around. As night fell on 10 August 1823, the ship dropped anchor just out of gunshot of the batteries guarding the city.

The following morning, to the astonishment of the unsuspecting townspeople, the *Maranhão* raised the green-and-yellow flag of the Brazilian Empire and fired a gun salute, while the letters which Grenfell carried were rowed ashore under flag of truce and delivered to the authorities. The Junta – overawed, as intended, by the size of the force Cochrane had apparently deployed against it, and coerced by the demonstrations in favour of Independence which had been stimulated by the appearance of the *Maranhão* – immediately called a council of the civil and military authorities. Meeting in the comparative cool of the evening outside the Palácio do Governo, and later in the building itself, the delegates learnt of the blockade of Pará and the proximity of the Imperial forces. Cochrane's letters confirming the declaration of Maranhão for the Brazilian Empire, and his firm but courteously phrased demand that Pará too should embrace the cause of liberty, were produced, together with his guarantee of the lives and property of all Portuguese citizens who declared allegiance to Dom Pedro. After the briefest discussion, the meeting decided by an overwhelming majority that Cochrane's terms should be accepted, and that the province should adhere immediately to the Brazilian Empire.[2] The only opposing voice was that of the wily Brigadier Maria de Moura, who expressed deep suspicion as to whether any blockading force actually existed, and on being outvoted immediately resigned his post. But an opponent of Maria de Moura's shrewdness was too dangerous to be allowed to remain free when Pará's future remained so finely balanced and, at Grenfell's request, he was arrested three days later on suspicion of fomenting unrest and confined out of harm's way on the *Maranhão*.

Accordingly, without opposition and amid scenes of wild rejoicing, on 15 August 1823 the Province of Pará officially became part of the Brazilian Empire. The frigate in the dockyard, the batteries and the ships in the roadstead, hoisted the Imperial ensign, Independence was solemnly proclaimed at the Palácio do Governo, a *Te Deum* was celebrated in the cathedral, and the city was illuminated for three nights. Oaths of loyalty were administered the following day, and on 17 August a new Provincial Junta was elected with Geraldo de Abreu as President. But from the beginning it was clear that the patriot party, both in the Junta and outside it, were divided into two hostile factions: the 'extremists', led by Baptista Campos, who expected independence to yield solid dividends at the expense of Portuguese jobs and property; and the 'moderates' led by Geraldo de Abreu, who were opposed to the dismissal of Portuguese office-holders or the seizure of property, and favoured harmony and reconciliation. Through the sweltering heat of September and into October the latent hostility simmered beneath the surface as the two groups manoeuvred for power and popularity.

Independence secured and a Brazilian administration installed, Grenfell busied himself with the second part of his orders. In accordance with Cochrane's wishes, the frigate so recently completed in the dockyard was incorporated into the Navy and renamed *Imperatriz*. She proved a useful acquisition. A strong and well-built vessel of the largest size, comparable to the *Piranga*, she carried 28 cannon on her main deck and mounted a total of 50 guns. When Grenfell took over, however, the ship was little more than a bare hull. Only the lower masts had been rigged, and the whole was in a state of extreme neglect through having been left open to sun and rain. To equip and prepare the vessel was a long and difficult task, and Grenfell was forced to strip the dockyard of stores, remove items of gear and rigging from prizes, and send to Maranhão for additional supplies of rope and cable. He also recruited officers and men for the Imperial Navy in order to supplement his slender forces, and armed a schooner which was sent to patrol the sea lanes off Pará commanded by James Watson.[3]

In accordance with his orders, Grenfell also seized all vessels and cargoes belonging to Portuguese non-residents, together with the 22-gun transport *Gentil Americana*. On arrival, he found six merchant ships flying the flag of Portugal in the harbour: the ships *Astrea* and *Diligente*, the brigs *General Rego* and *Nova Iphigenia*, and the schooners *Lucrecia* and *Andorinha*. Their number was soon augmented by four more Portuguese vessels which sailed innocently into Belém, in ignorance of the change of government, and the brig *General Noronha*, which was captured making its way up river with a cargo of gunpowder. Because of the impossibility of transporting all these prizes to Rio, Grenfell persuaded the Junta to establish a local Prize Court, by which they were promptly and formally condemned.⁴ They were then sold for 49,850 milreis (£10,000) by Grenfell's agent, a prominent local British merchant named James Campbell, and part of the proceeds were distributed among his crews as prize money as a reward and encouragement for their efforts.

As he carried out his professional duties, Grenfell was well aware of the deteriorating political situation in Pará. On the night of 21 August as he crossed the harbour, he himself was stabbed in the ribs by a Portuguese seaman who proved to be part of a larger group preparing to attack the *Maranhão*.⁵ Over 150 conspirators were swiftly rounded up and deported and on 26 August Brigadier Maria de Moura, whose continued presence in Belém clearly constituted a dangerous rallying point for dissidents, was sent back to Europe in a Gibraltar-bound merchant vessel. With the Portuguese threat removed, the tensions between the two Brazilian factions reached new levels of acrimony, and on 13 September Grenfell reported to Cochrane that only the presence of the Navy was preserving a fragile peace. He recommended that the Imperial Government should send representatives to Pará urgently to mediate between the two groups.⁶

On 15 October 1823, three days after celebrations marking the Emperor's birthday, this delicate balance was broken. Troops from the garrison rose against their officers and marched on the Palácio do Governo, where they deposed Geraldo de Abreu and his 'moderate' colleagues and installed Baptista Campos as President. Next day, he decreed the wholesale dismissal and deportation of Portuguese and moderate-Brazilian officers and public employees. Mutinous troops, joined by the mob, then went on the rampage, breaking into liquor stores, looting property, burning shops and houses, and killing or imprisoning those who resisted. For a night and a day the city of Belém witnessed an orgy of violence and plunder. Finally, on the evening of 17 October, members of the old Junta begged for help from the only disciplined force remaining in the city, the officers and men of the *Maranhão*. Grenfell armed his crew, led them ashore, rallied the few loyal troops, cleared the streets, and restored order. The three regular infantry battalions and the units of cavalry and artillery which had joined the revolt were then disarmed, and their weapons taken under heavy naval escort to the arsenal. The guards were strengthened and their commander was ordered to use grapeshot and grenades if any hostile mob attempted to force an entrance. Three hundred rioters were arrested and, in an act of swift retribution, the five ringleaders of the mutiny were shot as an example after a drumhead court-martial. With the city once more tranquil and a series of signals agreed with the Junta so that urgent assistance from the ships-of-war could be requested at any time, by day or night, Grenfell returned with his men to the *Maranhão*.

The citizens of Belém had been horrified and shocked by the events of the 15, 16 and 17 October, but worse was to follow. On 18 October, the Junta wrote to Grenfell explaining: 'the prisons in the town are filled with those arrested ... and a large number of militiamen are needed to guard them. Our other jails are too weak to be used and could be easily broken into, but the Junta considers that the brig *Diligente* could be used as a prison ship to which those arrested could be kept with only a small guard as long as the vessel remains among the ships-of-war.'[7] Grenfell agreed to the suggestion, and on 20 October 256 prisoners were ferried out to the *Diligente* and secured in the hold.

As night fell black and stifling over the river, sounds of violent hammering and muffled shouting were heard from below. Water was lowered to the prisoners, but when the noise increased the nervous young Brazilian lieutenant in charge, fearing an attempt to overwhelm his tiny force, ordered the hatches to be battened down as a precautionary measure, and the clamour slowly subsided. Through the heat of the day and night of 21 October, the brig swung languidly at its anchor in the brown water. At dawn the following morning the hatches were taken off, to reveal a horrifying spectacle. The hold was filled with piles of corpses, many of them bloody and disfigured after a day of agony in those fetid confines. Of the 256 men who had been imprisoned in the

Diligente, only four remained faintly alive; the rest had been suffocated or trampled to death.[8]

The Junta, shocked by the rioting and the tragedy on the prison ship, attempted to rally the province behind it in a strongly worded proclamation:

> Citizens, the fatherland is in danger. A small number of criminals managed to deceive a large part of the armed forces and led them in rebellion: you yourselves were witnesses of the horrible deeds committed during which our houses were broken into, looted and robbed. Our very existence was in danger and in the last resort we were saved only because Providence had brought to this port the *Maranhão*, to whose illustrious commander we owe the greatest gratitude for his energetic action in protecting the cause of the Brazilian Empire, our own independence and the preservation of this city....[9]

The stratagem failed. The patriot faction denounced the legal Junta as being partisans of Portugal, accused it of deliberately murdering the detainees on the *Diligente*, and set up a rebel headquarters at Cametá, a small town some miles up river from the capital. Disaffection rapidly spread through the adjacent area, and before long other settlements in the region had joined the revolt.

With Grenfell's help, the Junta in Belém sent waterborne expeditions against the rebels. The revolt was contained, but the problem was essentially a political one, and no military solution could be effective in a province so vast and thinly populated as Pará. Grenfell, recognizing this, wrote to Cochrane on 3 November reporting on his activities, asking for reinforcements, and recommending once more that they be accompanied by a person in the confidence of the Imperial Government who would be able to mediate between the opposing factions. He also reported that the turbulent priest Baptista Campos, whose restless and able mind had inspired the extremist camp from the beginning, had been found guilty of fermenting the revolt of 15 and 16 October and was being sent under arrest to Rio de Janeiro in the *Gentil Americana* under the command of Sublieutenant Watson.[10]

As the civil disputes and turbulence within the province continued, so the Junta's attitude to the rebels hardened. The regular troops who had been deprived of their weapons were rearmed, and a flotilla of gunboats was organized to protect the cargo-carrying canoes and launches which plied the river from attack. Then, at the end of January 1824, there were rumours of a Portuguese plot to overthrow the Junta. Dismissal of Portuguese public servants, imprisonments and mass deportations were once again the order of the day in Pará. Grenfell, mindful of the terms offered to Portuguese citizens at the time of the province's adhesion to Brazil, protested against such harsh treatment, but obtained nothing for his pains except the enmity of the Junta and its supporters. That accomplished, on 14 February the Junta decided to launch an attack on the rebels in Cametá. The regular troops were alerted, and Grenfell was ordered to prepare transports and provide a naval escort which would both convoy the troops to their destination and assist in the assault.

On 23 February, Grenfell reported that his preparations were complete and that three transports, two armed-ships and three schooners were ready to embark the expeditionary force. But the second paragraph of his letter turned the Junta's optimism to consternation:

> Having completed the task which Your Excellencies entrusted to me, I would like to take this opportunity of informing you that the frigate *Imperatriz* is now ready, and that in obedience to the instructions which I have from the First Admiral, I intend to leave Pará shortly in order to join the Imperial Squadron in Rio de Janeiro. I would therefore like to thank Your Excellencies for the assistance you have given me in discharging the Imperial orders with which I was charged, and for the courtesy with which I have been personally treated....[11]

The news came as a bombshell. The Municipal Council of Belém addressed an urgent letter to the Junta on 26 February protesting that the departure of the brig and the frigate would leave the city unprotected. Two days later the Junta wrote to Grenfell at length, stressing that it was vital for the ships-of-war to remain in Belém until the rebellion had been crushed. To abandon the province in its hour of need threatened disaster: the attack on Cametá would have to be abandoned if Grenfell's forces were not present to defend Belém; the English merchants would close their businesses and leave; and the industrialists and capitalists in the city would soon join them. 'The services you rendered to the Emperor in uniting this province with the Brazilian Empire were great and important', they concluded, but what does this signify if it is not preserved and if all is ruined and destroyed because you abandon it before the assistance requested from HIM has arrived? ... The service of HIM and the integrity of the Empire demands that all available land and sea forces, which are counted to include the frigate *Imperatriz* and the brig *Maranhão*, are employed in the defence of this province: and because of this, the Junta orders you, together with the squadron you command, to remain....[12]

But Grenfell, by now heartily sick of the political squabbles in which he had been thanklessly involved, and with some 40,000 milreis' (£8000) worth of prize money in the hold, was unmoved. On 3 March 1824, oblivious to all protests, the *Imperatriz* and the *Maranhão* weighed anchor, sailed down river, and disappeared over the horizon bound for Rio de Janeiro. The Junta, left without its strong right arm, sent a blistering letter to the Emperor denouncing Grenfell's political interference and his abandonment of Belém, then patched up an uneasy compromise with the rebels.

CHAPTER 9
VICTORY

In Rio de Janeiro, May 1823 marked the watershed of a momentous year. The opening of the Brazilian Constituent Assembly and the visit of an emissary from the British Government in the form of Lord Amherst, on his way to India to become Governor General of Bengal, were the high points of an inspiring month. As returning warships and prizes brought news of Cochrane's victories to the capital, first from Bahia, then from Maranhão, the survival of the Empire became a reality, and public opinion as to its form of government and its relations with its erstwhile metropolis began to polarize. Within the Assembly, delegates found themselves divided into two hostile groupings. Both supported independence, but one, comprising native Brazilians who formed the rural aristocracy and the bulk of the lower orders, favoured an extreme anti-Portuguese line and a 'democratic' order of things that would counterbalance the influence of the Portuguese-born office-holders and merchants; while the other, made up of Portuguese adherents to the Imperial cause and wealthy Brazilians who were hostile to popular rule, supported a policy of national reconciliation, an absolute system of government, and the restoration of amicable relations with Portugal.

At first, the Government of José Bonifácio de Andrada e Silva, which had directed the destinies of Brazil so firmly during the struggle for independence, steered an unbending course between the two groups, arrogantly ignoring both. Then, in July 1823, the two factions combined to force its resignation by means, it was said, of a petition of protest about the tyrannical conduct of the Andradas in São Paulo which was slipped anonymously into the Emperor's correspondence. Another explanation was that Pedro had learnt the truth during public audiences held to allay public alarm after he had broken two ribs in a riding accident. But whatever the reason for their fall, out of office José Bonifácio and his brothers threw themselves on the side of the 'patriot' faction and devoted their considerable talents to sharpening the attack. Before long, both the press and the Assembly were openly proclaiming sentiments that were not only anti-Portuguese but anti-monarchical as well.

By November the Emperor had had enough. Spurred by the Andradas, the violence of the verbal attacks had reached dangerous proportions, and the latent Brazilian hostility to the Portuguese-born which was never far from the surface seemed likely to tear the Empire apart. Finally, on 12 November, in the confusion following the collapse of the new government, Pedro dissolved the Assembly, surrounded the building with troops and artillery, and ordered the delegates to disperse. After a final session which lasted for over twenty-four tense and exhausting hours, they accepted the inevitable. As the members filed wearily out between the bayonets, Antônio Carlos bowed towards the guns and expressed the feelings of them all. 'I obey the sovereign of the world', he said, 'His Majesty the cannon.' He, his brother Josè Bonifácio, and the other leaders of the 'patriot' party were immediately arrested and a new administration was appointed.

The new government was competent, but uninspiring and unmemorable. It was led by José Severiano Maciel da Costa as Minister of the Empire, with Luis de Carvalho e Melo as Minister of Foreign Affairs, and Francisco Vilela Barbosa – a special favourite – as Minister of Marine. To calm the situation further, the Emperor promised to produce a constitution even more liberal than the draft on which the Assembly had so fruitlessly laboured; decreed elections for a fresh Assembly; and nominated new Presidents to head the governing Juntas of the various provinces. All were Brazilians, all were respected figures, and many of them had pronounced liberal views. The continued presence of José Bonifácio and his brothers on Brazilian soil, however, remained both an embarrassment and a threat to the regime. Deportation to Europe seemed the only answer. Accordingly, on 20 November, the Andrada brothers, their families and servants were loaded on to the *Luconia* bound for France. But even then their adventures were not at an end. The vessel proved to be hardly seaworthy and, after a poor crossing, was forced into Vigo by stress of weather. There, she lay for weeks being refused repairs by an unfriendly Spanish government while two Portuguese warships cruised outside the port with orders to arrest the *Luconia* and its distinguished passengers when she emerged. Things looked bad for the patriarch of Brazilian Independence, but finally, after intervention by the French and British Governments, José Bonifácio's party were permitted to continue their journey to Le Havre overland while the unfortunate *Luconia* was sold for scrap.

Against the sombre political background of Brazil which followed the dissolution of the Assembly, Lord Cochrane's victories shone with even greater glory. On 17 July, Commander Antônio Freire Garção of the *Liberal* brought news of the fall of Bahia. On 1 October, Lieutenant Anderson in the prize *Mary* arrived after a 43-day voyage from S. Luis with despatches describing Cochrane's success in Maranhão and the adhesion of the northern provinces to the Empire. Three weeks later, on 26 October, Sublieutenant David Carter brought in the prize *Borges Carneiro* with news that Pará, too, had joined the Brazilian cause.

Each successive piece of news was received with mounting joy and acclaim. Rio was given over to days of rejoicing, the city was illuminated by night and gala performances were held at the theatre. In the south, the Portuguese continued to hold out in Montevideo, but from there the story was of continuous encirclement by land and victory by sea. The new commander-in-chief, Captain Antônio Nunes, had been blockading the city since 15 March 1823 with the brig-of-war *Real Pedro* and a handful of schooners. Five months later, the Navy's victories in the north allowed the Government to reinforce his flotilla, and on 12 August the corvette *Liberal* (Commander Antônio Freire Garção), the brig *Cacique* (Commander Antônio José do Couto), the brigantine *Leopoldina* and the schooner *Seis de Fevereiro* sailed to join him, followed a month later by the *Guarani*, now commanded by Lieutenant James Nicol.

On 21 October the Portuguese in Montevideo, who had been busy changing into armed-ships the three Brazilian transports that had been turned over to them in January, made one last attempt to break the naval blockade. The two squadrons sighted each other at dawn: the Brazilians lying off the port, the Portuguese sailing out in order of battle, the *Conde dos Archos* in the van, followed by the *Restauradora*, the *Liguri* and the schooner *Maria Teresa*. Antônio Nunes, flying his pennant in the *Liberal*, signalled for his division to stand along the coast so as to occupy the windward position, then, putting his ships about, he advanced on the Portuguese with the *Liberal* in the lead, followed by the *Cacique, Guarani, Real Pedro* and *Leopoldina*, and flanked by the schooners *Cossaka* and *Seis de Fevereiro*. A fierce and hard-fought engagement followed until the Portuguese abandoned the action and retreated to Montevideo. The Portuguese commander, Dom Álvaro da Costa, had already learnt of the fall of Bahia and the northern provinces, and knew that further reinforcement was impossible. The failure to break out by sea now convinced him that all was lost, and further resistance was useless. Negotiations began, and by the end of November 1823 Captain Nunes was able to report to Rio de Janeiro that outline terms for a surrender had been agreed. The War of Independence was over.

Brazil's military triumphs had been so stunning that the peace overtures made by the Lisbon Government following the overthrow of the Côrtes were received with little interest. General Luis Paulino da França was the first to arrive under flag of truce on 7 September 1823 in the packet *Treze de Maio*, carrying offers of a suspension of hostilities. He was given short shrift. At first, he was denied permission to land unless his instructions covered the recognition of Brazilian Independence – which they clearly did not – and the old man was eventually allowed to set foot on shore only when his health began to deteriorate. The Conde de Rio-Maior was next. He sailed into the Bay of Guanabara in the corvette *Voador*, foolishly flying the Portuguese flag. The new terms he offered were better, and included recognition of Brazil as a separate kingdom with its own administration, but they in no way included recognition of the country's independence. The Brazilian Government ignored the offer and sent Rio-Maior and his party packing in the *Treze de Maio*, leaving the *Voador* behind. She was seized as a prize of war, and added to the Brazilian Navy as the *Itaparica*.

The expectations and excitements of this time were captured in the daily Journal being written by Maria Graham, now happily installed in Rio in a house on the Gloria Hill close to an old childhood friend, William May, and his wife. May was a partner in the prominent local firm of May and Ludkin, which also acted as Lord Cochrane's agent. Prevented from returning to England by bouts of illness – for which she was treated by yet another close friend, Dr Dickson – Mrs Graham was making the most of her time in Brazil. With an intellectual curiosity which more than compensated for her poor physical health, she investigated every aspect of life, indefatigably visiting the commercial quarter, the warehouses, the arsenal, the dockyard, the foundling hospital, the botanical gardens, the library, the theatre, the forts and the churches as well as the sugar mills, great estates, Indian settlements and farms of the interior. In her Journal she left a detailed and colourful account of life, manners, food and social habits in the new Brazilian Empire. She also regularly recorded details of Cochrane's triumphs in the north as his ships returned to port bringing personal letters from friends in the Brazilian Squadron, including the First Admiral himself. Inevitably she also took advantage of the opportunity to study slavery at first hand, finding the practice both fascinating and repugnant. She went to the slave market and the plantations. She calculated the size of the Brazilian slave trade, finding that in 1822, 24,934 souls had been imported through Rio de Janeiro alone. She proved to her own satisfaction that slavery was not only immoral and degrading to all involved, but also profoundly uneconomic.

On the lighter side, Maria Graham was also establishing a modest place on the Rio social scene, renewing acquaintance with officers of the Royal Navy's South America Squadron and making friends among the British community. The only hitch was an initially cool relationship with Mrs Chamberlain, wife of the British Consul-General, over the etiquette of who should visit whom first, but intervention by Sir Thomas Hardy in his usual breezy and avuncular manner soon put that to rights. But on the Brazilian side there were no inhibitions, and Mrs Graham was soon mixing with the local aristocracy, making friends with Dona Ana Carvalho e Melo – wife of the new Foreign Minister – her mother, the Baronessa de Campos, and the family of the Viscondessa do Rio

Seco. She was received regularly and enthusiastically into their residences and visited the Imperial Court in their company on a number of occasions, noting the special attentions being paid to Lady Cochrane and forming a friendship with the Empress Leopoldina herself. Her admiration for the Empress knew no bounds. 'She is in all aspects admirable and respectable,' she recorded, 'and her conduct in both public and private justly commands the admiration and love of her family and her subjects. Her personal accomplishments would adorn a private gentlewoman; her temper, prudence and courage fit her for her high station.' Mrs Graham was a welcome visitor at Court, and her feelings seem to have been reciprocated. When she visited the Palace to pay her respects on the Emperor's birthday 12 October 1823 – eleven days before she was due to return to England as a passenger on the Packet *Chichester* – she was invited warmly to return in six months' time to become governess to the little Princess Maria da Glória. A chance remark by Sir Thomas Hardy had borne unexpected fruit. As she sailed for Falmouth, loaded with newspapers and happy anticipation, her major regret was that she would not be present to see Lord Cochrane's triumphant return.

On 9 November 1823, the *Pedro I* returned to Rio de Janeiro carrying a victorious First Admiral. At the harbour mouth he was greeted by the Emperor in person, who bestowed upon him the title of Marquis of Maranhão. Other honours swiftly followed – the Grand Cross of the Cruzeiro de Sul, a vote of thanks from the Assembly, membership of the Privy Council of the Empire. The honour and glory which Cochrane so richly deserved were his, and the officers of the Navy were not forgotten in the distribution of honours and promotions. In a brilliant campaign of only six months they had done all that had been expected of them – and more. They had blockaded and expelled a Portuguese army and a greatly superior naval squadron from its base in Bahia, and harried it out of Brazilian waters and across the Atlantic. They had then forced the Portuguese garrisons to evacuate Maranhão, Pará and Montevideo, leaving those provinces free to adhere to the Empire. As a result, the military stalemate which had threatened to frustrate Brazil's fight for freedom had been broken and the country cleared of Portuguese troops. For the Brazilian Empire and the Brazilian Navy, 1823 was the year of victory. Whatever the diplomatic position, the country was *de facto* independent, and the Government could enter into negotiations for peace and recognition with every certainty of success. For Cochrane and his men, there were all the pleasures of victory and public recognition. And in terms of more substantial reward, there were 73 captured ships and merchandise worth almost £250,000 awaiting the judgement of the Prize Courts.

CHAPTER 10

POLITICS AND PRIZE MONEY

The Ministers and Councillors of State who formed the new government after the dissolution of the Assembly were all native Brazilians, but politically they were supporters of the 'moderate' party and their policy, now that the war was as good as won, was based on reconciliation between Portuguese and Brazilian citizens and the restoration of friendly relations with Portugal. But there were problems in implementing this policy. Internally, the 'patriot' party remained a powerful force all over the country, stimulated rather than diminished by the dissolution and hostile to an administration it regarded as pro-Portuguese and liable to betray Brazilian national interests. Externally, foreign powers, led by Britain and Austria, were exerting pressure in favour of peace as a necessary preliminary to the recognition of Independence. On the one hand, therefore, the Government was faced with demands for the continuation of the war and the condemnation of enemy goods and prizes; while on the other, it was under pressure to suspend hostilities, to restore captured property and, even, to dismiss its British naval officers.[1] On the basic Brazilian position that fighting would continue until Independence was recognized, there could be no compromise; but in applying its other policies the Government had to tread so warily that it gave an impression of shiftiness which encouraged rather than removed suspicion.

The Emperor worked diligently to produce the promised constitution, and on 24 March 1824, he promulgated a Charter which was largely his own creation, and which was to remain Brazil's constitutional code for over 60 years. It was indeed a liberal document, balancing power between four branches – legislative, executive, judiciary and moderative – and providing for individual freedom and equality before the law. Unfortunately, the dominating issue of the day was the struggle for power between the 'moderate' and 'patriot" factions, and the theoretical niceties of the new Constitution neither mollified the antagonists of the regime nor prevented them from calling Pedro a despot and a tyrant.

In the military sphere, Lord Cochrane's achievements and reputation established him without question as the leader of the infant Brazilian Navy. As First Admiral, his opinion was sought on all maritime matters from broad issues of national defence to technical details such as the design of steamships or the availability of anchors or cables. As was the custom, all orders and communications between the Ministry of Marine and the ships and personnel under his command were channelled through Lord Cochrane. The only problem was when, on 19 December 1823, the Ministry directly ordered the brigantine *Atlanta* to the River Plate. Cochrane protested that he had not been consulted, and that the order was an infringement of his authority. Two weeks later he received an apology and the explanation that his original command extended only to the ships in Rio which had constituted the Squadron of Independence, and did not cover the River Plate flotilla.

Theoretically, the Government had at its disposal military and, particularly, naval forces strong enough to confront any challenge to its authority. But in reality, the Navy's efficiency was being undermined during the first months of 1824 by a bitter dispute between Lord Cochrane and the Ministry of Marine over the squadron's claims to prize money. From the prize as well as the military point of view, the independence campaign had been brilliantly successful – Cochrane had blockaded one port, captured two others, and pursued a heavily laden convoy for hundreds of miles. In all, the squadron had taken some 78 merchant ships and transports (of which 16 had been released or destroyed), three warships, including a brand-new frigate, eight gunboats, large quantities of merchandise, and considerable amounts of public and private property. Contemporary estimates put the total value at around 1260 contos of reis (or £252,000 at the prevailing rate of exchange).[2] Cochrane claimed that all this belonged by right to the captors – the ships taken on the high seas under the normal prize laws; the public property captured in Maranhão and Pará by right of conquest; and the private goods seized in the two ports under the Imperial Decree of 11 December 1822 confiscating enemy property. In January 1824, 24 ships and cargoes worth 600 contos of reis (£120,000) were already in Rio, and Cochrane was looking forward to their speedy condemnation by the Prize Courts according to law – which, as he well knew, awarded one-eighth of the value of all legitimate prizes to the commander-in-chief.[3]

Cochrane's preoccupation with pecuniary reward was notorious from the beginning, and any delay was liable to cause difficulties. As a precaution, Francisco Vilela Barbosa, who at the time had been Minister of Marine for only five days, went to the Admiral's house on 24 November 1823 to offer his personal respects and to assure an impatient Lord Cochrane that action on prizes would soon be taken. Three weeks later he instructed the Admiralty Judges to complete their examination of prizes with the greatest possible speed so that they could be sent to the Supreme Military Council for final judgement.[4]

Unfortunately, in the circumstances speed was hardly possible. The unusual nature of the conflict with Portugal and the lack of Brazilian prize laws produced legal complications, and months slipped by before the situation could be clarified. The difficulties were twofold. First, was a conflict between two coequal kingdoms under the Portuguese crown a 'war' in the internationally accepted sense? Second, if the two nations were truly at war, what laws applied to prizes taken by Brazilian naval vessels when the only Imperial legislation on the subject was a decree of 30 December 1822 controlling the activities of privateers? On 18 September 1823, the Supreme Military Council asked for guidance on these knotty points, and received the answer on 5 December. The ruling was that Brazil and Portugal were indeed at war: the decree of 30 December, which constituted the declaration, was still in force even though no privateering commissions had been issued; but its terms did not apply to warships, whose actions were to be regulated by the traditional Portuguese prize laws. These were contained in two Alvarás (or Royal Ordinances) dated 7 December 1796 and 9 May 1797. As in other countries, they set out in detail the formalities and conduct to be observed in the taking of prizes in time of war. Their basic principle was that legitimate prizes seized by warships were to remain the property of the takers. The only exception was in the case of military stores, where one-fifth of the value was to be retained.

Once the legal position had been settled, political problems came to the fore. To Cochrane and the men of the squadron, the quantities of enemy merchandise and the prizes riding at their anchors in the bay were concrete evidence of the victories they had won. But to the Government the very size of the Navy's triumph was an embarrassment. The restoration of captured Portuguese property was a basic plank in any policy of internal reconciliation or external peace, and ministers seem to have decided to secure the release of as many ships as they could by legal means. Thus, when the Supreme Military Council began to examine the cases before it, every loophole and technicality in the law was used to free the squadron's captures. A decision that no vessel taken in port or within two leagues of the coast was lawful prize liberated the majority of the merchantmen; the squadron's claims to captured warships were dismissed on the grounds that they were *droits* of the crown; and Cochrane's claims to public property seized in Maranhão and Pará were disallowed by a decision that the province had never been enemy territory – merely a part of the Brazilian Empire under temporary Portuguese occupation. By February 1824, the Superior Prize Court had dismissed the squadron's claims to over half of the ships and property it had captured, and claims for damages against Cochrane and his captains were already being filed by their aggrieved owners.

Lord Cochrane had been growing increasingly impatient at the delays in Prize Court judgements: now he erupted into anger. Openly expressed displeasure was supplemented on 10 February by a long letter to the Emperor in which he listed his services in the cause of Brazilian Independence, protested at the treatment to which he was being subjected, and offered his resignation. The open complaints of their commander-in-chief and the unaccountable release of their prizes inevitably caused a drop in the Navy's morale. Cochrane's public strictures in particular infected his men, who were already resentful at the way they were being treated on the question of pay. There was no real grievance over the speed or regularity with which crews were paid, but there were protests at the amounts that were offered. The monthly rates of the Imperial Navy in 1824 were 10 milreis (£2) for Able Seamen and

8 milreis (£1.60p) for Ordinary Seamen. The majority of the sailors recruited in England had enlisted for these amounts, but 150 out of the 450 British seamen had been engaged in Liverpool, where Vice-Consul Antonio Meirelles Sobrinho had dishonestly promised £5.50p. On their arrival in Rio the Government flatly refused to pay such an inflated figure and, in spite of Lord Cochrane's protestations on their behalf, declared that the men must accept the normal rate or go.[5] As a result many of them did just that, and by March over 100 much-needed sailors had left the service.[6] The officers, too, had a grievance, for they found that they were far less well off than General Brant had led them to expect. The spectre of a manpower shortage once again raised its head, and Cochrane reported that without some gesture to satisfy their prize claims and financial complaints, the effectiveness of the squadron would be seriously compromised.

The growing dissatisfaction of Lord Cochrane and his men was a matter of deep concern, for although ministers were dedicated to a policy of national reconciliation, they were equally aware of the need for a loyal navy. The vital contribution which Cochrane's ships had made to the liberation of Brazil was obvious, and alarming reports of Portuguese preparations for military reconquest and growing republicanism in the north-east made it clear that the Navy was crucial to the defence and unity of the Empire. The Government therefore found itself in a dilemma – its policy of reconciliation made the return of Portuguese property vital, yet the very act of restoring prizes to their owners was undermining the effectiveness of the Navy. There was also the problem of Lord Cochrane. His concern with financial gain was notorious, and the Government was not only reluctant to lose his incomparable talents, but fearful that he might offer them to a potential enemy.[7]

The whole problem was thrashed out in a meeting of the Council of State on 12 February 1824. After extensive discussion it was decided that the only answer lay in compromise – the policy of returning Portuguese property would continue, but to satisfy Cochrane and his men the National Treasury would not only pay them the value of all prizes, whether they were condemned or released, but would meet the claims for damages from aggrieved owners as well. Finally, as a special gesture of good faith, the squadron would be paid 40 contos of reis (£8000) on account for the frigate *Imperatriz*. Armed with these concessions, the Emperor interviewed Cochrane the same evening and quickly reached an agreement. The final terms were clear and concise, and were transcribed by Pedro in his own handwriting for the First Admiral's benefit.

The crisis now seemed to be over. On 14 February 1824 the Emperor reported the success of his negotiations to the Council, and on 23 February an Imperial decree was published giving official force to the terms of the settlement. On the same day, the process of reconciliation between the Government and its First Admiral was taken a step further in a decree which extended Cochrane's authority to all Brazilian naval vessels. Official documents no longer described him as commander-in-chief of 'the Imperial squadron in this port' but of 'the naval forces of this Empire ...'. The limitation which had caused friction over the *Atlanta* was removed. Unfortunately, the seeds of future arguments were sown by the qualification that the appointment would be effective only ' during the duration of the present war'. The decree was published in the official gazette five days later, on 28 February 1824. By 3 March, morale and confidence had been far enough restored among the officers and men of the Navy for a squadron comprising the frigates *Niterói* (Captain John Taylor) and *Piranga* (Captain James Norton), the brig *Bahia* (Commander Bartholomew Hayden) and the transport *Gentil Americana* (Lieutenant James Watson) to sail for Pernambuco, where rebellious tendencies had begun to manifest themselves.[8] On 15 March, orders were given for the process of arbitration on the value of the prizes to begin.

If the description written by John Cunningham, surgeon of HMS *Cambridge*, is anything to go by, then outside observers were highly impressed by the morale and condition of the Brazilian Navy at this time, and saw the prize money issue as a small and slightly amusing irritant. The *Cambridge*, a newly built 84-gun warship of massive size, had arrived in Rio de Janeiro on 22 February, after a dreadful voyage of two months from Portsmouth in which its equipment had been shown to be shoddy and its puny crew inept. All three topmasts had been carried away or found to be rotten, sails had split and simple manoeuvres had been bungled. The shame had been magnified by the fact that the *Cambridge* carried the entire British diplomatic corps for the newly independent states of South America. On board were three consul-generals, one consul and five vice-consuls who, together with their families and servants, made up a party of over seventy persons. As the *Cambridge* limped into Rio dockyard for repairs in full view of the smart little ships of the Brazilian Navy and a visiting French squadron, Consul-General Woodbine Parish, on his way to Buenos Aires, penned an acid despatch to the Foreign Office. The condition of the Royal Navy's vessels was so inferior, he wrote, that 'even the officers of the contemptible navy of this miserable government are laughing, not up their sleeves but openly, at such mismanagement, and the runaways from our own squadron on board the Brazilian ships dare say that Pedro I's ships-of-war are as well rigged and fitted as the King of England's!'

John Cunningham's reactions to the voyage and to Brazil were written into a massive and verbose daily journal. In 600 pages of neat handwriting, he described at length the breathtaking scenery surrounding the Bay of Guanabara, the attractions of the town, the harbour and the fortifications. From his own observations and from information supplied by Bartholomew Hayden, he went on to describe the Brazilian vessels and their commanders:

> It is impossible for ships of war to appear in higher external order than this little navy, but when we consider that all their captains, most of their officers and the greater part of their crews are Englishmen, it is not to be wondered at – especially with the immortal Cochrane as their chief.... As a reward for his splendid services the Emperor conferred on his lordship the rank and title of Marquis of Maranhão but we are given to understand that he wishes to deprive him of the more substantial fruits of his labour viz his *prize money*! It must be confessed however that His Majesty has a hard fellow to contend with when money is in the scale, and I daresay his lordship will press him hard ere he finally surrenders his claim to what is his just reward.[9]

Cunningham was not wrong in his estimation of Cochrane's attitude. In spite of all the assurances the Brazilians had given, his relationship with members of the administration remained at rock bottom. The agreement of 12 February seemed to satisfy all his demands, but the way in which it had been obtained had done nothing to mollify the First Admiral's obsessive mistrust in the government's good faith. Indeed, he seemed to be preparing to leave. Lady Cochrane had suffered greatly from the heat and humidity of the Brazilian summer, and had found the attentions of the Imperial Court trying rather than flattering. On 17 February she was sent back to England in the Packet *Marchioness of Salisbury* with her daughter and her servants to await the birth of Arthur Auckland Leopold Pedro, leaving her husband alone to press his grievances and threaten resignation. Cochrane remained convinced that ministers were partisans of Portugal who were deliberately trying to undermine his authority and weaken the Brazilian Navy by driving away its British officers with harsh and unjust treatment. Lord Cochrane's single-minded attitude to life prevented him from appreciating either the delicacy of the Government's position or the complex nature of its problems. The compromise over prize money, which had been stimulated partly by necessity and partly by a genuine desire to heal the breach, was seen as a reluctant concession torn from a hostile administration only as a result of Cochrane's personal appeal to the Emperor. A number of points had been settled, but the deep mistrust in his mind remained.

In his simplistic way Cochrane blamed all the problems encountered on the prize issue on deliberate Portuguese obstruction. For a man of the First Admiral's temperament, only concrete proof in the shape of faster prize adjudication and the rapid appearance of prize money could overcome his conviction that the ministers had deceived him. In the circumstances, neither was possible: first because of the nature of the legal processes involved; and second because of the Government's financial problems.

Compared to the administration of British prize laws, Brazilian procedures were lengthy and legalistic, and were complicated by the manner in which many of the prizes had been taken. The Alvarás of 1796 and 1797 had specifically laid down, for example, that prize cargoes were to be left untouched, and that all papers and at least two officers from each captured ship were to be detained to give evidence. The circumstances of the chase of the Portuguese convoy and the capture of S. Luis and Pará had been such that it had been impossible to observe these requirements – some ships had arrived in Brazilian ports without officers, some without prize crews, some loaded with merchandise which did not belong to them; and when Cochrane had run out of prize crews in Maranhão, he had taken the highly irregular step of demanding the value in cash of goods he could not remove. As a result, a naturally lengthy legal process was made even more prolonged by a host of technical infringements. Cochrane understood none of this. To his suspicious mind, all the delays were part of a Portuguese intrigue in which the Minister of Marine, Vilela Barbosa, was closely implicated. He did not know that the Minister was in fact applying pressure on the Prize Courts to produce faster judgements,[10] nor that the number of weekly sessions had been increased to speed up the procedure.[11] Indeed, on 13 November 1824, the Supreme Military Council protested to the Emperor that the haste forced on the Prize Courts had resulted in a number of clear miscarriages of justice.

In spite of the delays, it seems likely that Cochrane could still have been won over by the payment of an advance on prize money – but this, too, was hardly possible. Throughout its existence, the Brazilian Empire had been in a state of perpetual financial crisis, and until 1824 it had been deprived of the revenues of almost half the country. In 1821, government income had covered only two-thirds of expenditure, and the national debt had risen inexorably until it had reached 11,000 contos of reis (£2,200,000).[12] In 1824 the situation improved slightly, but the Government was still forced to save the situation by raising a loan of £3 million on the London market against the security of the customs revenues of Rio, Bahia, Pernambuco and Maranhão. With the threat of Portuguese reconquest, the spread of the north-eastern rebellion and the payment of arrears of salary being the first condition for the evacuation of the Portuguese troops still in Montevideo, the Imperial Government had no money to spare to mollify a suspicious Lord Cochrane.

Neither did the Ministry appreciate fully the reason for the First Admiral's obsession with prize money. In the Portuguese and Brazilian navies, prizes were a minor consideration: commissioned service was genuinely a 'career', and promotion to the senior ranks the rule rather than the exception. In the British Navy, where promotion depended on influence and overexpansion in war invariably led to fierce cuts and widespread officer unemployment in peace, prize money was a major inducement and an important factor in offsetting the uncertainties of the service. But just as the Brazilians failed to understand the British outlook, so Cochrane was unaware of the financial problems of the Government. To him, the non-payment of an advance of prize money was inexplicable – except by assuming double-dealing. And to Cochrane, accustomed to the rich prize harvests of the Napoleonic Wars, the sums involved – 600 contos of reis (£120,000) for the ships and goods in harbour, and perhaps another 400 contos (£80,000) for prizes outside Rio – seemed comparatively small. The appointment of a British commander-in-chief in the West Indies had been reckoned to be worth £100,000 during the war, and the frigate *Pallas* was said to have won prize money totalling £200,000 while under Cochrane's own command in 1805. To the Brazilians, however, the amount of money involved was enormous. The Empire's naval expenditure in 1823 had been 1100 contos of reis (£220,000) and was running at 100 contos per month during 1824.[13] In these terms, Cochrane was demanding prize money equal to the entire cost of the Brazilian Navy for a full year! Cash on this scale was just not available.

And so, in spite of the agreement of 12 February, relations between the Minister of Marine and the First Admiral continued to deteriorate. On 20 March, Cochrane submitted his resignation once more. On 30 March, he repeated his grievances in a long letter to José Severiano Maciel da Costa. Four weeks later, the Chief Minister replied in tones which, however polite, could hardly disguise the Government's growing weariness with Cochrane's continual complaints. He began by disclaiming any responsibility for maritime affairs, then went on to assure the First Admiral:

> the intentions of HIM and the members of his Council are, and always have been, to do pleasure to Your Excellency, and the proof of this is that the misunderstandings (so natural in the verbal undertakings arrived at with the late Ministry) have always been decided in a manner favourable to Your Excellency. The difficulties surrounding the question of the prizes have had origins so well known that it is melancholy to see them attributed to the ill-will of the Council of HIM, who have already dismissed two judges because they were not endowed with the requisite activity.... As to the ideas that the difficulties that you have met with in the arsenal and in other offices were commanded, or at least tolerated, by the Ministry, I believe them to be totally imaginary and having no other source than the sordid ambitions of some intriguer. And in a word, all that seems to me to be trifles unworthy to occupy the head of Your Excellency if it were not

forced on you by persons of bad intentions. For the rest, let Your Excellency reflect for a moment and it will be found that the Government of HIM, simply and entirely to do pleasure to Your Excellency, have incurred an enormous liability in the engagements made with you. It is unfortunate that in the place of thanks and satisfaction, Your Excellency should think right to reply by recriminations both bitter and violent. For myself ... I do not know in what manner we can content you; and do believe that your official correspondence, once made public, would prove it.[14]

But no reply, whether diplomatic or forthright, could make any difference. Cochrane refused to be mollified. A Memorandum on the Defence of Brazil submitted on 3 May provided another opportunity for him to repeat his complaints; the recommendations for the Development of the Navy submitted on 21 June and 3 July provided two more. He also mounted a serious attack on the Prize Court in a letter to the Emperor. He pointed out that nine of its thirteen members were Portuguese by birth, and accused them of perverting the course of justice in favour of their compatriots, and being openly antagonistic to the interests of the Navy and the country. He demanded government intervention. For its part, the administration continued to reject his charges, protested its good faith, and reaffirmed the undertakings on prize money that had been given in February.

The atmosphere in Rio was made even worse by the pronouncements of the Prize Court itself, which seemed to be acting with hairsplitting legalism. Infringements of the procedures laid down for the capture of prizes were penalized with complete disregard for the circumstances. Article 18 of the Alvará of 1796, for example, said that those guilty of tampering with prize cargoes should be fined four times their value and be liable to corporal punishment. Lord Cochrane had clearly transgressed this regulation in Maranhão, but for the Prize Court to draw attention to the penalties without regard to the circumstances was inexcusable, and provoked an understandable outburst of anger. Captain Taylor of the *Niterói* was sentenced to a fine of four times the value of the goods in question for having replenished the frigate's stores from the cargo of the *Prazeres e Alegria*[15] at a time when his ship had been at sea for three months and was in Portuguese waters 4000 miles from a friendly port.

The legalistic nature of Brazilian naval administration also took the British officers by surprise. Small infringements which in the Royal Navy would have been dealt with quietly by a ship's commander became the subject of lengthy courts martial. By the middle of 1824, over a dozen officers were being proceeded against. Although some charges were sufficiently serious to warrant dismissal – as in the cases of Sublieutenants Poynton and Sewell, who were sacked respectively for blatant insubordination and incompetence – the majority were not, and the defendants were either found innocent or promptly 'pardoned' by the Emperor and immediately re-employed. But the system was bad for morale, and three officers, Lieutenant Gillett and Sublieutenants Watson and Drummond, chose to desert rather than face the ordeal.

By June 1824, Cochrane was conducting a vitriolic and anonymous correspondence in the newspapers with Vilela Barbosa – the latter writing under the pseudonym 'Curioso'. By this time it had become impossible to satisfy the First Admiral: nagging complaints over his terms of service, the treatment of British officers, the release of prizes, his position after the war, went on and on.

The Grenfell affair was typical of the low ebb to which relations had sunk. Commander John Pascoe Grenfell arrived in Rio from Belém with the *Imperatriz* on 24 May 1824. While he was ashore, documents and prize money amounting to 40,000 milreis in silver were taken from the frigate, and he was ordered to report to the Ministry of Marine so that complaints against him by the Junta of Pará could be investigated.[16] Grenfell, alarmed by the atmosphere of antagonism in Rio, went into semi-hiding for two months while Cochrane reported that he had taken refuge on a British warship (information which was untrue, and caused an angry correspondence between the Brazilian and the British authorities).[17] Cochrane then refused to arrest Grenfell and, when he finally issued the necessary orders, refused to enforce them. Finally, in late July, Grenfell voluntarily gave himself up. He was eventually tried and acquitted of all charges.

Then, in June 1824, Cochrane was warned by Madame Bompland, wife of a resident French naturalist, that the authorities intended to use the excuse of a naval review on the fifth of the month to remove quantities of prize money from the *Pedro I*, which he had refused to turn over to the authorities for adjudication. As described graphically in his autobiography, Cochrane rode in the dead of night to the Palace of São Cristovão, interviewed the Emperor still clad in his nightshirt, and successfully secured the abandonment of the plan and the cancellation of the review. But the element of farce apart, the position of the Brazilian Government was becoming increasingly difficult. The autocratic traits in the Emperor's character and his predilection for the advice of Court favourites were already evident. His ministers were inexperienced in office and, caught between a host of conflicting pressures, lacked the will or the confidence to pursue a strong line. National unity and reconciliation remained the aim, and the Government chose to follow a policy of moderation in its dealings with the dissidents in the north-east, hoping that restricted military action in the shape of the naval blockade, accompanied by a spirit of compromise, would bring the wayward sheep back into the Imperial fold. In private conversations, the Emperor himself confirmed that if his compromise candidate, Mayrick Ferrão, were accepted as President of Pernambuco, he would offer a general amnesty and forget the past.

By June 1824, however, there was no doubt in the minds of Brazilian ministers that Pernambuco was treading a path which would eventually lead to open rebellion. Firm action was impossible, however, due to events on the international scene. All through April, May and June, reports from Europe told of massive Portuguese preparations for the reconquest of Brazil. On 4 April, the British packet-boat *Lord Herbert* brought copies of Lisbon decrees giving details of the proposed military expedition. Three weeks later, the *Princess Elizabeth* carried confirmation and more information. On 4 June, the packet *Cygnet* arrived with more alarming news, this time elaborated in despatches from Felisberto Brant and Gameiro Pessoa in London.

The Imperial Government took urgent countermeasures. Troops were raised, fortifications rebuilt and floating batteries placed at the entrance to the bay. Fortunately, the National Subscription for the Navy was still active, and on 1 June 1824 it stood at 132 contos of reis (£26,000). With its aid, Vilela Barbosa began a rapid expansion of Brazil's thinly stretched naval forces. During June and July, six of the prizes captured by the squadron and condemned by the Prize Courts were purchased for the Navy, their value being paid to Cochrane's agents, May and Ludkin. These were the 12-gun brigantine *Pará*, the 18-gun brig *Maranhão*, the *Leal Portuguêz* (which became the corvette *Carioca*), the *Carvalho VI* (which became the brig-of-war *Pirajá*) and the transports *Harmonia* and *Caridade*. On 17 July, General Brant in London – already assembling huge quantities of naval and military stores ordered in May – was instructed to buy two big 1200-ton East Indiamen, and to recruit 800 sailors.[18] Orders were sent to Bahia Arsenal on 4 June for the construction of a 74-gun ship, and to the dockyards of Rio and Pará on 31 May and 11 June for the laying down of two frigates and various gunboats.

Vilela Barbosa made one last effort to satisfy Lord Cochrane's complaints. On 4 June, he wrote to assure the First Admiral that the Government was determined to honour the prize agreement of 12 February, and to pay to the squadron the value of all prizes released. To ease the manpower problem, it was also decreed on 11 June that all foreign seamen were to be paid 50 per cent above the normal pay scales; and on 14 July, in recognition of their financial difficulties, it was decided that the officers contracted in London should receive 'embarked' pay rates whether serving ashore or afloat. On 19 June the Government wrote once more to Cochrane confirming the prize agreement and telling him that it had been decided to make 200 contos of reis (£40,000) available immediately as an advance of prize money and a gesture of good faith. On 12 July, the money was deposited in the iron chest of the *Pedro I*, and Jackson began to pay out prize money to the officers and men of the squadron. Finally, Vilela Barbosa settled a grievance that had exercised Cochrane since the decree of 28 February, which extended his authority to the whole of the Brazilian Navy, but limited the appointment to the length of the war. On 27 July a new Imperial decree announced that Cochrane could remain commander-in-chief for as long as he wished, but that when he chose to resign he would receive halfpay for the rest of his life, his widow enjoying the same privilege for as long as she lived.[19]

On 11 June 1824, the Emperor issued a proclamation calling the nation to arms against the Portuguese threat. 'Vigilance Brazilians!' it declared. 'Preserve valour, constancy and above all internal unity amongst ourselves. And may the God of Armies bless our legitimate struggle to preserve Liberty and Independence!' Further orders rallied the regular troops in Rio and recalled all naval units to the defence of the capital. Brazil's second line of resistance was to lie in the provinces, and Presidents were ordered to make arrangements for local defence. On 12 June, the schooner *Carolina* sailed for Pernambuco and Pará carrying orders for Taylor to lift the blockade and return to Rio with the ships under his command.[20] Any Portuguese attack was to be met with the maximum concentration of force.

CHAPTER 11

THE GATHERING STORM

The province of Pernambuco was one of the richest and most important regions of Brazil. Protected by a chain of parallel reefs which provided a natural breakwater against the Atlantic swell, its flat and fertile soil produced an abundance of sugar, cotton and coffee which made it the centre of a thriving foreign and domestic trade. From the sea, travellers found the prospect of Pernambuco enchanting. Its blue seas, palm-fringed beaches, great plantations and stone-built, whitewashed towns set among the richly wooded countryside excited both the eye and the senses. It was only on closer acquaintance that the oppressive heat and the fevers bred by the flat and well-watered landscape became painfully apparent.

But when the anonymous author of *Revolução do Brasil* wrote of 'the malignant vapours of Pernambuco' he was not only referring to the climate. The province had a reputation for turbulence and political radicalism, and its intellectuals were devotees of the principles of the American and French revolutions and of the Enlightenment, which they had acquired at the universities of Montpellier and Coimbra or at the local seminary of Olinda, for years the only institution of higher education in Brazil. The fact that the province was dependent on slavery, and that the proportion of black slaves in the population was one of the highest in Brazil, was in no way seen as being incompatible with these fine principles. The Pernambucanos had also inherited a fierce regional loyalty and a tradition of resistance to foreign rule, the last manifestation of which had been a violently extinguished revolt against the Portuguese crown in 1817.

The triumph of constitutionalism in Lisbon and the growth of the Independence movement in Rio de Janeiro put the governing

Junta of Pernambuco in a dilemma. On the one hand, although it was opposed to Portuguese domination, it realized that the Côrtes' policy of decentralizing the administration of Brazil favoured the cause of regional autonomy. On the other, although it was inclined to support the cause of Brazilian Independence, it had no desire to be subordinated to a monarchical government sitting in Rio de Janeiro. Thus, in the interests of Pernambuco, the Junta tried to steer a delicate course between the two alternatives.

The reasoning of the Junta, however, was too subtle for the masses. As relations between Rio and Lisbon deteriorated there were mass meetings, demonstrations and newspaper articles favouring independence. By August 1822, the momentum had become irresistible. A military coup in September put a more radical Junta in office, and the commitment of Pernambuco to the Brazilian cause became total. On 8 December, the accession of Pedro was enthusiastically proclaimed in Recife and in other towns, and on 15 December the new green-and-yellow flag of the Empire was raised and saluted in Pernambuco for the first time. The province's resolution was strengthened when the Portuguese warships *Dez de Fevereiro* and *Audaz* imposed a short-lived blockade on Recife. The Pernambucanos promptly retaliated by sending an expeditionary force to join the patriot army in Bahia.

Unfortunately, the new state of affairs did nothing to settle the disturbed and factious state of political life. There was hostility between the Junta and the military, between groups within the Army, and between individual members of the Junta itself. The republican faction steadily gained the upper hand, but the internal struggle for power continued to dominate the Pernambuco scene, and went on apparently oblivious to the overthrow of the Côrtes in Lisbon or of the expulsion of the Portuguese from Bahia.

It was into this confused situation that Commander Bartholomew Hayden sailed on 14 July 1823. Hayden had left the chase of Madeira de Melo's convoy on 7 July with orders from Lord Cochrane to convoy four prizes to Pernambuco and deliver letters to the provincial authorities. He was then to remain off the coast in the brig-of-war *Bahia*, seizing all vessels flying the flag of Portugal. On arrival in Recife, Hayden was treated cordially, but the suspicious Pernambucanos refused to allow his prizes to enter the port, fearing that they might be troop transports from Rio attempting to seize the province by *coup de main*.¹ There were ample grounds for further disagreement. The port of Recife was not under technical blockade, and in interpreting his orders Hayden decided to ignore ships which were already in the port or were leaving it, and to restrict himself to those newly arriving from Portugal or its colonies. On this basis, he began to patrol the sea lanes off Pernambuco, seizing in his first weeks the prizes *Alexander I* and *Deus te Guarde*, but keeping aloof from the political turmoil ashore.

Then, on 13 December 1823, came a political bombshell. The *Alexandre* sailed into Recife carrying eight north-eastern delegates with news of the dissolution of the Constituent Assembly by force of arms. In Pernambuco the reaction was violent and immediate. Within hours the provincial administration resigned, having lost, it claimed, both moral authority and public confidence. In an atmosphere of excitement and defiance a new Junta was elected, dominated by the extreme radical faction and headed by Manuel de Carvalho Paes de Andrade, one of the survivors of the 1817 rebellion who had spent years of exile in the United States. Colonel José de Barros Falcão, commander of the Pernambuco contingent which had returned from the victory in Bahia only the day before, was appointed military commander by acclamation.

The tone of the new Junta's public pronouncements was moderate, but a radical, anti-imperialist turn in Pernambuco politics was immediately evident. Urged on by the extreme views of the *Sentinella de Liberdade* and the *Typhys Pernambucano*, the old-style republicans of 1817 began to dominate the scene, especially Manuel de Carvalho – ambitious, shrewd, and with the gift of being able to communicate his extremism while seeming to favour moderation – and Father Joaquim do Amor Divino Rebelo, called 'Caneca', an eloquent and fanatical intellectual recently returned from post-1817 imprisonment with his revolutionary fervour undiminished. The *Bahia* and its 31-year-old commander were clearly seen as floating representatives of the Imperial mammon, and action was soon mounted against them. Manuel de Carvalho, who was also Intendant of Marine, refused to provide supplies for the brig, and the Junta ordered Hayden to send copies of his authority to take prizes off the port. On 17 December he was told to appear in person before the civil government to justify his action in seizing the Portuguese brig *S. Andre Diligente*, which had arrived the same day carrying 272 slaves from Angola. When he refused, the possibility of seizing the slaver by force was contemplated, but rejected. Hayden was in no doubt as to the real intentions of the Junta of Pernambuco. On 14 December 1823 he informed Cochrane of the growing violence in the province, and the republican tendencies of its government, in despatches carried by Lieutenant Cowan in the *Carvalho VI*, which had been captured a week earlier.[2] He brusquely refused to acknowledge the Junta's right to give him orders and, certain that it was planning to arrest him, refused to be tricked into going ashore. Meanwhile, his bag of prizes increased. On 20 December the *Incomparavel* was taken, on 24 December the *Dos Amigos*, on Christmas Day the hired Danish merchantman *Holstein*. All were sent to Rio for adjudication.

As Hayden watched, the situation in Pernambuco continued to deteriorate. At the end of December, the Junta decreed the expulsion of all Portuguese citizens who had not taken an oath of loyalty. Days later it seized the Imperial brigantine *Independência ou Morte*, dismissed her commander and replaced him with a local officer. It was rumoured that the main motive for this action was to attack the *Bahia* itself. Hayden feared nothing on that score, but with supplies, especially water, running low, and with most of his officers and half of his crew of 106 away on prizes, it was clear that he could not remain much longer.[3] Eventually, on 12 January 1824, the *Bahia* was forced to leave its cruising station and sail for Rio de Janeiro.

But before the *Bahia* departed, matters had reached the point of no return. On 8 January, the provincial electors of Pernambuco had gathered in the cathedral of Olinda to confirmed Manuel de Carvalho Paes de Andrade as President, and decisively to reject the claims of the Emperor's nominee, Francisco Paes Barreto. In normal circumstances the choice of Paes Barreto – a veteran of the 1817 rebellion, head of an important local family, and landowner of known liberal views – would have been a good one. But in the charged atmosphere of January 1824, it was not enough. The electors, while protesting that they were 'zealous, faithful subjects', went on to tell Pedro that Paes Barreto was incapable of solving the ills of Pernambuco, and that these were the result of 'the lack of confidence felt by all the inhabitants of the province aroused by the extraordinary events which took place in Rio on 12 November last, and who now fear with great concern the restoration of the ancient and equally detested despotism....'4

In early February, Francisco Paes Barreto arrived personally in Recife to take up the office of President. Manuel de Carvalho, ambitious and astute, was determined both to prevent his rival from assuming power and to evade responsibility for having done so. Superficially he remained neutral, but in secret his supporters were active and successful in their opposition. On 21 February 1824, representatives of the cities and towns of the province gathered in the Casa do Governo, decisively rejected Paes Barreto and demanded that Manuel de Carvalho be confirmed as President of Pernambuco. For the radicals it was a victory, but the issue had revealed a deep division of opinion in the province. Supporters of Paes Barreto began to rally. The army, like the civil population, was divided. There were arrests, counter-arrests, demonstrations and scattered fighting. Finally, Francisco Paes Barreto and his followers withdrew to the south, entrenched themselves in Barra Grande, and awaited help and reinforcements from Rio de Janeiro.

The withdrawal of his rival from the seat of government and his resort to arms left Manuel de Carvalho in undisputed command of Pernambuco. His supporters began to intensify their secret campaign to win the other provinces of northern Brazil to the anti-Imperial cause. Reactions were various. Maranhão was too involved in its internal struggles for power to be much interested. Piauí was still too weak after the 'Fidié' War to make any positive response. In Rio Grande do Norte the authorities arrested Manuel de Carvalho's agents as soon as they began to disseminate leaflets and propaganda, and deported them. In Alagoas the extremist doctrines found some support, but the President of the Junta quickly smothered the outbreak.

But in other provinces, the Pernambuco message fell on more receptive ears. In Paraíba, where there were strong social and political ties, the news of the dissolution of the Assembly was received with equal fury. Encouraged by Manuel de Carvalho's agents and by their own ejected deputies – who had also sailed from Rio on the *Alexandre*, and had participated in the protest at Olinda on 8 January 1824 – the province rallied strongly to the side of Pernambuco. In Ceará, news of the dissolution was carried

The Coronation of Pedro I, 1 December 1822. From Jean Baptiste Debret, *Voyage pittoresque et historique au Brazil*.

"Independence or Death" Pedro America's famous evocation of Dom Pedro's declaration at Ypiranga, 7 September 1822.

Rio de Janeiro in 1799 by Garneray

Rio de Janeiro from the north east by Cicéri and Benoist

The departure of Cochrane's Squadron on 1 April 1823. The *Predro* I in the lead is followed by the *Piranga*, *Maria da Gloria* and *Liberal*. A modern picture by Peter Davies, Commissioned by Lt. Cmdr Bernard Wardle (reproduction courtesy of the present owner, Mrs William Gough).

Lord Thomas Cochrane from the mezzotint by Ramsay and Meyer

John Pascoe Grenfell

Thomas Sackville Crosbie

John Taylor

James Norton

likewise by the province's own deputies, who had travelled via Pernambuco, where they had had long discussions with Manuel de Carvalho and his followers. The word spread like wildfire through the countryside, exciting the same violent reaction. On 9 January, the city of Campo Maior resolved to exclude Pedro from the throne and demanded a republic. Other towns quickly and enthusiastically followed suit. In February, the Cearense troops who had played such a notable part in the defeat of the Portuguese in Piauí and Maranhão arrived home, imbued with republican and radical enthusiasms. On reaching Fortaleza, their first act was to install their leader, José Pereira Filgueiras, as military commander of the province and his civilian mentor, Tristão de Alençar Araripe, as head of the Junta. Throughout March, the two Cearense leaders regaled the population with a spate of proclamations, on a printing press thoughtfully provided by Manuel de Carvalho, which extolled the cause of liberty and demanded solidarity with their neighbour province. On 31 March, they addressed a defiant letter to Rio expressing displeasure at the dissolution and the apparent threat to their rights, preferring 'death rather than accept the ancient yoke!'

By the end of April 1824, the contagion of rebellion had reached Pará at the mouth of the Amazon, where Manuel de Carvalho's agents were busy distributing leaflets and anti-Imperial propaganda. So effective were they that on 27 April President Geraldo de Abreu was deposed and a new Junta appointed which favoured the republican cause. The anarchy which was still prevalent in Pará clearly favoured the extremists, but the scatter of population prevented any concentration of popular support and gave the movement a flimsier basis than it had in other parts of the region. Nevertheless, open defiance from yet another province boded ill for both the unity of Brazil and the authority of the Imperial Government.

CHAPTER 12

TAYLOR BLOCKADES PERNAMBUCO

As news of the rising tide of resistance and republicanism in the north-east reached Rio de Janeiro, the Imperial Government decided on a show of force. As early as 30 December 1824 orders had been issued for the preparation of a naval expedition, but the disaffection of Lord Cochrane and his men over prize money had made any decisive action impossible. It was only when that issue had been settled by the agreement of 12 February 1824 that the Government was able to answer the challenge being posed to its authority in Pernambuco. Orders were given, and a fortnight later a flotilla of four ships was ready to sail under the command of Captain John Taylor. His instructions were to sail directly to Recife in the *Niterói*, with the *Piranga* (Captain James Norton), the *Gentil Americana* (Lieutenant James Watson) and the brig-of-war *Bahia* (Commander Bartholomew Hayden) under his command. If Francisco Paes Barreto had not been accepted as President, then Taylor was to put the province under strict blockade and to ensure that neither Manuel de Carvalho nor the other leaders of the rebellion could escape. On the way the *Bahia* was to visit the ports of Salvador, Sergipe and Alagoas before joining Taylor off Pernambuco, bringing with him the brigantine *Atlanta* (Lieutenant Samuel Gillett), which was ordered from Salvador to join the blockading squadron. On 3 March, the flotilla weighed anchor and sailed from Rio bound for the north-east.

Taylor's force reached its destination on 31 March 1824. On the surface the province was tranquil. All was calm, and the Imperial flag could still be seen flying over the forts and the principal buildings of the town. Taylor cautiously made contact. Diplomatically refraining from addressing the illegal civil authorities, he wrote to the military commander requesting an urgent meeting on board the *Niterói*, as his duties prevented him from going ashore. Colonel Barros Falcão de Lacerda replied with equal tact and caution, sending his compliments to the officers of the Imperial Navy, reaffirming his obedience to the Emperor, but regretting that bad health prevented him from accepting the invitation. Taylor wrote back, asking the military commander to distribute a proclamation urging the people of the province to accept the Emperor's nominee, Paes Barreto, as President of Pernambuco in order to avoid the evils of civil war. On 2 April Taylor wrote again, saying that in order to seek a solution to the problem without delay he had decided to send his second-in-command, Captain Luis Barroso Pereira, 'an officer who enjoys the particular confidence of His Imperial Majesty and of myself', to show Falcão de Lacerda copies of his instructions and to receive the latest information on the state of affairs. At the same time he established contact with Francisco Paes Barreto, entrenched in Barra Grande, asking him to rendezvous with the Imperial Squadron as soon as possible. The following day, Taylor sent copies of this correspondence to Falcão de Lacerda, trusting that this evidence of solidarity with Paes Barreto would make the evasive authorities in Recife show their true intentions while reassuring them of his moderate attitude should a compromise be forthcoming. In some measure he succeeded, for on 5 April Falcão de Lacerda wrote to say that a Grand Council would be held in two days' time to consider the political future of Pernambuco, in view of the Emperor's wishes and the arrival of the squadron. Taylor was cordially invited to attend. With equal courtesy the invitation was accepted, although due to ill health and lack of fluency in Portuguese, Taylor asked to be permitted to send Barroso Pereira in his place.[1]

On 7 April, the fragile cordiality was torn apart and the battle-lines were drawn. At 10 a.m., a Council of 300 people, comprising representatives of all the major cities and the military districts, met at the Casa do Governo. The atmosphere in the chamber was electric, with supporters of Manuel de Carvalho excitedly packing the public seating in the balcony. All began calmly. On request, Captain Barroso Pereira explained the presence of the naval division off Pernambuco; dwelt on the Emperor's moderation and desire to promote peace and harmony; and urged the acceptance of Paes Barreto as Provincial President. But the mood quickly changed as speaker after speaker, led by the vitriolic Frei Caneca, declared their support for Manuel de Carvalho and, amid cheering from the balcony, denounced the despotic acts of the Imperial Government and the forced dissolution of the Assembly. Amid scenes of wild enthusiasm, the presidency of Manuel de Carvalho was confirmed by acclamation and the claim of Paes Barreto contemptuously dismissed. It was resolved that a delegation of three should go to Rio to appeal to the Emperor in person. The official minutes of the meeting which were subsequently issued were moderate in tone, but Barroso Pereira had seen and heard the anti-Imperial panegyrics, the offers of blood, the cries for war and the mood of defiance. It was in this vein that he reported to his superior both verbally and in writing. The pretence was now over and the die cast. Taylor immediately put his orders into execution, and declared the port of Recife and the adjacent coast in a state of blockade.

Playing the game to its hypocritical conclusion, Falcão de Lacerda responded to the news with pained innocence, protesting at the blockade and claiming that no one in the Council or the population was lacking in fidelity to the Emperor. But Taylor, who was by now fully aware of the gap between what the Pernambucanos said and what they did, was neither convinced by the military commander's words nor deflected from his purpose. His despatch to Cochrane dated 8 April showed a shrewd and realistic grasp of the situation in the province. In Taylor's opinion, the hostility being shown towards the President nominated by the Emperor was motivated basically by Pernambuco's separatist ambitions, and Manuel de Carvalho and his adherents – far from being anxious for reconciliation with the Imperial Government – were actively spreading the 'fires of revolution' to other provinces, sending agents, propaganda and money.[2]

Manuel de Carvalho's open defiance of the Imperial Government, symbolized by the sight of Taylor's ships rolling at their anchors off Recife or patrolling offshore on blockade duty, strengthened rather than weakened his position in Pernambuco, and drove the politics of the province further in the direction of extremism. On 20 April, the blockade was relaxed to enable a hired brig to sail for Rio de Janeiro carrying the three Pernambuco delegates. Once they were safely on their way, however, the authorities in Recife adopted a markedly more belligerent attitude. On 23 April, Manuel de Carvalho issued a proclamation which bitterly attacked Taylor's attempts to bring the province to obedience, recalled the alleged persecution of patriots by Grenfell in Pará, and rejoiced in the spread of the rebellion to other provinces. On 12 May, Falcão de Lacerda, who had now committed himself wholeheartedly to the rebel cause by despatching a body of troops against the 'Imperialist' positions in Barra Grande, published a second and more vicious attack on Taylor's character. 'Who is this John Taylor,' he wrote,

> this second Nelson? A ridiculous officer of the British Navy who deserted the flag of his nation.... A lieutenant who sold himself for the rank of captain-of-frigate. Soldiers! A foreigner who has betrayed his country and sacrificed his honour for vile self-interest merits neither your trust nor your confidence. Remain alert against his seditions and deceits![3]

For John Taylor, the enforcement of the blockade off Recife was no easy task. His first problem was the sea. The onshore winds and the reef-fringed coast made naval activity off Pernambuco dangerous at the best of times, and the coral which was interspersed with the white sand on the seabed took a steady toll in anchors and cables. Bad weather during May made the situation worse, and the *Niterói*, with only one anchor remaining, was forced to stand out to sea in the interests of safety. Supplies, too, presented a problem. With the naval arsenal at Recife closed to them, the blockading ships were dependent on food and stores sent from Rio de Janeiro. By the end of April the Ministry of Marine had set up a system of regular supply, but the first weeks of the blockade were difficult, with stocks running dangerously low. Taylor solved the immediate problem by reprovisioning the *Niterói* from the brigantine *Atlanta*, which arrived under Lieutenant Gillett's command on 17 April, and from the *Bahia* and the *Piranga* before they were sent four days later to Barra Grande to support Francisco Paes Barreto's forces.

Through Vilela Barbosa in the Ministry of Marine, the Government gave Taylor's squadron sterling support. On 26 April – a fortnight after returning from Montevideo, where they had supervised the embarkation of the final contingent of Portuguese troops for Europe – the brigs *Cacique* (Commander F. Bibiano de Castro) and *Guarani* (Lieutenant James Nichol) and the brigantine *Leopoldina* (Lieutenant Rodrigo Teodoro de Freitas) were ordered north as reinforcements. On 7 May they were followed by the store ships *Meruí* and *Animo Grande* with anchors, cables and supplies, escorted by the *Leopoldina*, which had been forced back to harbour after losing its foremast and fore-topmast in a gale. On 3 June the *Maria da Glória* (Commander Teodoro de Beaurepaire) sailed for Barra Grande with anchors, cables, munitions and 10 contos of reis (£2000) to enable Taylor to pay his crews and purchase fresh provisions.

Taylor's main military objectives were to enforce a strict blockade of the rebels in Recife and in the adjacent ports of Serinhaem and Itamaraca, where Manuel de Carvalho had attempted to open customs houses, and to keep a close watch on the other provinces so that assistance could be given to the legal authorities if they required it. To this end the ships at his disposal were deployed with skill and decision. While the *Niterói* remained on watch off Pernambuco during April with the recently joined *Atlanta*, the *Piranga* and the *Bahia* were sent to Barra Grande to land munitions and a detachment of 150 seamen.[4] Paes Barreto's forces now totalled some 1600 men, and Taylor was busy writing to the Juntas of Bahia and Alagoas urging the despatch of reinforcements. In May the *Atlanta* was sent northwards to support the loyalist forces in Paraíba, while the *Piranga* sailed for Bahia to watch the situation there. Days later the *Cacique* and the *Guarani* appeared. The *Cacique* was immediately ordered south to Alagoas, where news had arrived that supporters of Manuel de Carvalho were attempting to raise the standard of rebellion.

The news which Taylor's ships gathered as they watchfully patrolled the coasts of north-eastern Brazil during April and May was disturbing, and the intelligence they regularly passed on to the Imperial Government in Rio was of a steadily deteriorating situation as the seeds of rebellion spread from Pernambuco to adjacent provinces. On 16 May Taylor reported that separatist ideas were spreading rapidly through the north-east, and that the Imperial authorities were under threat almost everywhere. In Pará, firm action and widespread arrests had saved the situation. Rio Grande do Norte was quiet, but showing increasing sympathy with the rebel cause. Alagoas was in ferment. The situation in Paraíba was dangerously balanced.[5] The news from Ceará was the worst. Only ten days after his arrival from Rio de Janeiro on 14 April in the *Gentil Americana*, the President newly appointed by the Emperor, Pedro da Costa Barros, had been abruptly overthrown in a coup organized by the two republican separatists, José Pereira Filgueiras and Tristão de Alençar Araripe. On 28 April the latter was elected as Provincial President, and the unfortunate Costa Barros was packed off to Rio in the hired ship *Mathilde*. There were arrests and deportations throughout the length and breadth of Ceará. A fortnight later, the rebel Junta issued a proclamation triumphantly announcing that the province was now part of a great alliance with Pernambuco, Paraíba and Piauí, and calling its citizens to resist despotism, whether it came from Lisbon or Rio.

In one sense the blockade of Pernambuco was a success, and the external trade of the province had been dealt a severe blow. But Taylor was aware that the impact of his activities was limited. The agriculture and internal commerce of Pernambuco remained almost unaffected. Communications by land were still open, and Manuel de Carvalho and his adherents were stockpiling munitions and sending agents and money to other provinces to fan the flames of discontent. At the end of April, Taylor reported that the rebels now had a 20-gun brig, *Constituição ou Morte*, and had mounted an attack on Paes Barreto in Alagoas. Two weeks later he wrote to report that troops from Pernambuco had marched into Paraíba to support the separatist faction there.

In accordance with his orders, Taylor had conducted himself with moderation in his dealings with those who had defied the Imperial authority. Indeed, his behaviour seemed so reasonable that Manuel de Carvalho and Falcão de Lacerda had both resorted to personal attacks to undermine his credibility. But Taylor was convinced that only vigorous action and overwhelming force could restore peace and order. On 8 April and 16 May he repeated his views to the Imperial Government, and on 17 and 29 May he urged the despatch of a military force to act in concert with the Navy and put an end to the outbreak before it was too late.[6]

Pernambuco's three emissaries arrived in Rio on 2 May after

a fourteen-day voyage from Recife. The Emperor was away in Minas Gerais, but on his return they were received in audience. The interview was long and stormy at times – the Pernambucanos attempting to justify the actions of their compatriots, Dom Pedro lamenting the province's disobedience. At length the emissaries withdrew and took ship for Recife, carrying assurances of Imperial magnanimity manifested in the nomination of a compromise candidate, José Carlos Mayrinck da Silva Ferrão, as new Provincial President. To the Imperial authorities, Mayrinck Ferrão's selection served both to confirm the Government's magnanimity and to allow the north-eastern dissidents to return to their allegiance without loss of face.

When the brig carrying the three delegates arrived back in the Pernambuco roadstead, it was intercepted by the blockading squadron. Two officers boarded the vessel, inspected the safe-conducts which Lord Cochrane had supplied, and allowed the delegates to visit the *Niterói* in order to report to Captain Taylor. The meeting, held in the frigate's great cabin, was cordial as the delegates told of their discussions with the Emperor and the nomination of Mayrinck da Silva Ferrão as President. Taylor received the news with pleasure and relief, and wished the emissaries success in their endeavours to bring peace. As a gesture of goodwill, he allowed the brig to pass through the line of blockading warships rather than making the delegates complete the rest of their journey in an open boat. In return, they presented the English captain with the remains of their fresh provisions: a wholesome present comprising eight chickens, five sucking pigs, a turkey, a ham and a barrel of biscuits. The *Cacique* had already arrived from Rio de Janeiro on 21 May with despatches which warmly approved Taylor's conduct of affairs off Pernambuco and officially confirmed the appointment of Mayrinck Ferrão as President of the province. If the nomination were accepted by the authorities and people of Pernambuco, then Taylor was ordered to lift the blockade and return to Rio de Janeiro.

Viewed from Rio de Janeiro, the appointment of Mayrinck Ferrão may have seemed an ideal solution, but in Pernambuco the nomination settled nothing and satisfied no-one. The supporters of Paes Barreto were unhappy to see their candidate abandoned, while Manuel de Carvalho and his adherents remained determined both to keep power and to resist the claims of the new Imperial nominee by subtle but potent means. Meanwhile, in his house in Recife, a nervous Mayrinck Ferrão felt no enthusiasm for the unexpected honour. On hearing the news, his first instinct was to refuse the appointment outright; his second, to request a long meeting with the rebel President in which he confessed his inability to settle Pernambuco's problems and asked Manuel de Carvalho himself to decide whether or not he should assume the presidency. Manuel de Carvalho, determined to keep power but equally anxious to hide his opposition behind a facade of obedience, urged Mayrinck Ferrão to accept the office but at the same time ensured that his supporters threatened dire consequences should he be foolish enough to do so. After a week of futile discussions, Mayrinck Ferrão nervously resigned himself to the inevitable and withdrew from the contest.

While these delicate manoeuvrings were taking place onshore, the blockading squadron waited anxiously for news. With all access to Mayrinck Ferrão prevented by the rebel authorities, Taylor wrote to Manuel de Carvalho on 27 May asking for a definite decision as to whether or not he intended to obey the orders of the Imperial Government and withdraw from the presidency. The letter was delivered by one of the *Niterói*'s midshipmen. Landing from a ship's boat, he was taken to the house of Manuel de Carvalho, whom he found in conference with some fifteen of his cronies. There, in contemptuous tones, he was given messages of open defiance both verbally and in writing, which he was told to pass on to Taylor and the Imperial Government.[7]

The pretence of loyal disagreement was now over. The authorities in Recife had shown themselves in their true colours as separatist rebels against the Empire. On 29 May, Taylor sent copies of the correspondence to Rio and reported on events. Manuel de Carvalho was now openly attempting to organize the northern provinces into a republic, he wrote, and his agents were fomenting disorder everywhere. Within Pernambuco, the planters and the wealthier citizens remained aloof, but the lower classes were enthusiastic in their support for Manuel de Carvalho and the frustrated intellectuals who surrounded him, while Falcão de Lacerda lacked the intelligence to perceive his revolutionary intentions. In Taylor's opinion, decisive measures and the despatch of Imperial troops now constituted the only answer. On 11 June, he wrote again. Manuel de Carvalho and his henchmen – Frei Caneca, the hard-drinking *mulato* poet José da Natividade Saldana, and João Soares Lisboa, editor of the latest republican broadsheet, *Desengano Brasileiro* – had interpreted the nomination of Mayrinck Ferrão as a sign of weakness, and become even more daring. Within the province, political opponents were being persecuted, while outside it the regime was planning aggressive moves against Alagoas and Bahia.[8] Taylor again urged immediate countermeasures, and meanwhile deployed his forces to contain the new menace. The *Cacique* was sent to Alagoas to support the Imperial authorities there. The *Piranga* sailed for Barra Grande with munitions for Paes Barreto whose forces remained on the offensive, supported by the *Bahia*. The brigantine *Rio da Plata*, sent on Norton's initiative as additional reinforcement, was ordered to Paraíba to join the *Leopoldina*. The squadron, as Taylor reported on 11 June, was active, in good spirits, and now provisioned for two more months at sea.

But it was not to be. The strategic situation had changed. Faced with the serious threat of a Portuguese invasion, the Brazilian Government was frantically concentrating its forces on Rio de Janeiro. On 28 June 1824 the schooner *Carolina* reached Taylor's squadron, carrying fresh orders. Next morning, when the citizens of Recife looked out to sea, the familiar white sails of Taylor's warships had disappeared. The blockade had been abandoned, and the squadron was on its way back to Rio de Janeiro.

CHAPTER 13

THE CONFEDERATION OF THE EQUATOR

News of the threatened Portuguese invasion and the withdrawal of Imperial naval and military units to Rio de Janeiro was received with derision in the northern provinces. Frei Caneca denounced the moves furiously in the columns of the *Typhus Pernambucano*, alleging that Pedro's concentration of force was being made not to oppose the Lisbon expedition but to unite with it, and jointly to reimpose Portuguese rule on hapless Brazil. A special supplement to *O Desengano Brasileiro* which was circulated throughout the north-east subjected the Imperial Decree of 11 June to a malevolent analysis, accusing Pedro of abandoning the provinces in order to save himself and hinting at a sinister plot whereby the Portuguese Army of the Englishman Marshal Beresford and the Imperial Navy of the Scotsman Lord Cochrane would combine to destroy Brazilian freedom. On 2 July 1824, President Manuel de Carvalho Paes de Andrade addressed a proclamation to the people calling for the establishment of a separate constitutional government. This was followed on 24 July by a lengthy manifesto aimed at Pernambuco's six neighbours – Paraíba, Rio Grande do Norte, Piauí, Ceará, Maranhão and Pará. It was no less than a Declaration of Independence – beginning with philosophical reflections on the nature of Man, Society and Liberty; going on to rehearse the despotic acts of the Imperial Government, its intrigues with Portugal and its abandonment of the people in their hour of peril; hinting at the mobilization of warships and of '12,000 bayonets' to defend the cause of liberty; and ending with the exultant cry 'Long Live the Confederation of the Equator'.[1]

Under the supervision of Manuel de Carvalho's secretary, José da Natividade Saldana, the administration was purged of the

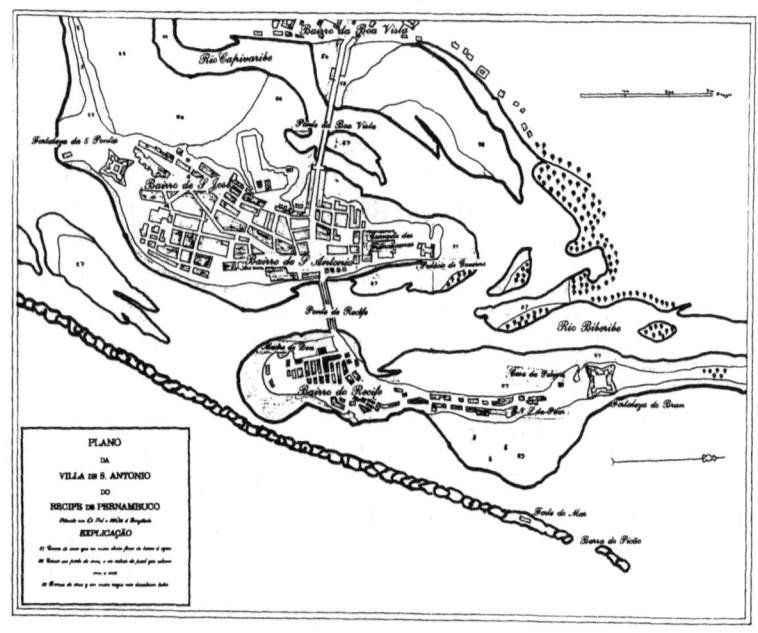

RECIFE 1824
After Antônio Bernadino Pereira do Lago

moderate and the lukewarm, and agents were sent to spread the word in other provinces. A flag was designed for the new state comprising a sky-blue field against which was placed a square shield containing a white circle with the words 'Religion ... Independence ... Union ... Liberty', and emblazoned with a complicated design featuring branches of coffee and of sugar, numerous white stars, a scarlet cross, a hand, the eye of Providence and, prominently located, the word 'Confederation'. Manuel de Carvalho had himself devised the Constitution of the new state, based on that of Colombia. There were also signs of American influence, which was hardly surprising for a man who had spent years of exile in the United States and whose three daughters had been baptized Carolina, Philadelphia and Pennsylvania.

Ceará responded eagerly to the call. On 26 August new flags were issued, a *Te Deum* was celebrated, oaths of allegiance were sworn and eight delegates were elected to attend the Assembly of the Confederation of the Equator at Olinda. Rio Grande do Norte adhered to the republican cause with equal speed, signing a political and military alliance by which it undertook to form a corps of troops with which to intimidate its neighbouring provinces. With varying degrees of enthusiasm, Piauí and Paraíba also rallied to the Confederation. In Pará, the development of a republican movement was promptly nipped in the bud by the arrival on 30 April of the *Gentil Americana* carrying a vigorous new President, Colonel José de Araujo Rozo. A few quick arrests soon restored the Emperor's authority. In Maranhão the republican issue hardly surfaced, being lost in the continuing struggle for power between the supporters of the military commander, Félix Pereira Burgos, and those of the President, Miguel Freire Bruce. Pernambuco could expect little by way of help from either province.

Manuel de Carvalho was fully aware that the survival of his Confederation would depend not on inspiring resolutions or popular enthusiasm but on military force. A realist as always, the rebel President had begun assembling arms and munitions, and orders for more were already being sent to Britain and the United States. As early as April 1824, the Brazilian Agent in London had expressed concern at the huge quantities of armaments being shipped to Pernambuco,[2] and his opposite number in Washington reported that almost every American ship sailing for Pernambuco was carrying illegal gunpowder.³ On 2 July, Manuel de Carvalho ordered two steam packets and large quantities of munitions from the British firm of James Burne & Co. As the supplies arrived, fortresses were reinforced, new militia regiments were raised and the military units in Pernambuco, now called the 'Constitutional Army of the Confederation of the Equator' were re-formed into two groups: the 'Division of the South', facing the loyalist forces in Barra Grande, and the 'Division of the North', operating in Paraíba.

The importance of sea power was not forgotten. Manuel de Carvalho made strenuous efforts to expand the arsenal in Recife and to assemble warships. Having served previously as Intendant of Marine in Pernambuco, he knew exactly how to do it. In July, he sent orders to the United States for six gunboats armed with 24-pounders for the defence of the port, and for a big 38-gun corvette. An 18-gun brig, *Constituição ou Morte*, was also fitted out and manned in Recife with a Maltese adventurer, João Metrowich, in command with the rank of Sublieutenant and a Portuguese, João Guilherme Ratcliffe, as his second-in-command. The 14-gun former Imperial brigantine *Independência ou Morte* and the schooner *Maria da Glória*, which had fallen into the hands of the rebel authorities in December 1823, were both now prepared for sea, the latter renamed *Goiana*. On 9 July, two more ships – the schooner *Independência* and the merchant brig *Guadiana* – were seized for the service of the new state and sent to various northern ports carrying Manuel de Carvalho's agents and bundles of separatist propaganda. The career of the *Guadiana* was brought to an abrupt halt a week later when it was seized in the harbour of Salvador by the provincial authorities.

Manuel de Carvalho did not wait for the Imperial Government to make the first move, but went immediately on to the offensive. Unfortunately for him, the enthusiasm of the rebels was not matched by military success. On 8 July the 'Division of the South' attacked Paes Barreto's positions in Barra Grande, but was driven off with heavy losses after a furious action which lasted all day. A similar assault by the 'Division of the North' on Imperial forces in Paraíba was repulsed a week later. At sea, Manuel de Carvalho was no more successful. On 17 July 1824, the *Constituição ou Morte* and the *Goiana* sailed from Recife with supplies, troop reinforcements and orders to co-operate with the 'Division of the South' against the loyalist forces. Their cargo safely landed, on 23 July the two warships began to blockade Paes de Barreto's main supply routes. Unfortunately for the Pernambucanos, the 26-gun Imperial corvette *Maria da Glória* (Commander Teodoro de Beaurepaire) and the 16-gun brig *Guarani* (Lieutenant James Nichol) were cruising in the vicinity looking for them. On 25 July, the topsails of the Imperial ships appeared over the horizon and the game was up. Recognizing that one broadside from the *Maria da Glória*'s 24-pounder carronades would blow their brig to pieces, the crew of the *Constituição ou Morte* ignored Metrowich's frantic orders to fight, and sensibly hailed down their colours. The *Goiana* tried to make a dash for it, but one shot from the corvette and she too decided to heave to and surrender.

The Imperial Government was fully alive to the danger to national unity posed by the deteriorating situation in the northeast, but in May and June it was the threat from Portugal which dominated its thinking. Then, on 30 June 1824, the arrival of the British packet *Sandwich* after a 49-day passage from Falmouth brought dramatic news. Letters, despatches and papers from Europe told a delighted Brazilian public of an absolutist counter-revolution in Portugal. In April, the King's vicious and devious youngest son Dom Miguel, egged on by his diminutive and equally unpleasant mother, had raised the Lisbon garrison, overthrown the government and seized power. The bewildered and corpulent Dom João had taken refuge on the British warship *Windsor Castle*. The situation was confused, but one fact was clear: the projected invasion of Brazil was now out of the question. Tension in Rio fell, and although some defensive measures continued, the Government was able to turn its attention fully on Pernambuco.

On 6 July, Vilela Barbosa in the Ministry of Marine ordered the resumption of the blockade of Recife. A week later, a squadron comprising the 20-gun corvette *Maceió* (Captain Antônio José de Carvalho), the frigate *Real Carolina*, recently renamed *Paraguassú* (Captain Mateus Welch), and the brigantines *Leopoldina* (Lieutenant Teodoro de Freitas) and *Pará* (Lieutenant William Eyre) sailed for the north-east. The expedition was under the overall command of Antônio José de Carvalho, whose orders were simply to reimpose the blockade and enforce it with the utmost vigour. If he met

Taylor's force on its return voyage to Rio de Janeiro, he was to take command of the smaller vessels but to allow the *Niterói, Piranga, Maria da Glória, Rio da Plata* and *Pará* to return.[4] These preparations had been made in ignorance of the foundation of the Confederation of the Equator. Then, on 23 July, the British frigate *Doris* arrived from the north bearing news of the rebellion and of Manuel de Carvalho's proclamations. The Imperial Government went immediately on to the attack. On 26 July, constitutional guarantees and habeus corpus were suspended in the offending provinces, and a military commission was appointed to try and punish the leaders of the rebellion. A newly promoted Brazilian Brigadier, Francisco de Lima e Silva, was named as President, military commander and head of the military commission for Pernambuco. The 3rd Brigade of the Imperial Army, comprising 1200 men under Lima e Silva's own command, was selected to form the expeditionary force, and on 27 July the Emperor held a grand review of the troops on the Campo da Aclamação. On the same day a defiant proclamation was issued:

> Comrades, National Honour and My Own have been offended by the incendiary proclamations and manifestos in which the so-called President of Pernambuco, Manuel Carvalho Paes de Andrade, and his faction have declared a Confederation! What greater insult could there be to the general opinion of the Nation? ... And what do such insults demand? Without doubt – exemplary punishment!

Naval preparations reflected the military bustle on land. On 31 July, Lord Cochrane received orders to sail in the *Pedro I* (Captain Thomas Sackville Crosbie) for the north-east with the corvette *Carioca* (Captain Antônio Joaquim de Couto), the brig *Maranhão* (Commander George Manson) and the transports *Harmonia* and *Caridade* with the expeditionary force on board. On arrival he was to tighten the naval blockade, act in concert with the Army in re-establishing Imperial authority in Pernambuco, and see to the pacification of the other rebellious provinces of the north. On that same day, with bands playing and flags waving, the Army was embarked: Lima e Silva and his staff on the flagship, the officers on the men-of-war, the troops on the transports together with their arms, equipment and, for a campaign where words were likely to be as lethal as bullets, a printing press. On 2 August, the squadron weighed anchor and sailed out to confront the rebels in the north-east.

With the expedition on its way, Vilela Barbosa turned his attention to providing reinforcements and supplies. Three weeks later, on 21 August, a second squadron sailed under the command of the American Commodore David Jewitt in the *Piranga*, with the *Niterói*, the brig-of-war *Cacique* (Commander F. Bibiano de Castro) and the transport *Animo Grande* carrying munitions. But this time the *Niterói* had a new commander, Captain James Norton. After eighteen months of evasion and delay, the Imperial Government had finally been forced by remorseless British pressure to dismiss John Taylor from its service. But nothing could prevent it from showing its reluctance to take such a step, and in announcing the news on 20 August 1824, the *Diario Fluminense* was allowed to carry a bitter attack on British persecution of a Brazilian hero.[5]

On 13 August, Cochrane's squadron made landfall at Alagoas and anchored in the shelter of Jaraguá Point, the nearest deep-water anchorage in Imperial hands to Pernambuco, where the Army was to establish its base before marching against Recife, 250 kilometres to the north. Three days later, after the troops had disembarked, Cochrane weighed anchor and set sail for Recife in the *Pedro I*, leaving the *Carioca* and *Maranhão* to cover the Army in its advance. Once on shore, Lima e Silva's first act was to issue a fierce and uncompromising proclamation whose words reflected both his attitude to the rebels and his single-minded conduct of operations: 'Evil ones tremble, the sword of justice is about to sever your heads: surrender yourselves or the brave troops that I command will treat your country as that of an enemy, for there are no enemies worse than revolutionaries. Expect no mercy; our fearful judgements admit of no appeal.'

For a fortnight the Army paused in Alagoas, collecting horses and guns, being joined by local militia units and re-formed into a 'Co-operative Army of Good Order'. Then, on 29 August, Lima e Silva's Army began its march northwards between the red cliffs and palm-fringed beaches of the coast and the rolling green countryside. On the second day it reached the low hills of Santo Antônio da Barra; on the third, São Miguel dos Milagres; on the fourth, Porto das Pedras, where the southern outposts of the rebel forces surrounding Barra Grande were attacked and captured; and on the fifth, 2 September 1824, Barra Grande itself where, amid congratulations and euphoria, the Army was united with Paes Barreto's veterans. The Imperial forces now boasted a combined strength of 2500 men. With typical energy, Lima e Silva then pushed northwards in a series of forced marches heading for Cabo. The following day he captured the fort and bay of Tamandaré, and on 4 September he reached Serinhaem, where the last of the supplies and munitions were unloaded. As the Imperial troops advanced, the rebel 'Division of the South' fell back before them, abandoning Cabo and eventually joining their main army under Falcão de Lacerda himself. Together they took up positions on the Jaboatão, a river running north to south some 30 kilometres to the west of Recife. It was on this line that the rebel commander, after much indecisive manoeuvring and wavering, had decided to stand and fight.

Lord Cochrane anchored off Pernambuco on 18 August 1824, finding the *Maceió* and *Leopoldina* on blockade duty. The *Maria da Glória* had been sent to Bahia. The *Guarani* was in Paraíba giving support to the authorities, and the *Paraguassú* and *Pará* were on their way to the same port with despatches and proclamations. Cochrane immediately sent in letters announcing his intention to bombard Recife as well as strengthen the blockade, and after anxious enquiries from the consuls of Britain and the United States, he gave neutrals eight days to remove their vessels and property before the attack should begin.[6] Unfortunately, Manuel de Carvalho refused to play the game according to the customary rules, and issued orders forbidding the departure of neutrals from the port. The foreigners went back to Cochrane in panic, but the First Admiral remained unmoved and refused to extend the time limit – even when Captain Hunn of the British frigate *Tweed*, brought in by Consul Parkinson to give added weight to his case, indicated that in the event of an attack Cochrane would be held personally responsible for the value of British property in the city, estimated at half a million pounds.[7]

Having brandished the iron fist, Cochrane then showed the velvet glove. He was in luck. On 20 August, the British packet *Reynaldo* arrived from Falmouth. On board was an old friend, Mrs Maria Graham, returning to Rio de Janeiro to take up her appointment as governess to the Emperor's daughter, the Princess

Maria da Glória. She was only too willing to act as peacemaker, and Cochrane used her to deliver letters to the rebel President offering lenient terms for a capitulation. Obedience to the Emperor was obligatory, but the First Admiral offered free pardons, guarantees of life and property, and permission for the leaders of the rebellion to leave Brazil at will. Manuel de Carvalho, however, was not impressed. He replied in a tone of carefully rehearsed nobility, stating that Pernambuco had no navy, troops or foreign mercenaries to fight for it, but that the strength of its cause lay in the devotion of brave, free men. Nevertheless, he was prepared to negotiate with Cochrane face to face. The First Admiral seized the opportunity and suggested a meeting on a neutral-ship-of war. Manuel de Carvalho, however, refused, explaining that the citizens of Recife had petitioned him to remain in the city lest he be arrested in a neutral vessel. As an alternative, he proposed a meeting in a small boat midway between the guns of the fortress of Brum and those of the *Pedro I*.[8] It was the First Admiral's turn to refuse, his honour seriously offended. Cochrane's pride was then injured even further when Manuel de Carvalho offered him a bribe of 400 contos of reis (£80,000) to change sides!

By this time, Cochrane was convinced that the rebel President had no serious desire for conciliation. He therefore abandoned the negotiations and prepared to carry out his threat of bombardment. The plan was for the *Pedro I* to drop down within range of Recife, and rake the town and the shipping with cannon fire. All the British seamen in the *Paraguassú* were transferred to the flagship in preparation for the demonstration, but on the day appointed, 27 August, the wind and the swell made it too risky to take a vessel of the *Pedro I*'s size so close to land. As a result, it was the *Leopoldina*, with the *Pará* in support, which eventually crept inshore and, with HMS *Tweed* anxiously observing, began to bombard Recife's white stone buildings and churches with mortar shells.[9]

But the demonstration was not a success, and the condition of the squadron was beginning to cause concern. The easterly wind and the unfriendly coast were already restricting Cochrane's freedom of manoeuvre, and the coral on the seabed had begun to take its toll in anchors and cables. The *Maceió* had already lost three anchors, and the *Pedro I* had lost two. The *Paraguassú* had only one left. New equipment and fresh supplies were urgently needed from Bahia, and in view of the navigation dangers, Cochrane decided to suspend the attack. In his estimation it would be many weeks before the Imperial Army appeared, and the strength of rebel support indicated that the campaign would be a long one. A tedious period of hazardous blockade duty off Pernambuco was not to Cochrane's taste, and at the end of August he sailed off in the *Pedro I* to find General Lima e Silva – withdrawing, as he did so, the most powerful ship in the squadron and the bulk of the British sailors. Behind he left the *Maceió*, *Paraguassú* and *Leopoldina*, with orders to maintain the blockade but no information as to his movements.

On 4 September 1824, the *Pedro I* met the Brazilian Army marching northwards along the coast near Serinhaem. Cochrane wrote to Lima e Silva advising him of Manuel de Carvalho's intention to withdraw into the interior if attacked and even to free the slaves, and gave his opinion that the war was likely to be lengthy. The following day the General replied. His reading of the situation was different: the aristocracy and the sugar magnates of Pernambuco were loyal to the Empire; the rebels consisted of a handful of adventurers; the masses would support whichever side was strongest. For this reason a massive show of military and naval strength was needed. The following day, 6 September, he intended to establish his headquarters in Cabo, 34 kilometres from Recife, and hoped to receive a visit there from the Admiral to plan the final assault on the city.[10] Cochrane's reply was cool. He did not agree with Lima e Silva's analysis but agreed to allow Captain de Couto and Commander Manson, with the *Carioca* and *Maranhão*, to continue under his orders. The First Admiral then sailed over the horizon – he had others matters to attend to in Bahia – while the Army continued its march.

The main body of the 'Constitutional Army of the Confederation of the Equator', by now a motley force of 1500 men, stood waiting for the Imperial Army on the Jaboatão river, its centre at the bridge of Carvalhos. But Lima e Silva was unwilling to play the rebel game, and decided to strike hard and fast at Recife rather than fight on Falcão de Lacerda's chosen ground. Detaching 400 of his troops to launch a diversionary attack on the main enemy position, Lima e Silva led the bulk of his force, amounting to 2000 men, on two rapid forced marches northwards through the rolling, verdant countryside inland of the rebel positions. On 11 September he launched a fierce attack, turned the rebel's right flank at the *engenho* of Santa Anna, turned eastwards and marched on headlong for Recife and the coast. In the afternoon his sweating troops reached the lowlands and, after slight resistance, successfully crossed one of the bridges and causeways which provided the only access to the city across the network of estuaries which were its natural defence. By the time night fell, the Imperial Army had seized one of the two islands on which Recife was built, capturing the Fort of Cinco Puntos, and was bivouacked safely among the tall houses and baroque churches of the Bairro de Santo Antônio. The same night, Manuel de Carvalho, having been driven ahead of the Imperial forces in their dash for the capital, fled aboard a fishing raft and found refuge on the British frigate *Tweed*.

Commodore David Jewitt had arrived with his ships in the Pernambuco roadstead on 10 September, finding the *Paraguassú*, *Maceió* and *Leopoldina* blockading the port. There was no sign of Lord Cochrane and no news of his whereabouts, so Jewitt decided to assume command and render what assistance he could to the approaching Imperial Army. On 12 September the sound of cannon and musketry could be heard from the west, and an army officer boarded the *Piranga* with a letter for Lord Cochrane. Jewitt read the contents and decided to provide the support requested. The *Cacique* was sent off to look for Lord Cochrane, while Captain Antônio José de Carvalho went ashore to liaise with the land forces and agree a plan of action for a joint attack. In spite of his victories, Lima e Silva's position was not yet secure. His troops were in possession of the Bairro de Santo Antônio, but were being attacked fiercely from all sides. From the east, they were being pinned down by a storm of musketry and cannon from the second of the city's two islands, the Bairro de Recife with its two fortresses of Brum and Buraco; from the west they were under attack from the third of Recife's Bairros, that of Boa Vista; and from the south they were under constant bombardment from the rebel brigantine *Independência ou Morte* and the gunboats moored within the reef. On 14 September, by previous arrangement, the *Piranga* and *Niterói* dropped down to within cannon shot and, under heavy fire themselves, began to bombard the enemy's vessels and positions in the city while Lima e Silva's men attacked and secured the Bairro of Boa Vista.[11]

Later that evening came a distraction. Captain Hunn of the *Tweed* visited the *Piranga* and offered to act as intermediary between the Imperial forces and the rebel regime. He carried terms for a capitulation from Manuel de Carvalho and revealed that the rebel President was in fact aboard the British frigate. Jewitt sent the terms immediately to Lima e Silva, who rejected them out of hand. Captain Norton of the *Niterói* was sent to the *Tweed* to demand that Manuel de Carvalho be given up to the Imperial authorities as a rebel, but was told that he was now under the protection of the British flag and could not be surrendered.[12] The rebel President was then hastily transferred to the newly arrived HMS *Brazen*, and was soon on his way to England.

The speed and success of Lima e Silva's advance and the news of Manuel de Carvalho's apparent desertion stunned both the civil and the military authorities of the Confederation of the Equator. The rebel army, outflanked and outmanoeuvred on the Jaboatão, had at first followed Lima e Silva towards Recife, where they had been repelled by his rearguard. Then, having marched round the city, the commanders held a Council of War. Rather than attack the Imperial troops in Recife, they decided to retire and defend the old colonial capital of Olinda, situated on a low hill five kilometres to the north. The Municipal Council of the city, on whom the responsibilities of government had fallen following the disappearance of Manuel de Carvalho, were pessimistic and sent emissaries to negotiate terms. At first, Lima e Silva insisted on unconditional surrender, but learning from Falcão de Lacerda that the rebel army would fight to the death rather than accept the dishonour of submitting without terms, he relented and offered the minimum possible – submission to the Emperor, amnesty for troops and civilians, and trial and punishment for the leaders of the rebellion.

While the authorities in Olinda considered these grim proposals, the final assault on Recife was mounted. On the night of 16 September, 400 men from the squadron under the command of Captain James Norton were rowed silently ashore in the rear of the enemy positions in the Bairro de Recife. At dawn the army launched a frontal assault, while the naval division attacked from the seaward side. The action was a complete success. Norton and his seamen stormed the Fortress of Brum and the Fort of Buraco to the north, then took possession of the shipping in the port while the army occupied the rest of the city.[13] With his customary energy, Lima e Silva then pursued the retreating rebels northwards towards Olinda. At 8 a.m. the Imperial troops entered the old capital, and by noon it was all over. The authorities capitulated, the leaders of the rebellion fled or sought exile overseas and, with the exception of a number of hard-core units which disappeared into the interior, the troops laid down their arms. On 18 September, a *Te Deum* was held in the cathedral of Olinda in celebration of the Imperial victory, and the city and the harbour reverberated to the thunder of gun salutes. The Confederation of the Equator was dead.

Lima e Silva hastened to inform the Imperial Government and the neighbouring provinces of the capture of Recife and the suppression of the revolt. With Jewitt's consent, the *Pará* was despatched to Bahia, the *Cacique* to Maranhão and Pará, and the *Guarani* to Rio with Lima e Silva's despatches. In these he reported on his operations, allocating praise – or blame – where he felt it was deserved. 'It is my duty to make known to Your Excellency,' he wrote in a secret letter to Vilela Barbosa,

> the harmony which has existed between myself and the commander of the naval forces, Commodore Jewitt. He has been zealous and untiring and assisted the capture of Pernambuco by every means in his power. Captain Norton is also worthy of mention. He landed at the head of the seamen and marines ... and played an important part in the restoration of Recife. How different, however, was the conduct of the Marquis of Maranhão! He appeared before Serinhaem while the army was passing ... and on that occasion I requested his return to Recife; and later when I reached Suassana I requested his assistance in the assault and even gave the time and the date on which I would need his help. However, when I attacked Recife there was no flagship and no news of the First Admiral.[14]

Jewitt's despatch to the Minister of Marine was less directly critical, but he made no bones about his attitude to Cochrane's careless and erratic behaviour.[15] There is no doubt that Cochrane had been guilty of an unusual and serious error in his judgement of the strategic situation and of Lima e Silva's abilities. Naval stores were urgently needed, and the despatch of the *Pedro I* to Bahia was justified – the flagship was not only one of the fastest vessels available, but its size made it the most difficult to manoeuvre in the dangerous waters off Pernambuco. But there was no excuse for Cochrane himself to quit the scene of the action, and his mistake was made worse by his removal of the squadron's best seamen. While Lima e Silva and Jewitt were recapturing Recife, Cochrane was anchored in Bahia busily paying out prize money with Henry Dean, who had been installed in the port to represent his prize interests.[16]

The news of the fall of Recife was received with enthusiasm in Rio de Janeiro. The victory of Imperial arms over the rebels was celebrated with gun salutes, and the city was illuminated for three nights. Lima e Silva's despatches were avidly read in the pages of the *Diário Fluminense*, and congratulations were heaped on the Imperial commanders. There were two points, however, which were noted with displeasure – one was the escape of Manuel de Carvalho in a British warship, the other the absence of Lord Cochrane at the moment of the assault.[17]

Cochrane returned to Recife in the *Pedro I* on 25 September 1824, to find the city and the province already in Lima e Silva's hands. There were also signs of additional enthusiasm, for the previous day news had been received that the United States had formally recognized Brazilian Independence, and three days of rejoicing had been ordered. While the church bells of Olinda and Recife rang out in celebration and the smoke of daily gun salutes drifted into the blue Pernambuco skies, Jewitt reported to Lord Cochrane on events in his absence.[18] Pointing out that he had been left without orders, the Commodore sent copies of his official correspondence and the logs of the ships for the First Admiral's inspection. The conduct of the squadron, he reported, had been generally good, but there had been problems which, in his usual prim and humourless style, Jewitt went on to elaborate. Antônio José de Carvalho of the *Maceió* had not been an efficient intermediary between the land and sea forces. There were rumours that some officers (including Norton, with whom Jewitt seemed to have felt some personal animosity) had been guilty of looting. He hinted that other senior officers, notably Captain Welch and Commander Kelmare of the *Paraguassú*, had not done their utmost, but omitted to mention that this had been because Cochrane's removal of 76 British sailors had left them undermanned and incapable of assisting.[19] The only real blemish had been the conduct of Sub-lieutenant Gore Whitlock Oudsley and Master's Mate John Rogers Molloy. They had both been so drunk during the assault on Recife that they had fired prematurely and nearly compromised the attack.[20]

Lord Cochrane's first act was to write to Lima e Silva offering cordial congratulations on his victory; but relations between the two remained cool and awkward. Lima e Silva was Acting President of Pernambuco, and was clearly the Imperial Government's chosen representative, yet he was a mere Brigadier and far beneath Cochrane in military rank. The First Admiral, who always resented superior authority and was never comfortable unless he was in complete command, found the situation irksome and was quick to complain of any action which seemed to undermine his own position. He was annoyed by the Brigadier's demand for ships to carry despatches. He complained at the tardy attempts being made to pay his crews. He was scornful at Lima e Silva's refusal to supply even a small force of troops to buttress the Imperial authorities in Pará. The Brigadier replied with cold and even-tempered politeness. Continuous contact with Rio de Janeiro was politically necessary, he explained, even if it meant sending ships on successive days. The Provincial Treasury was empty, but the Navy would be paid by raising loans. And as for Pará, Lima e Silva was confident that the appearance of Cochrane alone would be enough to restore the situation.[21]

With Pernambuco back under Imperial control, Lord Cochrane turned his attention to the disposition and condition of the squadron. On 1 October the *Leopoldina* was sent to Rio with despatches. The *Paraguassú* followed. Captain Welch had orders to make the repairs his frigate needed in Salvador dockyard, then to patrol the sea lanes off Bahia. Cochrane's next task was to deal with outbreaks of fever on the overcrowded decks of the *Pedro I* and *Piranga*. It took a week to hospitalize and redistribute the crews and to fumigate the two vessels.[22] That concluded, the First Admiral set about deploying the remaining ships at his disposal. On 7 October, Norton and the *Niterói* were ordered back to Rio de Janeiro. Commander Bartholomew Hayden, recently arrived with the new brig *Pirajá* (having been pardoned by the Emperor after court-martial for a trivial offence), was sent to cruise off Pernambuco with carefully worded instructions to intercept any vessel carrying illegal munitions for the erstwhile rebels. He promptly caught the American schooner *Exchange* filled with contraband gunpowder, and sent the vessel into the Prize Court in Bahia for adjudication.[23]

Cochrane was now ready to continue with the rest of his mission. The corvettes *Maceió* and *Carioca* were left in Pernambuco with orders to defend the port should the warships which Manuel de Carvalho was said to have purchased in the United States actually appear. The rest of the squadron, comprising the *Pedro I*, the *Piranga*, the brigantine *Atlanta* and the schooner *Maria da Glória*, was prepared for sea. On 10 October 1824, Cochrane weighed anchor and the flotilla sailed out from the Pernambuco roadstead to complete the pacification of the remaining provinces of the north.

CHAPTER 14

COCHRANE SAILS NORTH

On 12 October 1824 Cochrane and the squadron anchored off Natal, capital of Rio Grande do Norte, to hear the latest intelligence and pass on the happy news of the capture of Pernambuco and the recognition of Brazilian Independence by the United States. The President of the Province, José de Moraes Navarro, reported that all was well and offered congratulations; and the following day the ships weighed anchor and sailed on to Ceará.

The republican euphoria which had accompanied the adhesion of Ceará to the Confederation of the Equator on 26 August 1824 was short-lived. In the deep south of the province, supporters of the Empire were hostile to this turn of events, and in early September news arrived in Fortaleza, the capital, that Imperial troops were about to mount an attack on Ceará from the east. The rebel military commander, José Pereira Filgueiras, decided to act decisively and marched into the interior at the head of all the troops he could muster. On 22 September Filgueiras established his base at the city of Crato on the Pernambuco border, then set out to contain the incursion of the Imperial troops (nicknamed derisively 'the turkey-cocks') from Paraíba. That done, he was back in Crato on 8 October. Ignorant of the capture of Recife and the end of the Confederation of the Equator, Filgueiras took the offensive again in response to a recently received appeal for help from Manuel de Carvalho and led his men against the Imperial units across the border in Pernambuco. The campaign was not a success. Service in the parched scrubland of the interior was unpleasant at the best of times, and the Cearense troops found their advance grinding to a halt in the face of growing opposition. They were attacked by militia units, shot at by guerrillas and harassed every inch of the way. Discipline began to deteriorate into looting and desertion. Finally, Filgueiras abandoned his plans and led his dusty, depleted and disheartened force back to Crato.

Meanwhile, in his absence, news had arrived in Fortaleza of the capture of the town of Aracatí and the establishment of a loyal Provisional Junta by invading Imperial troops from Paraíba. Filgueiras's republican confederate, now Provincial President Tristão de Alençar Araripe, took personal command. On 12 October he handed over the presidency of the province to José Félix de Azevedo e Sá, marched against the town with all the troops he could raise, and captured it after a brief bombardment.

Then, on 17 October 1824, the sails of the *Piranga* appeared over the horizon and the big frigate sailed boldly into the Fortaleza roadstead. Commodore Jewitt sent Cochrane's letters ashore and the stunned authorities learnt of the capture of Recife, the reconquest of Pernambuco, and the arrest or flight of the rebel government. In typical Cochrane fashion they were also treated to an exaggerated account of the strength of the seaborne forces now confronting Ceará – a squadron of warships commanded by the legendary First Admiral in person, well furnished with arms and carrying 3000 men.

In the face of such a threat, adherence to the Empire was the only sensible course of action. Acting President Azevedo e Sá quickly changed sides. The Emperor was once more proclaimed in Fortaleza, oaths of loyalty were sworn, and the green-and-yellow flag of Imperial Brazil was rehoisted on the city and the forts.[1] The following day, the massive bulk of the *Pedro I* sailed into harbour with its two diminutive attendants, the *Atlanta* and the *Maria da Glória*. Cochrane was greeted by popular rejoicing and assurances of welcome from the Acting President. The First Admiral replied in cordial terms, congratulating the authorities on their zeal for the Imperial cause and offering a complete amnesty to all who laid down their arms and adhered to the Empire within fourteen days.[2]

Azevedo e Sá despatched proclamations to the four corners of the province informing the military commanders and the councils of the cities and towns of the restoration of Ceará to the Brazilian Empire, and ordering the acclamation of Pedro I. On 21 October, a separate despatch ordered Filgueiras to disband his troops and return to the capital forthwith. No one, least of all Azevedo e Sá, thought that this tactic would have much effect, and Cochrane had already begun to organize the defence of Fortaleza against an attack by the rebel armies in the interior. On 19 October, Commodore David Jewitt was ordered ashore with a landing party of 84 men and took command of the city. The Commodore was alarmed at what he found. The garrison consisted of no more than 40 'miserable creatures', and the place was in such a poor state that it was incapable of resisting an attack by 50 men, let alone a rebel army of 1200 which was thought to be within three days' march of the city.[3] But the supposed strength of the squadron, combined with Cochrane's offer of amnesty, seemed to be doing the trick. Supporters of the Empire who had hitherto remained silent began to give open support, and former rebels began to change sides. Declarations of loyalty from the towns and cities began to flow into the capital, and both individual soldiers and whole units began to desert from the ranks of the rebel armies.

On 28 October, Cochrane reported to the Minister of Marine on his activities in Ceará with some satisfaction. In his opinion the province was now almost completely restored to the Empire. Only José Pereira Filgueiras and Alençar Araripe, operating deep in the interior, still constituted a threat, but their forces were rumoured to consist of no more than a few hundred men. So certain did the Imperial victory seem that Cochrane announced his intention to sail shortly for Maranhão to examine the situation there.[4] Jewitt and Azevedo e Sá, however, were less confident. In their opinion, the presence of Alençar Araripe and Filgueiras was always dangerous, and their influence might dominate the province once more if the squadron were withdrawn. It was decided to go on the offensive. A proclamation was issued which excluded Alencar Araripe from the terms of the general amnesty, and put a price on his head; and on 2 November, 300 loyal troops and 400 Indian guerrillas marched out of Fortaleza to find the rebel units which were said to be regrouping in the south. But by this time there was no enemy left to confront. On 31 October, Imperial cavalry had caught up with Alencar Araripe's remaining followers at Santa Rosa and forced them to flee after a brief skirmish in which Araripe himself had been killed. The Imperial force then scoured the interior in search of Filgueiras. But there was no more fighting. Stunned by the news of the death of his confederate, on 8 November 1824 the rebel commander wearily laid down his arms and surrendered with what was left of his men.

Three weeks later it was all over. After the fall of Recife, the tattered remnants of the 'Constitutional Army of the Confederation of the Equator' had been driven deeper and deeper into the interior by two columns of Lima e Silva's pursuing veterans. In November they reached Ceará. There, ragged, defeated and demoralized, they finally surrendered. The rank and file were disbanded and the leaders, including the turbulent priest Frei Caneca, were rounded up and sent back to Recife for trial and punishment.

With Ceará now restored to Imperial control, Cochrane continued with his mission of pacification. On 3 November, having sent the schooner *Maria da Glória* to Rio with despatches, he set sail for Maranhão in the *Pedro I*, accompanied by the *Atlanta* and the recently arrived *Cacique*. The *Piranga* followed a few days later. Behind them the air over the Palácio do Governo of Fortaleza was hazy with smoke. But this time it was not caused by gun salutes. Acting President Azevedo e Sá was carefully burning the Junta's correspondence so as to destroy all evidence of previous disloyalty by Ceará and himself.[5]

The province of Maranhão had taken no part in the Confederation of the Equator, but there was a state of anarchy and open warfare between the President, Manuel Ignacio Bruce, and the opposition factions. In other words, nothing much had changed since Cochrane had left it a year earlier. The First Admiral's return was greeted with relief and joy. His first act was appoint Commodore Jewitt as military commander of the province, and to send him ashore to restore order with a party of seamen under Sublieutenants March and Drummond. A hail of petitions from respectable citizens and the foreign consuls, backed by Jewitt's own investigations, revealed that the cause of the trouble lay in the tyrannical conduct of the President. Within a week Jewitt's men were in control and had begun to disarm the troops which Bruce had recruited from freed slaves and the dregs of the population to impose a reign of terror in the capital.[6] Even then the situation remained dangerous. On 10 December spies reported that the black units had been secretly rearmed, and there was a plot to seize the Palácio do

Governo and murder Cochrane and the loyal troops backing him. Confronted with the evidence, Bruce did not even attempt to deny it. Jewitt made his dispositions and reported on the situation almost hourly. His men were armed and ready. He had cannon in the streets.[7] Cochrane quickly nipped that one in the bud. The rebel troops were rounded up and deported, and Bruce was suspended from office and shipped off with his family and domestic slaves to Rio de Janeiro in the merchantman *George*. The Imperial Government wrote warmly to approve Cochrane's actions. Indeed, on 4 December it had already written to inform him that the Emperor had decided to dismiss Bruce and appoint a new Provincial President. It was to be Pedro da Costa Barros.[8]

After two months Maranhão was at peace, but Cochrane was aware that only the presence of the squadron was preventing a return to anarchy. On 31 December, he wrote to the Minister of Marine to say that he felt it necessary to remain in S. Luis until the situation had settled down and his nominee as Acting President – Antônio Teles Lobo – had taken firmer control. Moreover, news from Pará indicated that although the iron hand of President José de Araujo Rozo continued to be effective and the province remained generally calm, regular visits by the *Cacique* and the *Atlanta*, the latter now under the command of Sublieutenant Alexander Reid, were needed to nip any republican tendencies in the bud. Cochrane was also anxious to fit out the 14-gun brigantine *Dona Januária*, which had been recently been launched in Pará, and in January 1825 he sent Lieutenant Clarence and a contingent of seamen to Belém to complete the task. The need to communicate with Rio also solved another problem. Jewitt had been concerned for some time at the increasing hostility being shown by the *Piranga*'s second-in-command, Captain Joaquim de Moraes Delamare (brother of Commodore Rodrigo) towards the English officers – probably caused by frustration at the lack of achievement in his own career. Carrying important mails to the capital conveniently removed that source of friction.

By this time Cochrane's nerves were beginning to be affected by the exertions on which he had been engaged for the last four months, by his constant bickering with the Government and by the injustices which he believed were being inflicted on him. On the first day of 1825 he celebrated the New Year by writing to the

Emperor outlining his grievances yet again, and submitting his resignation. But even then the First Admiral had not finished with Brazil – his voyage to Maranhão had other aims besides the restoration of public order. On 11 January 1825 his other purpose was revealed in a letter to the Provincial President in which, ignoring the known ruling of the Prize Court and the instructions of the Government, he repeated the squadron's claims to prize money resulting from the capture of S. Luis in 1823, and demanded payment. As he explained further on 20 January, the amounts involved included public property and funds totalling 254 contos of reis (the squadron's by right of conquest) and private property valued at 170 contos of reis (which, he claimed, was owing to his men as a result of the Emperor's agreement on 12 February 1824 that they should retain the value of all captured enemy goods and prizes). The total was 424 contos (£85,000), but Cochrane offered to accept a mere 106 contos (£21,100) if it were paid within 30 days.[9] The Junta met on 26 January to consider the demand, but was unable to form a quorum. It met again on 3 February and agreed – partly because it was unable to question Cochrane's arguments, partly because of the force at his disposal – by four votes to two to provide the sums demanded.[10]

All seemed to be going well for Cochrane's plan, but on 5 February 1825 the *Animo Grande* dropped anchor in S. Luis carrying the new Provincial President, Pedro da Costa Barros. Two days later he was ceremonially installed in office. But Costa Barros was as unlucky in Maranhão as he had been in Ceará ten months earlier. Cochrane had no intention of having his plans spoilt by the substitution of the pliable Teles Lobo by a new man who was known to be in the confidence of the Rio Government. When Costa Barros began to ask questions, Cochrane suspended him from office and, using the technicality that he bore no sealed Imperial Patent, prevented him from carrying out his functions until confirmation had been received from Rio. Then, when supporters rallied to Costa Barros's aid, the First Admiral declared martial law, accused him of fomenting public disorder and shipped him off to the mouth of the Amazon with Commander Manson in the *Cacique*.[11]

Then there was another problem. On 10 March one member of the Junta changed his original vote on the prize issue to a negative. Cochrane demanded an immediate interview, and on 14 March he met the Junta in a lengthy session in which he forced it once more to agree to meet his terms and pay the money demanded.[12] The first payment of 33 contos of reis (£6600) was handed over in silver and letters of credit two days later, and by the middle of May the whole of the 106 contos (£21,100) had been delivered. Henry Dean had been left behind to safeguard Cochrane's prize interests in Bahia, so on this occasion William Jackson acted both as secretary and as treasurer. As the money came in, so Jackson added it to the balance of what was left from the 200 contos received in Rio de Janeiro and paid it out again in prize money, bonuses and back pay to the ships of the squadron as they put into S. Luis. Those whose duties took them elsewhere were not so lucky. Eyre and Taylor, for example, received nothing for their efforts, and had to wait decades before receiving any reward. For his extra duties Jackson himself received 1000 milreis which, as he noted in his diary, was one half of one per cent of the sum available.[13] He was also busy on Cochrane's behalf shipping over £10,000 worth of cotton back to England in four merchant ships as part of the Admiral's profits on the voyage.

Cochrane's behaviour in Maranhão showed clearly that his obsession with prize money, his conviction that he was being persecuted by an 'anti-Brazilian' administration and his refusal to accept any assurance of the Government's good faith had not changed one iota. In fact, private letters from Maria Graham confirmed his worst suspicions. Mrs Graham had arrived in Rio on 4 September 1824 aboard the packet *Reynaldo*, and had taken up immediate residence at the hillside Palace of São Cristovão as governess to the young Princess Maria da Glória. But things had changed since her last visit. Far from being welcoming, the Palace was a nest of intrigue and gossip, with access to the Emperor being effectively controlled by a group of Portuguese-born cronies, domestics and chamberlains. Hostile to the arrival of a foreigner, they made life as difficult as possible for her, ensuring that her baggage was detained in the customs, refusing to provide transport and lodging her among cooks and maids in the noisiest and most unsuitable part of the palace. Mrs Graham lasted a month. After a series of arguments, the last one triggered by the practice of bathing the six-year-old princess naked in front of servants and sentries, she gave up her duties and moved out. First she took a house in the Rua de Pescadores, then another in the leafier suburb of Laranjeiros. From there she and the unhappy Empress, whose life was being made increasingly difficult by the open presence of the Emperor's mistress, Domitilia de Castro, began a long and intimate correspondence.

Mrs Graham's adventures were viewed with concern by the British community. Some, led by Dr John Dickson, rallied round. Others were cold and unsympathetic. Her situation was worsened by her vigorous support for Lord Cochrane, whose activities were a source of growing speculation in the capital. In this context she found herself in difficulties with the pompous British Consul-General, Henry Chamberlain. But her access to Imperial circles had given her inside information, and it was on this basis that she wrote to warn Lord Cochrane that the Portuguese faction was secretly intriguing against him, and talking of dismissing the Navy's British officers and prosecuting their commanders.[14]

His fears confirmed by Mrs Graham's information, Cochrane wrote to his wife in England in December 1824 complaining of Portuguese persecution and claiming that he could never return to Rio de Janeiro, as he was now liable for Prize Court damages totalling £70,000. Lady Cochrane was so alarmed at the tone of this letter that she went straight to the Brazilian Agent, General Felisberto Brant.[15] On 30 January 1825 Cochrane addressed a long catalogue of complaint to Rio, and on 22 March, in a private letter to Luis Carvalho e Melo, the one minister he regarded as a friend, he listed his grievances, stating – with some accuracy – that his 'action in Maranhão will be represented as an outrageous robbery', and adding: 'it is not from the Portuguese faction in Rio that I expect either credit or justice: their object is sufficiently clear – namely the expulsion of every foreign officer from the service by means of privation or insult'.[16] Jewitt, who had always been coldly critical of the commander-in-chief, reported in a secret but contradictory letter to the Emperor on the same day that Cochrane was hatching dangerous plots, and had even suggested that the squadron should blockade Rio de Janeiro until the 400 contos of prize money were paid.[17]

Living now in greater comfort in the Bishop's Palace, Cochrane began to make his plans. His first task was to get rid of Jewitt, and at the end of March 1825 he and his officers were transferred to the *Pedro I* and ordered back to Bahia, while Crosbie and their most trusted lieutenants moved to the *Piranga*. Cochrane attributed these changes to the fact that the flagship needed repairs, while his presence was still needed in Maranhão.[18] With the Brazilian stage of his life clearly coming to an end, Cochrane was also anxious to make his peace with the British authorities and present his activities in Brazil in the best possible light. While he appreciated Maria Graham's inside information, he was alarmed by the news that her efforts on his behalf was causing trouble with the Consul-General. On 31 March 1824 he wrote to Dr Dickson asking him to restrain her enthusiasm, but to do so with the utmost delicacy in view of her good intentions and her tendency to become irritated over small issues!

Then he wrote to Henry Chamberlain. It was a careful letter, disowning Mrs Graham's well-meaning activities on his behalf, underlining that his only association with her was the natural sympathy for a naval widow which had inspired him to offer her passage from Chile in the *Colonel Allen*, and confiding that the Consul-General's wisdom and good judgement would enable him to put things in perspective. He had sent all his private papers to Chamberlain for safekeeping, and hoped that this would not be inconvenient.

Cochrane went on to make his main points with care and skill, clearly in the hope that they would be passed on to London. The police actions the Brazilian Navy had carried out in the north of Brazil, he explained, had been of enormous value to British trade, and commercial relations with Maranhão were now at an 'unprecedented' level. Indeed, as a patriot, it had been a factor he had always borne in mind. Likewise, although he had held 'the destiny of Brazil and of South America in [his] hands', he had acted with responsibility and honour. He deserved credit for his efforts and for his moderation, but so far he had received only persecution and injustice from the Brazilian authorities, and was filled with horror at the prospect of putting himself once more at the mercy of the Portuguese faction in Rio. He felt that Chamberlain, as the representative of a great and friendly power, should know the truth.[19]

Two months later, Lord Cochrane judged that the situation in

Maranhão was safe enough for him to leave. The decision was opportune, for the heat and humidity of the northern coast had been taking a heavy toll on the health of his officers and crews. So, on 19 May 1825, leaving George Manson of the *Cacique* in S. Luis to keep the peace, he weighed anchor in the *Piranga* and headed north on what he hoped would be a healthful cruise. Cochrane later claimed that he was taking the quickest – though longest – route to Rio de Janeiro by working the frigate across the equatorial zone, picking up the trade winds and sailing north-east with them as far as the Azores, then south to the Canaries and the Cape Verde Islands. It was a similar route to the one he had followed on his first return from Maranhão in 1823, except that on the previous occasion he had sailed only as far as 8 degrees north before heading westwards to catch the south-east trades.

As the *Piranga* ploughed resolutely northwards, at 35 degrees north near the Azores, it was discovered that her running rigging was rotten, her main topmast was sprung and her spare spars were useless. In view of the frigate's condition, Cochrane decided to make for the nearest friendly port for urgent repairs and fresh provisions. For political reasons France and Spain were obviously out of the question as havens for a revolutionary frigate; so he set course for England. Challenges to their seamanship apart, it was a routine voyage. The major touch of excitement came at the end of May, when Cochrane yielded to the persuasion of his two closest companions and agreed to promote them. Thus Crosbie became a commodore, while Jackson became a captain-of-frigate in the administrative branch. But the rejoicing did not last long. The Imperial Government, in whose name all this was done, took a dim view of these personal promotions and refused to endorse them.

On 11 June the *Piranga* passed the Azores, and two weeks later – six weeks after leaving Maranhão – those on board sighted the Lizard – the first glimpse of England the British sailors making up the majority of the crew had had for years. The frigate sailed boldly up the Channel, ignoring the sanctuary of Plymouth, passing Bolt Head, Portland Bill and St Catherine's Point on the Isle of Wight. At last, on 27 June 1825, Cochrane brought the *Piranga* to anchor in Spithead and, in a historic moment, the Brazilian flag was formally saluted for the first time by a European power in its own waters.

CHAPTER 15
THE PARTING OF THE WAYS

The Confederation of the Equator was no more. By the time Cochrane sailed from Maranhão in the *Piranga*, its leaders were either in prison or had fled to exile overseas. Under the presidency of Lima e Silva, the Military Commission for Pernambuco was already trying the leaders of the revolt for treason. Eleven, including the intransigent Frei Caneca, were executed, and thirteen were condemned to death in their absence. These included Manuel de Carvalho Paes de Andrade, who had fled to England, Barros Falcão de Lacerda, who was in hiding in the United States, and José da Natividade Saldanha, who had escaped to Colombia.

In Fortaleza, a second Commission under the presidency of Colonel Jacob Conrado de Neimeyer, the defender of Barra Grande, had begun its work in April 1825. Ignoring Cochrane's promised amnesty to the rebels of Ceará, eight were condemned to death, of whom five were executed and three reprieved. Finally, in Rio de Janeiro, Ratcliffe and Metrowich, the officers of the *Constituição ou Morte*, together with the commander of the rebel *Maria da Glória*, were condemned and shot for bearing arms against the Empire. There was one more fatality – José Pereira Filguieras, rebel military commander of Ceará and conqueror of Major Fidié in Caxias, who died of natural causes while under arrest on the journey to Rio de Janeiro.

Just as the guilty were punished, so the virtuous were rewarded. Francisco Paes Barreto was elevated to the Brazilian peerage as the Visconde do Recife. José Felix de Azevedo e Sá was confirmed as President of Ceará, and made a Commander of the Order of Christ. Special medals were struck for the troops and sailors who had served in the campaign, while their officers were rewarded with promotion and decorations. Only two commanders failed to gain rewards for their contributions to the victory. One was Lima e Silva, who was out of favour with the ruling party in Rio and was regarded as having been 'soft' on the rebels after the fall of Recife. The other was Lord Cochrane.

In Rio the bad impression created by Cochrane's absence during the capture of Recife had been partly erased by his quick and effective action in pacifying the northern provinces. But as news of his activities in Maranhão began to trickle into the capital after the two-month voyage from the north, the Imperial Government began to feel uneasy. And when, in June, the arrival of his own despatches confirmed that Cochrane had prevented President Costa Barros from taking office, set the Prize Court's decisions at nought, and was effectively holding Maranhão to ransom, its worst fears seemed to have been realized. A sharp order of recall was sent on 27 June 1825, but no one, from the Emperor downwards, seriously expected him to return.[1] The person most surprised was Henry Dean, who was still dealing with Cochrane's prize business in Bahia, loyally carrying out his instructions and raising loans in the Admiral's name. Learning with astonishment of Lord Cochrane's arrival in England from officers of HMS *Doris*, Dean had to sell everything he possessed in order to meet his obligations and hastily take passage back to London with his family.

The England to which Lord Cochrane returned after six years of exile had changed but little. Peel and Huskisson had begun to overhaul the more archaic elements in the laws regulating trade and public order, but the authoritarian instincts of the Tory Government remained unchanged. While on the continent of Europe the political situation had deteriorated even further as the monarchs of the Holy Alliance ruthlessly extinguished every spark of liberalism in one country after another. Freedom and constitutional principles were everywhere in sharp retreat.

Against this sombre backdrop, the sudden return of Lord Cochrane, fresh from his victories in the liberation struggles of Latin America, was the signal for rejoicing by lovers of freedom and romantic liberals alike. Everywhere he was treated as a conquering hero, cheered in the streets by enthusiastic crowds and fêted by radical friends eager to discuss his next scene of revolutionary triumph. In Edinburgh, when a reference to South America was added to the dialogue of a play Lord and Lady Cochrane were attending, the whole audience turned to the box where the tall, red-headed hero and his young wife were sitting, and broke into prolonged and spontaneous applause. Sir Walter Scott, as overcome with emotion as was Lady Cochrane by the scene, attempted to capture the moment in a somewhat unfortunate poem.

Not everyone shared the enthusiasm. Foreign Secretary George Canning may have been following liberal overseas policies in his opposition to the Holy Alliance and his support for the independence movements of Latin America, but the attitude of the Tory Government to internal affairs was firmly reactionary. To Lord Liverpool, the Duke of Wellington and other Cabinet colleagues, the arrival of Cochrane as a focus for radical enthusiasm was highly unwelcome. Some saw him as both a dangerous demagogue and a fraudster. Feeling in ruling circles was so strong that the Government took legal advice as to whether he was liable for prosecution under the Foreign Enlistment Act. Manuel Gameiro Pessoa, who was acting as Brazilian Agent in London during Brant's absence in Rio attending the peace negotiations, was horrified to hear of the possibility, and fearful that any prosecution of an Imperial officer would be a serious blow to national honour.[2]

Cochrane's appearance also caused a flurry of international concern. In January 1825, to spur the peace process forward, the Emperor Pedro had threatened to send the Brazilian Navy to attack the coasts of Portugal.[3] And five months later, Lord Cochrane suddenly appeared in European waters with a big Brazilian frigate! Alarming conclusions were drawn. It took time to establish that the First Admiral's appearance was purely accidental, and was unauthorized by the Rio Government.

To Gameiro, the arrival of Lieutenant March with a letter from Cochrane announcing the *Piranga*'s arrival at Spithead was equally surprising. Nevertheless, he acted quickly. Two months' backpay, amounting to £2065, was produced for the crew of the frigate, and a further £2291 in pay and prize money for the seamen who had been transferred from the *Niterói* and *Paraguassú*. Fortunately, Cochrane provided a contribution of £2000 from the balance of the money he had received in Maranhao. Gameiro then made arrangements for the *Piranga* to be repaired in Portsmouth

Dockyard, so that Cochrane and the frigate could return to Brazil without delay.[4] The First Admiral, however, proved elusive, and it soon became clear that he was in no hurry to go back. Gameiro eventually ran him to ground in Tunbridge Wells, to be told ambiguously that Cochrane intended to stay in England until the peace negotiations which Sir Charles Stuart was pursuing in Lisbon and Rio had been concluded.[5]

By August it had become clear that Cochrane was playing for time. The reason was easy to deduce – indeed, was being widely talked about. In 1825 the attention of liberal England was focused not on the liberation of South America, but on the Greek struggle for freedom from Turkey. The classical tradition and the study of Ancient Athens which formed the basis of the education of all European gentlemen made them deeply and romantically partisans of the Greek cause. Stories of Turkish cruelty and of massacres, and the example of idealists such as Lord Byron, inspired them further, and committees to raise funds and give active support were formed in every European capital. In London, such supporters included many of Cochrane's political friends – radicals like Francis Burdett, John Cam Hobhouse and Joseph Hume. There was no doubt in their minds that it was to the noble cause of Greece that the Admiral should next turn his attention. Indeed, no sooner had Cochrane arrived in England than the London Committee offered him command of the Greek Navy in the struggle against the Turks.

Lord Cochrane was flattered and interested. All through the summer of 1825 he negotiated his terms of service, and worked on the specifications of six 200-ton armed steamships whose construction for the Greek Navy formed part of his conditions. All was finally agreed in secret on 16 August. Cochrane accepted the offer of command of the Greek Navy for a salary of £57,000, which – learning from experience – he insisted should be paid in two instalments and in advance. His only condition was that he would formally take up the appointment only when his position in the Brazilian service had been settled. News of these negotiations was openly carried in the newspapers, and Gameiro, who by now was becoming desperate, demanded to be told the First Admiral's intentions in writing.[6] Cochrane, who was in Scotland being received like a hero by his fellow countrymen, clearly had no intention of returning to Brazil, but was unwilling to resign his position as First Admiral lest it weaken his claims against the Imperial Government. His reply of 24 August was therefore a masterpiece of evasion, stating that he would not leave the Brazilian service until his work had ended, but he had not refused the Greek offer. Unfortunately, Gameiro's translator failed to perceive all the nuances of the First Admiral's carefully phrased ambiguity, and the letter appeared to confirm that he intended to leave the Imperial service. Gameiro immediately acknowledged the supposed resignation with glowing tributes to Cochrane's contribution to Brazilian Independence, and the First Admiral was forced to reply in haste from Edinburgh on 6 September to disabuse him.[7]

Three weeks later, the diplomatic pouch from Rio de Janeiro contained a copy of the letter of 27 June from the Minister of Marine to Lord Cochrane – then thought to be in Maranhão – ordering him to return to the capital. Gameiro forwarded the letter to him in Scotland on 27 September. It produced another evasive reply in which Lord Cochrane repeated his intention to await the result of the peace negotiations before returning. Gameiro was now convinced that Cochrane had no intention of ever going back to Brazil, and decided that even if he remained, the *Piranga* should return without further delay. Repairs had been completed, the expenses of maintaining the frigate in idleness were mounting, and the English seamen in the crew, now that they had received their pay and prize money, were beginning to desert.[8] Thomas Sackville Crosbie, whose knowledge of Cochrane's intentions was clearly greater than Gameiro's, had already left Portsmouth for his London home in Wellington Street, where he was preparing to resign his Brazilian commission in order to follow his leader to Greece.

The command of the *Piranga* now devolved upon Captain James Shepherd. On 8 October he was interviewed by Gameiro, who demanded that the frigate be put under his orders and prepared for an immediate return to Rio de Janeiro. It was a stormy meeting at which Gameiro brutally pointed out that Cochrane would never return to Brazil with £60,000 worth of prize claims filed against him, and that if Shepherd valued his future in the Imperial Navy, he had better do as he was told. The Captain nevertheless refused to accept any orders other than those of the First Admiral, and reported the whole incident to Cochrane in a private letter.[9] In desperation Gameiro then tried to persuade the British authorities to seize the frigate. When this failed, he cut off all pay and supplies to the *Piranga* and, on 7 November, informed Captain Shepherd that they would be resumed only when he and the other officers put the frigate at the disposal of the Legation, and no longer regarded themselves as being under the orders of Lord Cochrane.[10]

In the event, such a disavowal proved unnecessary. In late October 1825, Cochrane returned to London to check on the boilers for the steamships he had ordered for Greece, and to confuse Gameiro further by informing him that the *Piranga* would sail with the first favourable wind after 10 November. In his house in Regent Street, Cochrane and Jackson were finalizing their Brazilian accounts and meeting some old friends. On the pleasant side, there was a call from Maria Graham, who had just returned from Rio. But less agreeable was a reunion with a newly arrived Henry Dean, who was suspected of selling the squadron's prize property on his own account but had called to claim £1653 which, he said, Cochrane owed him for the costs and commission on his prize work in Bahia.

Then, to his horror, Cochrane learnt from his friend Sir Francis Burdett that the British Government had decided to prosecute him for a breach of the Foreign Enlistment Act. Instant flight to the continent to avoid arrest until his Greek arrangements were ready seemed the only possible course of action – but how could he free himself from his Brazilian obligations without weakening his financial claims? Fortunately for Cochrane's plans, his arrival in London coincided with news that peace negotiations had been successfully concluded, and Portugal had finally accepted the fact of Brazilian Independence. This happy news gave him the excuse he needed to leave the Imperial Service without putting himself in the wrong by formally resigning. Cochrane offered his version of events in a courteous letter dated 5 November in which he informed the Minister of Marine that the *Piranga* was now ready to return, congratulated the Imperial Government on the conclusion of peace, and pointed out that as the Decree of 28 February 1824 had restricted his period of service to the end of the war, he now regarded his appointment as First Admiral as being at an end.[11] The fact that this decree had been superseded, at his own insistence, by another dated 27 July 1824 which allowed him to remain in the Imperial Navy for as long as he chose was conveniently overlooked. And so, having convinced himself, if no one else, as to the justice of his case, on 9 November 1825 Lord Cochrane and his family embarked hurriedly at Tower Hill on a steamer bound for France, there to await the summons to Greece and his next field of military glory.

Back in Rio de Janeiro, Vilela Barbosa had been watching Cochrane's antics through the medium of Gameiro's despatches with mounting frustration. On 20 August 1825, Cochrane was ordered once more to return to Brazil. On 30 December, in astonishment at the contents of his letter of 5 November, the instruction was repeated and his salary was suspended until he came back to face an enquiry. This reached him early in 1826 in Brussels, where he was then living to avoid prosecution in France for his seizures of French merchant ships in South America. There Cochrane wrote two letters to Vilela Barbosa dated 10 February and 16 March, in which he repeated his story that the decree published on 28 February 1824 had limited his command to the end of the war and asked to be paid his salary from 1 August until 10 November 1825, when that event had occurred. For good measure he added a claim for £1000 to cover the cost of Lady Cochrane's trip to Brazil in the *Sesostris* which, he said, the Emperor had promised to refund![12] Increasingly annoyed, Vilela Barbosa sent another order of recall on 9 June 1826. This one was delivered to Leghorn by Gameiro, and finally reached Lord Cochrane in Geneva on 22 December 1826. It stimulated an infuriatingly courteous reply in which he expressed his deep desire to return to Rio, but regretted that the 28 February decree made it impossible![13]

Finally, the Minister of Marine gave up. On 10 April 1827 the Brazilian Government dismissed Lord Cochrane from the Imperial Navy in a decree which was as terse as the original invitation had been fulsome.[14] In the period between these two documents, Cochrane had probably made a greater contribution to Brazilian Independence than any other single individual apart from Josê Bonifácio and the Emperor himself. And he had made it with skill, dash and astonishing success. Unfortunately, as so often in his career, his achievement was temporarily obscured by bickering and controversy, but it was so great that it would never be forgotten.

CHAPTER 16

RECOGNITION AND AFTER

The victories at sea, the expulsion of the Portuguese troops and, now, the suppression of the Confederation of the Equator, confirmed the authority of the Imperial Government over its far-flung national territory. By 1824, Brazil was in every practical sense an independent country. All that remained was for that fact to be internationally recognized – and for that, a treaty of peace and reconciliation between Portugal and its erstwhile colony was a necessary prerequisite.

The young Emperor Dom Pedro I was as anxious as anyone that a settlement should be reached. The Empire was new and fragile, and beneath the euphoria of victory lurked political tensions and incipient republicanism. None of its provinces possessed any natural or economic superiority over the others, and the dominance of Rio de Janeiro could be accomplished only by political will backed, if necessary, by force. And it was clear to the Emperor that the longer Brazil remained in international limbo and in a state of armed conflict with the mother country, the more difficult would be the task of uniting its diverse provinces under his rule. Worse still, the deepening hostility between Brazil and Portugal threatened to undermine what both Pedro and his Royal Father, King João VI, saw as their sacred duty – namely, the preservation of the position of the House of Braganza in both the old world and the new.

Common sense and self-interest both favoured reconciliation and a graceful Portuguese acceptance of the inevitable, but the situation was charged with emotion and national pride. Behind each monarch were ranged political forces with apparently irreconcilable viewpoints. The Portuguese, humiliated by their defeats and by the pretensions of the Brazilians, saw negotiations as being about the cessation of hostilities, the restoration of captured property and compensation. Discussion of some form of regional autonomy could follow, but strictly within a formula which would assert the superiority of Portugal and acknowledge Dom João VI as 'senior' Emperor of Brazil. The Brazilians, however, triumphant after generations of colonial subordination, saw things differently. To them, recognition of their independence from Portugal and from its king was the starting point of any negotiation. Only after that was agreed could hostilities be terminated and property claims considered.

From the perspective of Britain's international interests, a peaceful settlement of the dispute between Portugal and Brazil was an important objective. Portugal was her oldest ally, and the Foreign Secretary, George Canning, was determined to remain loyal to these obligations, especially as the monarchs of the Holy Alliance, having successfully crushed liberalism in Spain, were now trying to meddle in Portuguese affairs. On the other hand, an important consideration was that Brazil was a major trading partner, and the value of her commerce to Britain was as great as that of the rest of Latin America put together. The cause of colonial liberation which Dom Pedro represented was also one which had received Canning's consistent support, and like Castlereagh before him, he judged it politically important to ensure the survival of the institution of monarchy in the New World. Unlike his predecessor, however, he did not believe in a 'European' formula for recognition and was taking a unilateral British line, though discreetly colluding with the United States, whose own Monroe Doctrine had been announced in December 1823. There was also the fact that Brazil, as Wilberforce had said, was 'slavery personified'. The abolition of the slave trade was a political imperative in Britain, and the possibility that the recognition of Brazilian independence could be connected to abolition was an attractive one. Indeed, the need for such a linkage had been made clear to the Imperial Government from the beginning, first through Brant in 1822 and then during Lord Amherst's visit to Rio in May 1823.

In March 1824, after putting out initial feelers, the Portuguese Minister in London, the Count of Villa Real, passed on a request that the British Government should mediate between the contending parties. Canning was only too pleased to accept, and preparations began. There were delays due to infighting on the Portuguese side as they hammered out their negotiating position, but finally on 12 July, pressure from Canning and from the Austrian Government brought the two sides to the conference table, Villa Real representing Portugal, Caldeira Brant speaking for Brazil. The talks got nowhere. The distance between the two sides was so great that progress was impossible, and discussions alternated with backstairs intrigues. The French complicated matters further by secret manoeuvres aimed at gaining commercial advantages in Brazil. After six months the talks had run into the sand, with both sides putting the blame at the feet of the British. The Brazilians even threatened that when the present Commercial Treaty ran out in 1825, British goods would lose their 15 per cent preferential tariff.

By January 1825, the British had had enough. Canning abruptly terminated the mediation and took matters into his own hands. With a series of diplomatic initiatives, he checkmated the intrigues of other powers, forced King João to get rid of his most intransigent advisers, and then sent the patrician diplomat Sir Charles Stuart to negotiate directly in Lisbon and Rio. Sir Charles carried out his task with skill and aplomb, and after six months of exquisite diplomacy mixed with persuasion and threats, the two sides had been successfully manoeuvred into agreement.

The treaty of peace and reconciliation was signed on 29 August 1825 and immediately sent to Europe in HMS *Warspite*. By its terms, Portugal recognized the Independence of Brazil in return for the restoration of all confiscated property; a 'most favoured nation' trading clause; and a (secret) payment of £2 million as compensation for Portugal's war debt and for the value of royal properties in Brazil. Finally, in a necessary act of filial piety, Pedro formally acknowledged his father's right to the honorary title 'Emperor of Brazil'. That concluded, Sir Charles Stuart then busied himself with negotiating draft treaties aimed at abolishing the Brazilian slave trade and extending Britain's commercial privileges. The terms of the treaty were, however, highly unpopular in both Portugal and Brazil, and to cover themselves both governments announced them in a manner which was insulting and highly critical of each other. The role of Britain in the negotiations was fortuitous. Both sides were able to attribute blame for the less acceptable clauses of the treaty to impositions forced on them by an arrogant foreign power.

Mistrustful of both the abilities and the motives of his ministers, Dom Pedro dominated the independence negotiations. With a mixture of pragmatism, courage, common sense and cunning, he played one side off against the other, resorting to rehearsed but apparently spontaneous outbursts of anger or emotion, and taking advantage of the jealousies and animosities of both his subjects and his relations. Sir Charles Stuart, no mean negotiator himself, was impressed by the performance but failed to understand the reason for the apparently anti-British posture of the Brazilian authorities.[1] Personalities friendly to Britain – such as General Brant who had travelled from London to be present – were kept out of the discussions, and there were regular and intemperate leaks in the newspapers.

Looming behind the negotiations lay the threat of a resort to armed force – or to be more precise, the fear that the Brazilian Navy might be unleashed to wreak further havoc on Portuguese commerce, or to attack her colonies in Africa. There was even concern that it might be used against the coasts of Portugal itself. Distance and logistics would have made such a thing impossible, but the threat was nevertheless believed. Indeed, one of Canning's main arguments was that Britain's guarantee of protection to Portugal applied only to attacks from foreign powers, not from colonies in revolt. The Portuguese Government did not have to be reminded of what the Brazilians could do on the high seas if they put their minds to it. It also understood perfectly why the Imperial Navy was so formidable. When Villa Real requested Canning's mediation in March 1824, one of the four major demands he presented was that all British subjects serving with the Brazilian Navy should be either discharged or recalled.[2] It is small wonder that the possibility of British officers being dismissed was a constant source of speculation and gossip among the Portuguese cliques in Rio de Janeiro.

It is no less surprising that neither the Emperor nor his ministers had any intention of obliging the Portuguese by doing such a thing. On the contrary, the Navy was a trump card which was deliberately produced whenever they felt it necessary to stimulate the peace process. In October 1824, rumours were allowed to circulate in Rio that Cochrane's purpose on leaving Pernambuco was to attack Portuguese colonies in Africa.[3] Again, in January 1825 there were stories that Cochrane was to be sent against Portugal itself. And in the same month the Emperor, impatient with the failure of the London mediation, announced that he intended to strengthen the Navy and to recruit more British sailors – both of which he did.[4]

Dom Pedro and his ministers may have felt it necessary to be scathing and critical of the terms of the treaty with Portugal in order to mollify public opinion, but secretly they knew that it was a triumph and a milestone. Now that Portugal had recognized Brazilian Independence, other European powers would follow suit. Britain was the first, and in January 1826 Manuel Gameiro Pessoa was received as the Empire's first Ambassador in London. Within three months Austria, France, Sweden, Holland and Prussia had also formally recognized the new state.

With Brazil's international status confirmed, the Emperor and his ministers set about providing the monarchical focus which they felt the prestige and unity of the country required. There were processions, parades, elaborate ceremonial. The organs of government and the social structure were elaborated on the model of the courts of Europe. The crowning point was the creation in October 1825 of an indigenous nobility consisting of one count, 17 viscounts, 21 barons and innumerable lesser grandees. To emphasize the unique qualities of the only monarchy in Latin America, the new nobles luxuriated in territorial titles of native Brazilian, frequently Indian, origin. The Minister of Marine, Vilela Barbosa, was transformed into the Visconde de Paranaguá. Felisberto Brant became the Visconde de Barbacena. Even the humble Gameiro in London, after an anxious wait, found himself Barão Itabayana.

During the years of the Royal residence in Rio there had been a rage for decorations among the urban Portuguese, and the sale of stars and crosses had been a lucrative source of state revenue. But the native Brazilians were immune to the lure of aristocracies. The creation of this mass of nobility therefore both offended their egalitarian principles and seemed vaguely ridiculous. The fact that the glittering titles had been bestowed with little regard to either the importance or the merits of the recipients only made things worse. José Bonifácio de Andrada e Silva, in exile in Europe and defiantly unennobled, was scathing in letters to friends in Rio. 'Who would have believed it possible in the present situation in Brazil' he wrote, 'that the Great Duck could hatch so many eggs in one go as to produce 19 viscounts and 22 barons! Not even King João at the height of his autocratic powers could give birth to such progeny'![5]

The ministers of the Empire had more to be pleased about than their new patents of nobility. For the first time in its history, the Government found itself free from financial crises. With the country now united, the revenues and expenditures of the whole of Brazil were at last within its control, however haphazard and inefficient the methods of collection. It also had cash in hand with which to pay for the consolidation of the Empire. In April 1824, Felisberto Brant had been authorized to raise a loan of £3 million on the London market. So great was the faith of European capitalists in the future of Brazil that in spite of Portuguese opposition, the loan was fully subscribed in four months. The first instalment of £300,000 in coin and gold bars arrived in Rio de Janeiro in the hold of HMS *Sparrowhawk* on 2 August 1824 – passing, ironically enough, Lord Cochrane's outward-bound expedition for Pernambuco as it entered the harbour. The cutter *Sir William Curtis* brought another 500,000 dollars in silver on 16 November; and a third instalment was received in Rio six weeks later. By the end of 1824, There was £600,000 in the bank awaiting the Government's instructions.[6]

Of all the instruments of state power at its disposal, it was the Navy which most deserved and demanded investment. The lessons of the Independence campaign and its aftermath were clear to see. The Navy may have expanded to 39 warships and armed schooners, but the events of 1824 had shown that it was still too small to confront two enemies simultaneously. It was equally obvious that only a strong naval force could ensure the unity, the internal peace and, indeed, the communications of a diverse country like Brazil, scattered along a coastline of 4700 miles. On the other hand, the north-eastern rebellions of 1824 had also shown the limitations of sea power. In dealing with the Confederation of the Equator, the Imperial Navy had successfully sealed the external communications of the offending provinces and caused serious damage to the external trade of their coastal cities, but while communications by land remained open, agriculture and internal commerce went on more or less as usual The Navy could hold the ring and ferry troops swiftly to the point of conflict, but in a huge continental landmass like Brazil it could never deliver the knockout blow. Only land forces could do that.

But in deciding naval policy, there was also the question of national prestige to be taken into account. In the euphoria of victory and the pride of independence, Dom Pedro and his ministers were keen to see the Navy at a level which would adequately reflect the glory and magnificence of the only monarchy in the Americas. A navy which would not only police the lagoons, bays and estuaries of Brazil's extensive coastline but would also have a prestigious 'blue water' image – a navy, in short, which was made up of ships-of-the-line and modern heavy frigates, as well as schooners and gunboats. Thus it was the prestige factor as much as any other which determined the naval policy of the Imperial Government, driven forward, it must also be said, by threatening clouds which were gathering on Brazil's southern border. In 1816, Portugal had taken advantage of the chaos which had reigned in the old Spanish Empire to seize the Banda Oriental – modern Uruguay – and annex it to Brazil. Local resistance had remained dormant during the Independence period, but in 1825 the Uruguayan patriot Juan Lavelleja had raised the standard of revolt, and the countryside had responded with enthusiasm. The United Provinces of Buenos Aires had rushed to provide encouragement and military help. War seemed inevitable.

All this provided a pressing justification for the expansion of the Brazilian Navy. Using money from the London loan and the National Subscription – which by the end of 1825 had raised 208 contos of reis (£41,400) – seven more ships were commissioned during the year. Two were the results of Grenfell's capture of Pará: the 44-gun frigate *Imperatriz* and the newly launched brigantine *Dona Januária*. Three had been taken – or retaken – from the defunct Confederation of the Equator: the brigantine *Independência ou Morte*, the schooner *Maria da Glória* and the 18-gun brig-of-war *Constituição ou Morte* (renamed *Beaurepaire* after the captain who had seized her). The other two were purchases. One was Cochrane's prize brig *Cerqueira*, the other an American brigantine called *Berefin*. These came into service under the names *29 de Agosto* and *Empreendador*.

Military stores remained a problem, and the Government fell back once more on foreign sources. On 10 August 1824, General Brant in London received orders to buy huge quantities of armaments and supplies. With his credit good and his links with manufacturers well established following his purchases of the previous year, he was able to act quickly. On 14 and 30 September the merchantmen *Old Maid* and *Bride* put to sea carrying the first consignments of iron chains, hemp cables, copper plates and spars costing £13,948.[7] Over the next 18 months, 35 ships sailed from British ports with military stores for the arsenals of Brazil. Both the range and the value of their cargoes were enormous. They varied from anchors, cables, canvas, spars, steam pumps and cannon to muskets, tools, ramrods, bayonets, surgeon's instruments and buttons. In 1825 alone, the cost to the Brazilian Government was over £93,000 even with favourable discounts.[8]

In London, Brant and Gameiro were feverishly busy. Their diplomatic duties ranged from handling the negotiations for Brazilian Independence to dealing with the tricky situation posed by Lord Cochrane's sudden arrival at Portsmouth in the *Piranga*. At the same time they were purchasing, insuring and despatching huge quantities of military stores, and anxiously trying to carry out their orders to buy two East Indiamen for conversion to warships and two steamships to act as mail packets along the Brazilian coast.

They could find only one East Indiaman for sale, and that was the newly built *Surat Castle*. Gameiro bought the ship in the name of a bogus firm and arranged for her to be converted into a frigate by Wigram-Green of Blackwall.[9] The task of rebuilding the vessel proved to be enormous, and the eventual cost of £75,390 was substantially more than that of a new frigate. But the ship was ready in six months, and on 10 July 1825, she set sail for Rio de Janeiro under her new name, *Dona Paula*, armed with 18-pounder guns and flying the Brazilian flag. She carried a cargo of military stores, and was manned by a crew of British sailors. Gameiro was perhaps conscious of the cost of the vessel and gave Captain Doveton, the master contracted to deliver her to Rio, careful instructions so that she would look her best on arrival. He was to ensure that the frigate was repainted, run man-of-war fashion, and ready to receive the Emperor with appropriate honours were he to come on board.[10]

The steamships were more difficult to find. The first, a vessel of less than a year old called *Hibernia*, was bought through the Liverpool firm of Cropper, Benson & Co. for £18,718. She was a 300-ton paddle steamer of 140 horsepower with auxiliary sail. Gameiro's problem was to get insurance for what was the first voyage of such a ship to the South Atlantic. But the difficulty was overcome, and at the beginning of May 1825 the newly named *Correio Imperial* sallied forth under the direction of Captain John Pease and a team of five contracted engineers.[11] After a slow and careful voyage of 149 days via Pará, Maranhão, Pernambuco and Bahia, the steamer triumphantly reached Rio de Janeiro in September 1825. She was taken immediately into service under the command of Sublieutenant R.N. Murphy.

The second steamer, originally the *Britannia*, had to be built at Liverpool to the same specifications at a price of £16,308.[12] All went well, and after a slight delay in Cork caused by engine trouble, the ship was well on her way to Brazil in January 1826 under the command of a Danish officer, Herman Randolf, recently recruited into the Brazilian Navy as a captain-of-frigate. Armed with an 18-pounder gun and two 24-pounder carronades, the steamship had a good record and was still in service under her new name, *Correio Brasileiro* ten years later.

It was inevitable that the Brazilian Government would also look to the United States in its search for naval vessels. American yards were famous for the size and speed of their products, and were known to be building warships on contract for Mexico, Colombia and other South American republics. Indeed, it was the Brazilian Agent in Washington, Gonçalves da Cruz, who suggested that the Government in Rio should follow suit. Ministers agreed, and on 21 January 1824 ordered his successor, José Silvestre Rebello, to begin negotiations for the building of two frigates.[13] In September a naval constructor, José Joaquim Faustino, and a carpenter were sent to help him. Six months later, fresh orders arrived to buy eight brigs with nine guns a side.[14] This was easier said than done. The search for suitable vessels went on for months, but eventually, on 26 September 1825, Silvestre Rebello was forced to report failure. There were no brigs-of-war available for purchase, and the merchant vessels they had found were too weak to carry artillery. The Brazilians toyed with the idea of building, but American woods were soft, the cost was high and the life of the vessels too short to justify the expense. The idea was dropped.

Work on the frigates, however, went ahead smoothly. In January 1825, a contract was finally signed with Henry Eckford for the construction of two ships, one in New York, the other in Baltimore.[15] At 350 pesos (£70,000) each, the asking price was high and caused last-minute doubts in Rio, but by August the work was well ahead and the frames were in place. They were both 1768-ton frigates of the largest size comparable to the USS *Brandywine*, 177 feet long by 46 feet wide by 15 feet in the hold with rounded sterns, and carrying 62 guns with 32-pounders on the maindeck.

The New York frigate, named *Isabela*, was launched in April 1826. Fully fitted, she sailed on 1 April 1826 for Rio, where she was commissioned with Captain Teodoro Beaurepaire in command. The second, called *Principe Imperial*, was launched in May and was fitted out by her new captain, James Thompson, assisted by Lieutenants Craig, Newton and Fubbs before sailing from Baltimore on 7 September 1826. Both vessels were received rapturously by the Brazilian Government, and were in service by the end of the year.

The Government's opponents were highly critical of Imperial naval policy, and their strictures were passed on by contemporary observers such as the English merchant and historian John Armitage. They argued that the Emperor was following a policy of naval ostentation and waste, and that instead of building ships-of-the-line and buying massive American frigates, he should have been concentrating on shallow draught schooners suitable for service among the estuaries of the coast and the mud flats of the River Plate. As it confronted the threat from Buenos Aires, it is difficult to judge whether the Brazilian Government was so dazzled by the apparently easy victories and the boundless confidence of the Imperial Navy that it formed an unrealistic view of what the Empire could achieve in the military sphere. The extent of Brazil's huge coastline and its position across the trade routes of South America seemed to justified a mixed naval force. And once it had begun, the nature of the war with Buenos Aires fully justified the Imperial

Government's naval policy. The Brazilians finally prevailed at sea because the size and weight of the squadrons overwhelmed their opponents. If Commodore Norton and his Anglo-Brazilian force had confronted Admiral Brown and his Anglo-Argentinean squadron with identical ships of modest size, the result would have been different. And, off the Brazilian coast, the Empire needed frigates and corvettes to frustrate the depredations of the swarm of big privateers which sailed under the flag of Buenos Aires, most of them manned by foreigners thirsty for loot.

The expansion of the Navy over this period from 28 to 48 warships and armed schooners was certainly spectacular.[16] It also meant that once again the Government was short of junior officers and men. The experience of foreign recruitment for the Navy in 1823 had, however, been highly satisfactory. There had been desertions by seamen, it was true, but that was only to be expected. And of the 59 British officers or aspirant officers recruited in England and locally, only twelve had gone. Cochrane and Crosbie had left to follow their fortunes to Greece; James Watson and Samuel Gillett had deserted; Joseph Sewell and Thomas Poynton had been dismissed; Benjamin Kelmare and Sub-lieutenants Blakely and Macreights had quietly left the service, to no one's regret; and Lieutenants Chester, Challes and Mosselyn had died or been invalided out – a small proportion, taking into account the diseases prevalent in overcrowded ships in the tropics. The rest remained in service, having played vital roles in the blockade of Bahia, the liberation of Maranhão and Pará, the fighting off Montevideo which concluded the War of Independence, and the suppression of the Confederation of the Equator.

John Taylor was also back. Dismissed from the Imperial Navy in August 1824 as a result of remorseless British diplomatic pressure,[17] Taylor took Brazilian nationality and, in December 1825, was reinstated with the rank of commodore. An immediate and brutally worded British protest was passed on by a nervous Gameiro in London, but the Emperor stood firm in support of the hero and Taylor remained in the Navy until he died, reaching the rank of Vice Admiral.

Encouraged by the success of the foreign recruiting campaigns of 1823, the Brazilian Government decided to try again in 1824–25. Pay rates had improved by this time. It had been decreed on

11 July 1824 that foreign seamen should receive 50 per cent above the normal rates – an attractive increase which gave Able Seamen 15 milreis (£3) a month, almost double that paid in the Royal Navy – and on 2 April 1825, the pay of officers was increased by between one-third and a half. Lieutenants serving afloat, for example, were now to be paid 60 milreis monthly (£12) instead of the old rate of 36 milreis (£7.20p).

Alas, these inducements were not quite enough. Attempts to raise men in Genoa and in the United States failed, although London – once again – proved fruitful. On 2 October 1824, Caldeira Brant received orders to recruit 800 seamen.[18] On 5 May 1825, he was told to find 18 officers below the rank of commander. But this time it was more difficult. Thanks to Lord Cochrane, there were stories in the press of British sailors receiving poor treatment from the Brazilian Government, and the Portuguese consuls were alert and ready to denounce any illegal recruitment. General Brant managed to find eleven officers, but this time only two – Lieutenant Thomas Haydon and Midshipman Louis Brown – were British; the rest were French or Scandinavian.[19] Seamen were easier to find. Two hundred sailed on the *Surat Castle* on 11 July 1825, another 50 in the steamships which left in the months that followed, and 150 in the *Piranga* when it eventually sailed from Spithead in November. The total was less than needed, but nevertheless provided a valuable addition of experienced manpower.

Meanwhile, the situation in the Banda Oriental deteriorated into open rebellion, with the Uruguayan patriots receiving military help from the Argentinians. The Brazilian Navy geared itself for war. Dockyards and arsenals once more bustled with activity. New ships were commissioned and old ones prepared for sea. The armaments, naval stores and sailors arriving from England were redistributed, and warships ordered south to reinforce the Imperial squadrons in the River Plate or escort troop reinforcements to Montevideo. Finally, on 10 December 1825, the Imperial Government declared war on the United Provinces of Buenos Aires. Brazil's first military test as an independent nation had arrived.

CHAPTER 17

EPILOGUE

The war with Buenos Aires went on for two years. It was not a popular conflict. The Brazilian Army was beaten on land, and the Navy had difficulty in maintaining its blockade and frustrating the skill and ingenuity of the Irish-born commander of the Argentinian forces, Admiral William Brown. It was a messy war, fought out by small squadrons in the channels and mud flats of the River Plate and by individual warships engaging the big Argentinian privateers which were unleashed along the Brazilian coast. At length, the two sides wearily agreed to a compromise peace, and the modern state of Uruguay was born.

It was the British who once again mediated in the dispute. This is hardly surprising. Not only had Canning's influence in securing the independence of Latin America given Britain a political stake in the region, but the war was effectively strangling the substantial trade which Britain carried out in the River Plate. As Woodbine Parish, HM Consul-General in Buenos Aires, pointed out in his despatches, it was maddening to see this vital commerce being jeopardized by the action of two navies both of which were commanded and manned substantially by subjects of the King of England.

The British officers of the Brazilian Navy were certainly active and frequently prominent throughout the war with Buenos Aires. It was Commodore Norton who commanded the inshore squadron in the River Plate and led it to minor victories at Los Pozes, Lara-Quilmes and Monte Santiago, losing his arm in the process,[1] while John Pascoe Grenfell, William James Inglis and George Broom distinguished themselves as commanders in single-ship actions. Not all survived. Lieutenant John Rogers Gleddon was killed during the first action of the war in February 1826 while commanding the brig *29 de Agosto*. Captain James Shepherd died a year later leading a disastrous attack in Patagonia. Commander Alexander Anderson, Lieutenant James Taylor and Sublieutenant Charles Yell were all badly wounded in naval engagements. On the debit side, the Navy quietly dispensed with the services of four more of their number – Sublieutenant Gore Whitlock Oudesley and Lieutenant David Carter for being drunk during the capture of their corvette *Itaparica* in 1827; Lieutenant Vincent Crofton, described by his commanding officer as 'a madman and a drunkard'; and Commander Alexander Reid for incompetence in beaching the *Maceio* off San Blas. There was one worse case. In 1827, Sublieutenant Robert Mackintosh seized control of the schooner he commanded with the help of Argentinian prisoners and sailed it to Buenos Aires, where he sold it to the Government and pocketed the proceeds.

Inevitably the war served as a powerful stimulant to the growth of the Brazilian Navy, and neither officers nor men were difficult to find. On 3 May 1828, Minister of Marine Jorge de Brito reported to the Legislative Assembly that the Navy had grown to one ship-of-the-line, nine frigates and 66 smaller warships and armed schooners carrying 875 guns, with one ship-of-the-line, two frigates and six other vessels building. In his judgement, this was the minimum number needed to protect Brazilian territory, fight the war and provide the anti-slavery squadron which the country was now obliged to station off the coast of Angola. In terms of manpower, the Navy had also grown to reach a total strength of 8419 officers and men, of whom between a half and a third were foreigners. In terms of expense, the cost of this naval might in 1828 was a staggering 3500 contos – one-third more than what had been voted for the purpose, and three times as much as had been spent in 1823.[2] It was small wonder that the war plunged the Government into a series of serious deficits which could be cured only by slashing exchange rates and flooding the country with paper money.

Within three years, a minor liberal revolution had changed all this. In spite of his pivotal role in Brazilian Independence, the popularity of the Emperor Pedro had been steadily on the decline ever since. The unpalatable clauses in the treaty of recognition with Portugal, the bungled and expensive war with Buenos Aires, the deteriorating economy, the unsavoury personalities in his household, a merry-go-round of inept ministries and the death of the lonely but popular Empress Leopoldina in 1826 – all contributed to the disenchantment. Worst of all, at a time when Brazil's identity was being aggressively asserted, there remained the fact that Pedro was Portuguese not only by birth but, many suspected, by sentiment and interest as well. Finally, he gave up. Frustrated by public protests at the dismissal of a popular ministry in 1831, and accurately sensing the public mood, Pedro abdicated in favour of the only Brazilian-born member of his family, his five-year-old son. Then, leaving the patriarch of independence, José Bonifácio de Andrada e Silva, as the child's guardian, he sailed away to devote his still considerable energies to the dynastic struggles of the House of Braganza.

The problem was that the death of King João VI in 1826 had caused a succession crisis. Pedro, the heir, was clearly unacceptable to Portugal, while his brother, Miguel, was still in exile in Vienna following the failure of his coup attempt. But there was an ingenious solution. The idea was that Pedro would renounce his right to the Portuguese crown in favour of his daughter, the Princess Maria da Glória – Maria Graham's pupil – who would marry her uncle to safeguard his dynastic position. Miguel readily agreed then, true to form, treacherously seized the throne for himself and plunged Portugal into decades of civil war. It was in the cause of his daughter, Queen Maria II, that Dom Pedro was to spend the rest of his life until his premature death on campaign at the age of 35.

The events of 1830–31 brought to power in Brazil a government which believed in a policy of cuts in expenditure and political realism. The 'blue water' policy and the pursuit of international prestige, was abandoned and Brazil was recognized for what it was – a continental country of vast resources and regional tensions which had the sea as an easy but vital means of communication and trade. The logic of this position was ruthlessly applied to the Navy. Within two years it had been cut to one-fifth of its former size, boasting no more than 17 warships, the largest of which was a medium-sized frigate, and 1500 officers and men.[3] Its success in the Independence campaign and in the war with Buenos Aires were seen as a glorious but temporary flash in the pan, and the Navy was firmly recast into the role it would occupy for the next two decades – that of regional policeman and coastguard. And when it eventually went to war – first against the Argentinian dictator Rosas in 1852, and then against Paraguay as part of a Triple Alliance with Argentina and Uruguay in 1865 – its field of glory lay not on the ocean but in seizing control of the great internal rivers of South America. This abrupt change in the Navy's role and fortune was not easy on its officers. Promotion was effectively frozen and, as a result of a law of 15 November 1830, all foreign officers were discharged unless they had fought actively in the War of Independence. By this time, 25 of the 52 British officers who had been recruited for the Brazilian Navy in 1822–23 had already left the service and returned to England, either voluntarily at the end of their contracts or as a result of dismissal or desertion. Five years later, the Navy List of 1835 still contained the names of 22 British veterans.[4]

Economies may have been made, but the Navy was still needed. The smouldering regionalism of Brazil, its extensive lines of communication and growing economic hardship, resulted in a spate of rebellions. There were the 'Cabanos' in Pernambuco (1832–35) and in Pará (1835–36); the 'Sabinada' in Bahia (1837–38); the 'Balaiada' in Maranhão (1839–40); and the 'Farrapos' in Rio Grande do Sul and Santa Catarina, which dragged on for a decade from 1835. These crises caused a partial mobilization. In 1836 the number of ships in commission was increased to 30, but a rapid expansion in manpower proved as difficult to achieve as it had been in 1823. As before, the Government mounted a recruiting campaign in Britain, and managed to contract over 100 men in the Orkneys and Shetlands.[5] Coincidentally, the arrangements were made by Caldeira Brant – now Marquis de Barbacena – who was back in London attempting to renegotiate the unfavourable trade treaty.

The Brazilian Navy was inevitably prominent in the suppression of all these outbreaks, and so were its remaining British officers. William James Inglis was in command of the naval station during the bloody 'Cabanos' rebellion in Pará, and was killed during its early stages. Lieutenant R. N. Murphy died in the same campaign. Commodore John Taylor led the force which restored order, assisted by Captains William Eyre, George Manson and Bartholomew Hayden. In the south, it was likewise Commodore John Pascoe Grenfell who directed the naval units deployed against the 'Farrapos', with Captains William Parker, Richard Hayden and George Broom under his command.

Of the original British officers contracted in 1823, the names of six stand out in the naval history of the period. Commodore James Norton, the hero of the war with Buenos Aires, died prematurely in 1835 at the age of 46 on a voyage to New Zealand, having established himself in his new country with his wife and family. Others, too, settled in Brazil, married local girls and stayed on in the Navy to be entrusted with important commands and to reach the highest ranks of the service. John Taylor, although he was reappointed as a commodore when he adopted Brazilian nationality in December 1825, was not employed during the war with Buenos Aires. In favour again after 1831, he served as aide-de-camp to the Minister of Marine, was port commander of Rio de Janeiro in 1832, and commanded the forces which fought the Pará rebels in 1836. He retired to his coffee plantation at Cantagalo near Rio, and died a vice admiral in 1855.[6] Bartholomew Hayden was in almost continuous command of ships until 1840, distinguishing himself in the Buenos Aires war, commanding the anti-slavery Squadron of the East, and fighting the rebels in Pará in 1836. He died a commodore in 1857 at the age of 65 while on sick leave in Portsmouth.[7]

The most turbulent career was enjoyed by George Broom. In continuous employment until he died, he was decorated for outstanding bravery on numerous occasions, captured the Argentinian privateers *Liberdad del Sud* and *General Dorrego* after fierce hand-to hand-engagements, escaped from a prisoner-of-war fortress once, and was court-martialled no fewer than three times. Broom contributed to the history of Italy as well, for it was he who was in command of the blockade of Laguna in 1839 during the 'Farrapos' rebellion, when Garibaldi evaded the vigilance of the Brazilian patrols and escaped to find greater glory in Europe. Broom died a commodore in 1860 at the age of 63.[8] The longest and steadiest career was that of William Parker. Born in Dumfries, Parker was 22 years old when he left the *Lapwing* to serve as a midshipman and sublieutenant in the *Pedro I*, *Paraguassú* and *Niterói* during the

Independence campaign and the fighting off Pernambuco. He was subsequently in command of warships and small squadrons from 1825 to 1844, and in the twenty years that followed he served successfully as officer commanding Brazil's three main naval stations – Rio Grande do Sul, Bahia and Rio de Janeiro. He retired an admiral in 1867 and died in Montevideo at the age of 82 in 1883.[9] Parker was the last British survivor of the War for Brazilian Independence.

The most distinguished of these men, however, was John Pascoe Grenfell. From the beginning to the end, his career was spectacular and his abilities and personality were admired by all who met him. He lost his right arm serving as one of Brazil's most outstanding frigate captains in the Buenos Aires war; fought the 'Farrapos' in the late 1830s, was in charge of the naval stations in southern Brazil during the 1840s; and in 1851–52 commanded the Brazilian sea forces during the war with Argentina, achieving a famous victory when he forced the passage of Tonelero.[10] Grenfell died an admiral in 1869, having spent his later years as Brazilian Consul-General in Liverpool. It was in that capacity, and as his government's chief representative, that he attended the funeral of his old chief, Lord Cochrane, in Westminster Abbey on 14 November 1860.

Lord Cochrane's post-Brazilian career in Greece was neither happy nor distinguished. The military situation was chaotic, and the Greek forces were in a state of anarchy. In two years even Cochrane could achieve little. His return to Britain coincided with the replacement of the Tories by a government made up of his political friends. There then began a process of rehabilitation which ended with Cochrane being fully restored to his rank and privileges, and established as one of the monuments of Victorian Britain. In 1832 he was given a free pardon for the Stock Exchange conviction, and was restored to the Navy List as a rear admiral. Between 1848 and 1851 he was commander-in-chief of the Royal Navy's North America and West Indies Squadron. In the interim he devoted himself to scientific experiments with steamships, poison gas, bitumen and new weapons and, like his father, spent much of his fortune in the process. In 1854 he volunteered his services for the Crimean War, but was refused by a cautious

Admiralty which feared that his impetuosity might get them into difficulties. He was then 79 years old.

By 1855, Lord Cochrane was an institution. He was now the 10th Earl of Dundonald, an Admiral of the Fleet, Rear Admiral of England, an Elder Brother of Trinity House, a Knight Grand Cross of the Order of the Bath, and the holder of innumerable foreign decorations. As a hero and a legend, his stories and complaints were listened to with a respect and incredulity bordering on the naive. Nothing he said or did seems to have been doubted or questioned.

Unfortunately, fame, reputation and public recognition of the astonishing achievements of his life were not enough. The old obsessions with injustice and money revived and, if anything, intensified. By the middle of the 1840s Cochrane had convinced himself that he was owed £200,000 by the governments of Britain, Chile and Brazil, and for the next 30 years he and his heirs devoted themselves to getting the money.

Aided and egged on by a group of friends and hangers-on, who included his former secretary William Jackson, Cochrane set about producing a series of petitions and memorials which related at enormous length his various services and claims. In February 1845, a Memorial to the President of Chile was on its way to Valparaiso. In April 1846, the British Admiralty and Prime Minister were treated to 'Observations on Naval Affairs, including Instances of Injustice experienced by the Author'. And in October 1847, a Petition to the Emperor Pedro II of Brazil was ready for delivery. Cochrane attempted to have it sent through the British Legation in Rio, but Lord Palmerston in the Foreign Office refused on the grounds that the government could not be associated with his use of the title 'Marquis of Maranhão' as it had not been authorized by the Queen.[11]

With official channels closed, Cochrane appointed the Liverpool firm of Bramley Moore & Co. and its Rio subsidiary, James Moore & Co., to press his claims. Alas, the timing of his initiative could not have been worse. In 1845 the British Government, frustrated by continued inaction on the question of slavery, had passed the Aberdeen Act – properly the 'Slave Trade (Brazil) Act' – which authorized the Royal Navy to treat captured Brazilian slave ships as if they were pirates, and relaxed some of the earlier more stringent requirements regarding proof. The result was that the next five years saw a bumper crop of seizures in which over 400 slavers were condemned by the British Vice Admiralty Courts. Then, in 1850, Lord Palmerston suddenly announced that the Royal Navy's operations in implementing the Aberdeen Act need not be restricted to international waters or the high seas. The decision led to a spate of incidents in which British cruisers of the South America Squadron began to pursue slavers deep into Brazilian territorial waters. Ships were driven ashore or carried off from the very ports themselves, and in one incident there was an exchange of fire between HMS *Cormorant* and the shore batteries guarding Paranaguá. By the 1850s, a series of high-handed actions which the Imperial Government was powerless to prevent had made both Britain and the British the objects of loathing through the length and breadth of Brazil. Fortunately, Lord Cochrane's attention during this tense period was taken up by his duties as commander-in-chief of the Royal Navy's North America and West Indies station, which lasted from 1848 until 1851, and he was too preoccupied to devote much energy to the cause. From the point of view of the Admiral's standing in Brazil, it was perhaps also fortunate that his appointment in 1848 had been to the Royal Navy's North and not its South America station!

In the event, it was the Brazilian Government which took the initiative by deciding in the 1850s to tidy up some of the unfinished business of the Independence campaign and the war with Buenos Aires. Its main problem was with the complicated prize claims which still remained unresolved from both conflicts, but it was agreed at the same time to look into the case of Lord Cochrane. Encouraged, the Admiral and his allies set about producing a detailed 'Description of Services' which was completed in March 1854, to be followed up a year later by a 'Memorial to the Legislature of Brazil' and a second Petition to the Emperor, both supplemented with an annexe of quotations from selected documents. This time, the Petition was delivered in June 1855 via the British Legation in Rio.[12] Copies of the 'Memorial', however, were sent in bulk to James Moore & Co. who spent June and July distributing copies to every Senator and Deputy.

These documents included a detailed account of Cochrane's operations during the War of Independence and in the pacification of the Northern Provinces. They also enumerated his financial claims against the Brazilian state. Cochrane's argument was that his original appointment in March 1823 had been *permanent*; that the decree of 28 February 1824 had therefore been illegal without his consent (which he had never given); and that the decree of 27 July had permitted him to remain in the Brazilian Navy until he chose to resign (which he had never done). Thus, Brazil owed him 30 years' back pay – a sum which he estimated to be £75,000 at the appropriate rate of exchange!

Cochrane's narrative of his adventures in Brazil arrived just in time for the debate in the Senate which had been scheduled for 26, 27 and 28 July 1855. James Moore & Co. reported that Cochrane's story had had an enormous impact, and had done much to ensure that the favourable motion tabled by the Government had been passed. On 11 August, the firm wrote announcing what they regarded as a great victory. In a law dated 16 August 1855, the Government had been authorized to pay Cochrane what was owing on his salary up to 10 November 1825 and a half-pay pension for the 30 years since that date. In addition, the sum of 640 contos had been voted to meet the prize money claims of the two wars, part of which would clearly go to the Admiral. Unfortunately, not all the news was good. There had been no mention of interest on Cochrane's back pension, and it looked as if payment would be made at the current rate of exchange, and not that agreed in 1823.[13]

Rather than feeling pleasure at this news, Cochrane was incensed. Not only would a settlement on these terms reduce the payments to a quarter of what he had in mind, but a Ministry of Marine report submitted during the debate had contained criticisms of his behaviour. He and his supporters returned to the attack. In June 1856 a new 'Exposition' was on its way to Rio, and by 1857 yet another was in production. James Moore & Co. distributed the first, but urged Cochrane not to send another, since more long-winded protests were likely to do more harm than good.[14]

More successful was a third Petition to the Emperor, this time delivered personally in October 1856 by the incoming British Minister, Mr Scarlett. In it, Cochrane referred mildly to his bid for full pay, but concentrated his arguments on the question of exchange rates. He pointed out that both his letter of appointment dated 21 March and the Imperial Patent issued under the Great Seal of the Empire on 22 November 1823 had explicitly stated that he was to receive 'the same emoluments he had received when in Chile'. To him this meant that any payments should be calculated in 'hard' Chilean pesos rather than in Brazilian paper milreis, which had suffered twice as much in terms of devaluation since the 1820s. He even quoted from a letter from Cunha Moreira (no original copy of which could or can be found) which promised him his pay in 'metallic money' and his subsistence 'in paper notes'.

Dom Pedro gave the Judgement of Solomon. Tactfully ignoring the claims to full pay, he ruled that the Admiral should indeed receive his pension converted at the advantageous Chilean rate.[15] It still took a year for the final details to be settled. The pay books of the *Piranga* had to be examined to discover exactly what Cochrane had paid himself in 1825; then an outbreak of yellow fever temporarily halted the work as officials abandoned Rio and took to the hills. Then the heirs to the owners of two prizes ruled illegal in 1823 tried to prevent any payments to Cochrane until he had settled their claims. But finally, the Ministry of Marine paid up. On 23 February 1857, James Moore & Co. triumphantly remitted bills of exchange to Lord Cochrane worth £34,000, being his back pay and his pension from 10 November 1825 to 31 December 1856. From that date until his death in 1860, the Admiral received a pension of £310 promptly every quarter; and his widow, Kitty Lady Dundonald, continued to receive it until she too died in Boulogne five years later.

That was not the end of the matter. Cochrane remained aggrieved by a host of financial details and claims, of which prize money remained the most important. On that issue, it had been decided that the sum available to the officers and men who had captured prizes in the two wars should be split, with 250 contos of reis (£28,000 at the prevailing exchange rate) being set aside for the Independence campaign. By December 1855 the rules by which the money would be distributed had been determined, and a Commission had been appointed to do the work. Advertisements were put in British and Brazilian newspapers, and a period of six months was given for the receipt of fully documented claims.[16] But it was years before the commissioners got anywhere.

They decided first to deal with claims relating to Buenos Aires, and when they eventually got round to the War of Independence, the incomplete nature of the records caused endless delays. Cochrane, who (according to the published rules) now expected to receive up to one-fifth of the amount available as commander-in-chief, became more and more frustrated.

With a mass of documents at his disposal, a team of eager confederates and the bones of his thesis already contained in innumerable petitions and memorials, Cochrane decided to capture his version of events in a book, and in 1859 his *Narrative of Services in the Liberation of Chile, Peru and Brazil* appeared. At that time he was 84 years old. Although the Admiral undoubtedly contributed to this work in terms of half-remembered reminiscences, the book was substantially the work of a professional author, G.P. Earp, writing with the clear purpose of demonstrating that Cochrane was right in every controversy and was justified in all his financial claims. Indeed, Earp was promised a percentage of any payments the book might stimulate. The strongest influence, however, was that of Cochrane's former secretary, William Jackson, who supplied carefully selected documents and whose own thin and highly imperfect journal forms its basic framework.[17] Cochrane's letter books were meticulously examined so that any disagreement could be extracted and presented as a grievance – however unimportant it may have seemed at the time – and inconvenient correspondence was suppressed. The Admiral's letter to Vilela Barbosa of 5 November 1825, announcing his departure from the Imperial Navy, for example, was carefully omitted since its inclusion would have undermined Cochrane's claim that he had been effectively dismissed by Gameiro on the orders of Rio.

In these circumstances it is not surprising that the *Narrative of Services* is neither a just nor an accurate account of what took place. As in Jackson's journal, there are glaring errors in dates and geography, and excessive concentration on minor financial transactions. The motives of Cochrane's antagonists are invariably misunderstood, and the actions of his friends are often omitted to bring him greater glory and, presumably, a bigger share of prize money. A year later, in 1860, the Admiral's two-volume *Autobiography of a Seaman*, which recounted his adventures and feuds during the Napoleonic Wars, appeared. In England the books were read avidly and uncritically. The dramatic quality of his story, the nobility of the causes for which he fought and, indeed, the element of betrayal by lesser men, confirmed Cochrane as the archetypal Victorian warrior-hero.

In Brazil the Portuguese version of the *Narrative* was reported as being a 'sensation' and provoked renewed energy in the Prize Commission, whose members were still ploughing through the complications of the Buenos Aires conflict. At last they reached the War of Independence, and began to untangle the incomplete documentation and the contradictory versions of events, promises and payments. Nevertheless, the commissioners finally felt able to pronounce on the Admiral's prize claims, and in 1865 they awarded him a total of 84,069 milreis – or £9450 at the prevailing rate of exchange. Alas, the judgement came too late to benefit Lord Cochrane, who had died five years earlier, in 1860; but both the money and the grievance passed to his son, Thomas Barnes Cochrane, 11th Earl of Dundonald.

Dissatisfied with the size of the award, Dundonald returned to the attack, and on 12 October 1865 he petitioned the Brazilian Government claiming, as Lord Cochrane's heir, additional compensation to the value of 699,775 milreis or £77,750. This time there was a ragbag of demands, many of them dubious, most of them questionable. As amended in a second petition dated 7 December 1869, they finally boiled down to six. First, he claimed the 40,000 milreis promised for the frigate *Imperatriz*, captured in Pará; second, the return of the £2000 given to Gameiro by Lord Cochrane in 1825 for the provisioning of the *Piranga*, which was now claimed to be a loan; third, the Admiral's share on all prizes taken during the war, whether they were lawful captures or not; fourth, interest on Cochrane's pension payments; fifth, a large sum in return for estates which had been promised by Pedro I but never given; and sixth, 67,000 pesos which Cochrane said Brazil had promised to pay in 1823 on behalf of Chile. On this occasion the Brazilians were accused not only of breaking promises and delaying payment, but of consistently treating Cochrane in a harsh and unreasonable manner.

As before, Dundonald's petitions (paralleled by a similar campaign in Chile) were accompanied by extensive local lobbying. In Rio, most of the work was done by his legal representative, British

Consul Lennon Hunt, variously assisted by a Mr Scully. The Earl, who had mortgaged his estates to fund the campaign, paid personal visits to the Brazilian capital on four occasions between 1865 and 1872 to apply additional pressure, receiving the help of a friend in the British Legation, Minister George Buckley Mathew, who mobilized his staff in support.

The Brazilian Government issued a rebuttal of Dundonald's claims in July 1872, but under strong British pressure, and anxious to arrive at a settlement lest the embarrassing dispute drag on for another 20 years, it decided to go to arbitration. In February 1873 the Minister of the United States, Mr Partridge, and the Minister of Italy, Baron Cavalcanti, agreed to carry out the task with their Belgian colleague standing by in case of a disagreement. In the event his assistance was not called on, as the findings were unanimous.

After six months of detailed investigation, the decision was announced on 6 October 1873.[18] In a fair and detailed analysis, the arbitrators found no evidence of 'harsh and cruel' treatment. On the contrary, they concluded that the Brazilian authorities had dealt with Lord Cochrane with 'indulgence and generosity' throughout. There was, on the other hand, plenty of evidence of delayed payments and partial fulfilment of promises. Turning to the detailed demands in Dundonald's petition, they decisively rejected the second, fifth and the sixth of his claims. There was not a scrap of evidence that the Brazilians in 1823 had either promised to assume the debts of the Chilean Government or awarded Lord Cochrane an estate to match his title as Marquis of Maranhão. Indeed neither claim had been mentioned before they appeared in *Narrative of Services* in 1859. Likewise, on the question of the £2000 paid by Lord Cochrane for the *Piranga* in Portsmouth, there was ample evidence that the money was not a loan but had come from the amounts paid over by the Maranhão Junta. They also rejected the claim for interest on the pension payments, pointing out that Cochrane had never asked for it in his lifetime and supporting the Brazilian argument that the Admiral had been largely responsible for his suspension of pay and the delays which had resulted by his persistent refusal to return to Brazil.

On the favourable side, the first claim – which was now for a

EPILOGUE   185

one-eighth share of the value of the *Imperatriz* – was supported, and an award of £4125 was made. Indeed, it had never been contested by the Brazilians. The bulk of the judgement, however, was devoted to the complicated question of prize money. The final tally of vessels captured was calculated at 126, of which 33 had been condemned. The remaining 93 had either been ruled unlawful, or proceedings had been abandoned for lack of documentary evidence. The arbitrators were perplexed. They agreed with Cochrane's estimate that the value of the whole was about 2000 contos (or £400,000 at the 'hard' peso exchange rate, of which the Admiral's share would have been £50,000), but had to admit that whatever prejudices may have been shown by the Prize Courts, it was likely that a number of neutral vessels had been seized illegally, and it was therefore unreasonable to hand over the total sum to the captors.

To solve this dilemma, the arbitrators fell back on an offer made by Lord Cochrane to the Brazilian Minister in London in 1860 that he would regard all his prize claims settled by a payment of £44,000. Deducting the £9450 paid in 1865, they therefore awarded the Earl of Dundonald the sum of £34,550. The Earl decided that this was the best offer he would ever get, and accepted the award as full and final settlement. The Ministry of Marine accordingly included the amount in its budget, and on 23 December 1874 Buckley Mathew wrote to report that the Brazilian Government had paid the sums due to Dundonald (plus the one year's interest) into the Legation's accounts.[19] By January 1875, the money had been transferred and the Earl was £40,298.5s.9d better off.

The long dispute was now over – but not quite. With the consent of the Foreign Secretary, Mr Lennon Hunt received a handsome gift of plate for his part in the business, but Mr Scully and the heirs of G. P. Earp had to take Dundonald to court to get their promised percentages. The Cochrane family also began to quarrel over their respective shares of the spoils, and it took the Court of Chancery to settle the resulting dispute between the Earl and his three brothers. But in 1878, 55 years after Lord Cochrane had sailed from Rio on the triumphant cruise which had assured the Independence of Brazil, the disputes which had followed his victories were finally and thankfully laid to rest.

How, then, can the contributions of the British officers who fought for the Independence of Brazil be summarized? As individuals, they were certainly a mixed group. Some completed their five-year contracts and returned safely home. Some died in action, or of the diseases which were endemic in overcrowded ships in the tropics, and never saw England again. Some were heroes whose achievements and audacity are remembered to this day. Others – to quote Brazilian Admiral Tamandaré's reflections in old age on the war with Buenos Aires – 'were immensely brave but not very bright'. Some had dubious careers, due to drink or incompetence, and were quietly retired; while others were dazzlingly successful as naval strategists and leaders of men, married locally, and stayed on in Brazil to reach the highest ranks in the Imperial Navy.

On their arrival in Brazil, those with suitable social origins were accepted as valuable additions to the local British community, and began to extend into the naval sphere the personal links which had already been created by resident British merchants. British officials – particularly senior officers of the Royal Navy's South America Squadron – were less certain how they should act towards their countrymen serving under the Brazilian flag. Lord Cochrane's fame and social position meant that he was treated with respect by all, but few of his subordinates had these advantages. Successive British commanders-in-chief – first Sir Thomas Hardy, then Sir George Eyre – behaved with distant and studied courtesy, but many senior officers were openly hostile. The letters of Consul-General Henry Chamberlain were full of indignation at the prestige enjoyed by John Taylor, and of his impudent social contacts with ministers. And Captain Hunn of the *Tweed*, which had been present at the capture of Recife in 1824, made the already strained relations he enjoyed with his officers worse by forbidding any fraternization with the British 'renegades' (as he described them) in the Brazilian Squadron. Buenos Aires Consul-General Woodbine Parish took the same attitude. Junior officers, however, felt differently. They were largely well disposed towards the British officers of the Imperial Navy, whom they either knew as friends or regarded with a touch of envy as colleagues who had been lucky enough to exchange half pay or humdrum naval life in peacetime for a spot of well-paid excitement; while the 'young gentlemen', like Midshipman (later Admiral of the Fleet) Henry

Keppel of the *Tweed*, regarded Cochrane and his band of brothers with wide-eyed admiration. Notwithstanding Captain Hunn, social visits to the wardrooms of the ships of the Royal Navy were not uncommon.

The British may have been uncertain how to treat their countrymen in the Imperial service, but on the Brazilian side there were no doubts. From the Emperor downwards, it was clear that victory at sea had played a decisive role in securing Independence, and that the strength of the Navy rested on the reliability, skills and audacity of its British officers. Jealousy or resentment on the part of their Brazilian colleagues was remarkably rare. The decisive effect of Lord Cochrane's incomparable military talents on the course of the war were obvious, but the contribution of its British officers to the consolidation of the Brazilian Navy as a fighting force was no less significant. Whatever their ultimate destinies, their presence – and that of the ordinary British sailors who accompanied them – was the crucial element which had decided the war. To Dom Pedro's government they offered the loyalty and leadership which were so needed at the time, and to the infant Brazilian Navy they brought not only technical skills and discipline, but many of the attitudes of the British service, notably a confidence in victory born of 50 years of unquestioned supremacy at sea. Together, they and their Brazilian comrades established in the Navy a tradition of duty and professionalism which was to serve it well in the years to come.

APPENDIX

BRITISH AND IRISH SEA OFFICERS RECRUITED FOR THE BRAZILIAN NAVY 1822-25

ANDERSON, ALEXANDER W.
Appointed as Volunteer 21 Jan 1823. *Piranga* then *Pedro I* during Blockade of Bahia. Sublieut 12 Oct 1823. Prize master of the *Maria* from Maranhão. Commanded *Rio da Plata* 1824-25. Lieut 12 Oct 1825. *Maranhão* 1827 at the Plate. Commander 12 Oct 1827. Wounded 14 Jan 1828.

APPLETON, C.J.
Appointed as Midshipman 1823. Sublieut 22 Jan 1824. *Piranga* during Confederation of the Equator. *Paraguassú* during Buenos Aires war 1826. Lieut 1828. Still in service as a Lieut 1835.

BLAKELEY, WILLIAM
Appointed as Acting Sublieut. To Brazil in the *Mary* May 1823. Sublieut Aug 1824.

BROOM, GEORGE (1797-1860)
Appointed as Sublieut 9 April 1823. *Piranga* during Blockade of Bahia. *Niterói* during Confederation of the Equator 1824; decorated for bravery for the attack on Recife. Lieut 12 Oct 1824. To River Plate in the *Pirajá* Mar 1825. Captured privateer *Liberdad del Sud*. Commanded *Bertioga* brig in the Flotilla of Uruguay. Captured at the defeat at Juncal Feb 1827. Escaped and promoted Commander for bravery Oct 1827. *Bertioga* during the capture of the *General Dorrego* Aug 1828. On leave in England 1829-30. Commanded Marine Arsenal Rio, suppressed mutiny of Marine Artillery 1831. *Olinda* 1832. To S. Catarina as *Desterro* 1839 during the 'Farrapos' rebellion. Blockade of Laguna. *Paraguassú* 1840. *Trez de Maio* 1842. Captain-of-Frigate July 1842. *Dona Francisca* 1850-52. Inspector of Timber 1852-55. Captain Dec 1854. Officer commanding disarmed vessels 1855. Commodore Dec 1856.

APPENDIX 189

Brown, Louis
Cousin of Field Marshal Brown, chief of staff of the Brazilian Army in the Banda Oriental. Recruited in London as Midshipman. To Brazil in the *Piranga* Nov 1825. Sublieutenant 12 Oct 1827. *Caboclo* at the Plate 1827.

Carter, David
Appointed as Volunteer 28 Mar 1823. *Piranga* then *Pedro I* during Blockade of Bahia. Sublieut 12 Oct 1823 Prize master of the *Borges Carneiro* from Maranhão. 1824–25 *Piranga*, 'the oldest in his rank'. Promoted Lieut Oct 1825. Commanded *Pirajá* at Battle of Los Pozes and Lara Quilmes, June and July 1826. Drunk during capture of *Itaparica* 1827. Reprimanded. In service 1835.

Challes, Ambrose
Appointed as Sublieut 9 April 1823. To Brazil in the *Emperor Alexander*. *Atlanta* 1823. *Piranga* during Confederation of the Equator 1824. *Imperatriz* 1825. Died on the *Niterói* 19 June 1825.

Chester, Samuel
Ex-RN midshipman. Sailed from Liverpool in the *Lindsays*. Appointed as Sublieut 9 April 1823. *Niterói* during Blockade of Bahia and chase of the Portuguese May–Nov 1823. Died on *Paraguassú* 3 Sept 1824.

Clarence, George
Ex-RN midshipman and officer of East India Company ships. Appointed as Lieut 9 April 1823. *Piranga* 1823. *Pedro I* 1824. Sent to Pará to fit out the *Dona Januária* 1825. *Paraguassú* 1826. Commanded *Niterói* 1827. Captain-of-Frigate Jan 1828.

Clewley, Stephen
From Chile with Cochrane. Appointed as Lieut 21 Mar 1823. *Pedro I* during Blockade of Bahia, capture of Maranhão and Confederation of the Equator 1823–24. Commander 9 Aug 1824. *Niterói* and *Pirajá* 1825. *Principe Imperial* and *29 de Agosto* 1826. Captain-of-Frigate 12 Oct 1828. Commanded *Baiana* 1833.

Clare, Francis
Ex-RN midshipman. Sailed from Liverpool in the *Lindsays*. Appointed as Lieut 9 April 1823. *Niterói* and *Pedro I* during Blockade of Bahia. *Pedro I* and *Piranga* 1824–25. Commander 9 Aug 1824. *Dona Francisca* 1826. Commanded *Independência ou Morte* at Battle of Monte Santiago April 1827, later wrecked at San Blas Sept. Captain-of-Frigate 12 Oct 1827.

COWAN, GEORGE

Appointed as Sublieut 12 April 1823. *Bahia* during Blockade of Bahia. Prize master of the *Carvalho VI* from Pernambuco 1823. *Niterói* during Confederation of the Equator 1824. Lieut 9 Aug 1824. *Niterói* at the Plate 1826. Commanded schooner *Rios* at Battle of Monte Santiago April 1827. Commander 1828.

CRAIG, THOMAS

Sublieut 11 June 1824. *Imperatriz* 1824. *Piranga* 1825. *Independência ou Morte*, then to USA to fit out the *Principe Imperial* 1826. Lieut 12 Oct 1827. Commanded *Niger* at the Plate 1827–28. At the burning of blockade runners at Salado. Decorated for his part in the capture of the *General Branzden* June 1828. In service 1829.

CROFTON, VINCENT G.

Ex-RN midshipman. Sailed from Liverpool in the *Lindsays*. Appointed as Lieut 9 April 1823. *Luiza* then *Real Carolina* during Blockade of Bahia 1823. *Piranga* 1824. 'A madman and a drunkard.' Fitting out *Imperatriz* 1825.

CROSBIE, THOMAS SACKVILLE

Ex-RN midshipman and Lieutenant 1806 to 1815. Served in the Channel, Lisbon, Mediterranean, S. America and the West Indies. Travelled from Chile with Cochrane. Appointed as Captain-of-Frigate 21 Mar 1823. Commanded *Pedro I* and Flag Captain at Blockade of Bahia, capture of Maranhão and Confederation of the Equator 1823–5. Captain 12 Oct 1823. Commanded *Piranga* to Portsmouth. Resigned Nov 1825.

DRUMMOND, FRANCIS

Appointed as Volunteer. *Niterói* in Blockade of Bahia and the pursuit of the Portuguese 1823. Prize master of the *S. Manuel Augusto*. Court martial for insubordination 1824. Sublieutenant 2 Aug 1824. *Piranga* 1824–25. Shore party at Maranhão 1825. Deserted to avoid court martial 1826. Joined Argentinean Navy. Became fiancé of Admiral Brown's daughter Eliza. Fought at Juncal. Killed while in command of the brig *Independencia* at Monte Santiago 1827.

EYRE, WILLIAM (–1850)

Ex-RN. Appointed as Sublieut in Rio 10 Nov 1822. *Pedro I* at Blockade of Bahia and capture of Maranhão 1823. Prize master of the *Pombinha*. Commanded *Pará* during Confederation of the Equator 1824. Commander 9 Aug 1824. *Bahia* and *Niterói* 1825. *Itaparica* at actions off Ortiz Bank and Los Pozes 1826. Captain-of-Frigate 12 Oct 1827. Second-in-command during attack on Patagonia privateer base Feb/Mar 1827. Captured. Flotilla ran aground at San Blas Nov 1827. Captured. *Niterói* and *Piranga* 1828. *Isabela* on voyage to Europe 1829. Commanded *Dona Amelia* escorting Dom Pedro to Europe 1831. Leave in England 1833. Commanded *Imperatriz* at Pará against the 'Cabanos' 1835. Captain 7 Sept 1837. *Sete de Setembro* in Rio Grande do Sul against the 'Farrapos' 1837. Commodore 1847.

FITZCOSTEN, JOSEPH
Son of Hipolito da Costa, recruited in London. Appointed as Midshipman 5 May 1823. *Paraguassú*. and *Pedro I* 1824-25. Lieutenant 1826. Captured following attack on Patagonia Feb/Mar 1827.

FUBBS, DANIEL
Appointed as Master's Mate 1823. *Piranga* off Pernambuco 1824 Sublieutenant 20 Dec 1826. To USA to fit out the *Principe Imperial* Oct 1826. *Dona Francisca* and *Niterói* 1827. In service 1829.

GILLETT, SAMUEL
Ex-RN midshipman. Appointed as Lieut 9 April 1823. Officer commanding *Atlanta* in the north and north-east July 1823 to Dec 1824. Deserted when threatened with a court martial.

GLEDDON, JOHN ROGERS
Ex-RN midshipman. Sailed to Brazil in the *Mary*. Appointed as Lieut 9 April 1823. *Piranga* and *Pedro I* in Blockade of Bahia 1823. Prize master of the *Bizarria*. *Pedro I* then *Maranhão* during Confederation of the Equator 1824 and capture of Recife. Killed at Battle of Corales 23 Mar 1826 when in command of *29 de Agosto*.

GRENFELL, JOHN PASCOE (1800-69)
From Chile with Cochrane. Appointed as Lieut 21 Mar 1823. *Pedro I* during Blockade of Bahia and capture of Maranhão. Secured adhesion of Pará 1823. Commander 12 Oct 1823. *Pedro I* during Confederation of the Equator 1824. Acquitted in court martial for conduct in Pará 1824. *Caboclo* 1825. Captain-of-Frigate Jan 1826. Battle of Corales and Argentinian attack on Montevideo Feb and April. Lost arm at Battle of Lara Quilmes 29 July 1826. Granted pension. England on leave 1827. *Maria Isabel*. Captured privateer *Peruano* off Capo Frio July 1828. Captain 18 Oct 1829. *Isabela* to Europe Nov 1829. Leave in Montevideo 1830-32. *Baiana* 1833. Commodore 12 Nov 1836. Commander of naval forces fighting the 'Farrapos' rebellion in Rio Grand do Sul 1836-38 and 1839. Officer commanding naval forces in the River Plate 1838 and 1843. Rear Admiral 25 Mar 1841. Consul in Liverpool 1846-50. Officer commanding naval forces in war with the Argentinian dictator Rosas 1851. Forced the Passage of

Tonelero carrying the Brazilian Army 1851–52. Vice Admiral 3 Mar 1852. 1852–60 Consul in Liverpool. Admiral 12 Dec 1862.

HAYDEN, BARTHOLOMEW (1792–1857)

Ex-RN midshipman. Brought Cochrane from Chile in the *Colonel Allen*. Appointed as Commander when his brig was purchased and renamed *Bahia*. Commanded *Bahia* in Blockade of Bahia 1823 and off Pernambuco 1824. *Pirajá* in north-east and River Plate 1824–26. Captured privateer *Liberdade del Sur*. Captain-of-Frigate 31 Jan 1826. *Liberal* 1826–27. Present at Battles of Quilmes and Monte Santiago. *Imperatriz* 1828. Officer commanding (Anti-slavery) Division of the East in the *Animo Grande* 1828–29. *Imperatriz* and *Campista* in campaign against the 'Cabanos' rebels in Pará 1835–36. Captain 22 Oct 1836. Leave to work in Steam Packet Co. 1839–40. Commanded *Campista* and Corps of 'Imperial Marineiros' 1840. Retired 1842. Commodore 14 May 1847. Restored to the Active List 1849. Member of Naval Armaments Commission 1851. Leave for health in England 1856.

HAYDEN, RICHARD

Appointed as Acting Sublieut Feb 1824. *Bahia* in the north-east 1824. *Pirajá* 1826 at the River Plate. Captured during raid on Patagonia April 1827. Lieut 12 Oct 1827. *Pirajá* in S. Catarina 1839. In service as a Commander 1842.

HAYDON, THOMAS

Ex-RN Lieut. Recruited London. Appointed as Commander 5 May 1826. Commanded *Independência ou Morte* 1826 at the River Plate. *Dona Francisca* 1827. *Defensora* 1830.

INGLIS, WILLIAM JAMES

Appointed as Sublieut 9 April 1823. *Piranga* then *Pedro I* during Blockade of Bahia and pursuit of the Portuguese. *Pedro I* during Confederation of the Equator 1824–25. Lieut 9 Aug 1824. *Caboclo* 1826 and *Independência ou Morte* 1827. Commander 12 Oct 1827. *Caboclo* at Battle of Monte Santiago April 1827. Escaped from grounding of the flotilla at San Blas Sept 1827. Captured privateer *Niger* and part of the squadron taking the *Gobernador Dorrego* Mar and Aug 1828. Captain-of-Frigate 1828. *Caboclo* during the burning of blockade runners at Salado Aug 1828. *Baiana* 1831. *Cacique* 1834. Officer commanding *Defensora* and naval station at Pará. Killed by 'Cabanos' 1835.

JANUARY, WILLIAM

Appointed as Volunteer to *Piranga* 1823. Sublieut 12 Oct 1823. *Pedro I* during pursuit of the Portuguese, the capture of Maranhão and

APPENDIX 193

Confederation of the Equator I July 1823 to April 1825. Lieut 12 Oct 1825. *Rio da Plata* 1827. Commander 12 Oct 1827. *Piranga* 1827. Still in service 1835.

KELMARE, BENJAMIN
Ex-RN Lieut. In Chile with Cochrane. To Brazil in the *Lindsays* from Liverpool. Appointed as Commander 9 April 1823. *Real Carolina* during Blockade of Bahia 1823. Prize master of the *S. José Triumphante*. Arrested for insubordination. Acquitted. *Paraguassú* during Confederation of the Equator 1824.

MACERWING, WILLIAM
Commissioned as Sublieut 12 Oct 1826. Commanded *2 de Julho* at action of Salado and capture of the *General Branzden* Aug and June 1828. Lieut 18 Sept 1828. Still in service 1935.

MACKINTOSH, ROBERT
Midshipman on *Maria da Glória* 17 May 1824. Sublieut Jan 1825. *Real João* at Playa Honda Jan 1827. Commanded schooner *Maria Teresa*. Deserted with his ship to Buenos Aires July 1827.

MACREIGHTS, DUNCAN
Appointed Sublieut 9 April 1823. *Piranga* 1823. *Atlanta* 1824. In service 1825.

MANSON, GEORGE
Appointed in Rio as Sublieut 12 Nov 1822. Lieut 14 Jan 1823. *Piranga* then *Pedro I* for Blockade of Bahia and capture of Maranhão 1823. *Pará* as Commander 12 Oct 1823. Officer commanding *Maranhão* during Confederation of the Equator 1824–25. *Cacique* in north-east 1825. Captain-of-Frigate 1826. *Maranhão* at Battle of Monte Santiago April 1827. *Cacique* when captured by *General Branzden* Sept 1827. *Bertioga* 1832. *Campista* during campaign against the 'Cabanos' in Pará 1835.

MARCH, WILLIAM
Appointed as Volunteer 23 Jan 1823. *Piranga* then *Pedro I* for Blockade of Bahia, pursuit of the Portuguese and capture of Maranhão. Sublieut 12 Oct 1823. *Pedro I* 1824. *Piranga* to Portsmouth 1825. *Dona Francisca* 1826. Lieut 12 Oct 1828 in *Maria Isabel*. In service 1832 but on sick leave.

MOSSELYN, CHARLES
Ex-RN midshipman. Appointed as Lieut 22 April 1823. *Piranga* during Blockade of Bahia. To *Imperatriz* June 1824. Discharged on health grounds Sept 1824.

Murphy, Richard N.

Appointed as Volunteer 1823. Acting Sublieut Feb 1824 (confirmed Aug 1824). Gunboat *Cayalaume* 1823. *Bahia* in north-east 1823–24. *Niterói* and *Paraguassú* 1825. Commanded steamship *Correio Imperial* Sept 1825 and *Duas Estrellas* at the Plate 1826. Lieut 1828. Killed during defence of Pará against the 'Cabanos' Aug 1835.

Newton, Edward

Appointed as Master's Mate 1823. *Piranga* off Pernambuco 1824. *Independência ou Morte* 1826. To USA to fit out *Principe Imperial* 1827. Sublieut 20 Dec 1826. In service 1835.

Nichol, James

Mate of the *Lapwing*. Appointed Lieut 9 April 1823. *Real Carolina* during Blockade of Bahia. In command of *Guarani* for the fighting off Montevido and Confederation of the Equator 1823–25. Commander 1825. Died 1827. Brazilian widow awarded a pension.

Norton, James (1789–1835)

Ex-RN and officer of East India Co. ships. Action against the Dutch and at the Cape of Good Hope. Assisted General Brant in London recruitment. Sailed from Liverpool in the *Mary*. Appointed as Captain-of-Frigate 9 April 1823. *Niterói* 1824. Prominent in the capture of Recife. Captain 9 Aug 1824. *Niterói* at the Plate 1826. Battle of Corales. Commander of the Inshore Squadron 1826–27. Battles of Los Pozes, Lara Quilmes and Monte Santiago. Loses arm at the capture of the *General Branzden* 1827. Commodore 1829. Awarded a pension. *Isabela* on voyage to Europe supporting claims of Princess Maria da Glória to Portuguese throne 1829. Inspector of Rio Arsenal 1831. Leave of absence 1832–33. Died on voyage to New Zealand.

Oudsley, Gore Whitlock

Appointed as Volunteer Feb 1823. *Piranga* 1823. Court martial 1824. Acquitted. To *Niterói*. Sublieut 9 Aug 1823. Drunk during attack on Recife. *Independência ou Morte* 1825. Drunk during capture of the *Itaparica* in the attack on Patagonia Feb 1827. Captured.

Parker, William (1801–83)

Mate of the *Lindsays*. Appointed as Midshipman 1 April 1823. *Pedro I* during Blockade of Bahia and capture of Maranhão. Sublieut 12 Oct 1823. Prize master of the *Feliz Ventura*. *Niterói* and *Pedro I* off Pernambuco. Prize master of the *Dom Domingos*. Lieut 12 Oct 1825. *Dona Paula* to the Plate 1825. Lieut 12 Oct 1825. Battle of Lara Quilmes. To Rio naval station with the *Dona Paula* 1826. *Carioca*. *Bela Maria* at the Plate 1827.

APPENDIX   195

Commander 12 Oct 1827. *Carioca* and *Constança* at Salado 1828–29. *Isabela* bringing the 2nd Empress Dona Amelia from Europe 1830. *Baiana*. *Leopoldina* against 'Farrapos' rebels in Rio Grande do Sul 1836–39. Captain-of-Frigate 18 Feb 1837. *Sete de Setembro* 1839–40. Captain 23 July 1842. River Plate naval station in *Euterpe* 1844. River Plate naval station in *Dona Francisca* 1848–51. Commodore 3 Mar 1852. Port Captain Rio 1855. Vice Admiral 2 Dec 1856. Officer commanding Bahia Naval District 1857–61 and Rio Naval District 1861–64. Admiral (rtd) 15 Jan 1867.

POYNTON, THOMAS
Appointed as Acting Sublieut. *Atlanta* 1823. Court martial. Dismissed for 'incorrigible insubordination' July 1824.

REID, ALEXANDER
Appointed as Volunteer. Sublieut 12 Oct 1823. *Bahia* during pursuit of the Portuguese. *Pedro I* during Confederation of the Equator 1823–24. Lieut 12 Oct 1825. Officer commanding *Atlanta* 1825. Commander. Commanded *Maceió* when wrecked as San Blas 1827. Arrested for incompetence.

ROSE, CHARLES
Appointed as Volunteer. Acting Sublieut 16 Feb 1824. *Real Carolina* 1823. *Niterói* during Confederation of the Equator 1824–25. *Niterói* during attack on Montevideo April 1826. Officer commanding *Principe Imperial* lugger 1827. Lieut 12 Oct 1827. *Principe Imperial* during capture of the *Honor* April 1828. *Brasileiro* in capture of Oyeras in Pará rebellion 1836. Commanded schooner *Amazonas* 1837.

SEWELL, JOSEPH
Appointed as Volunteer. Sublieut 20 July 1823. *Real Carolina* 1823–24. Court martial following disorder on board. Dismissed 9 July 1824.

SHEPHERD, JAMES
From Chile with Cochrane. Appointed as Lieut 21 Mar 1823. On *Pedro I* during Blockade of Bahia, pursuit of the Portuguese and Confederation of the Equator 1823–25. Commander 12 Oct 1823. Commanded *Piranga* on its return voyage from Portsmouth Nov 1825–Jan 1826. Captain-of-Frigate 31 Jan 1826. *Piranga* escorting the Emperor to Bahia 1826. Killed leading attack on privateer base in Patagonia 7 Mar 1827.

STEEL, ROBERT
Appointed as Volunteer 11 May 1823. *Real Carolina* 1823. Prize master of *Visconde de S Lourenço* July. *Guarani* off Montevideo. *Niterói* 1824. Sublieut 9 Aug 1824. *Piranga* then *Pedro I* 1825. Commanded yacht *12 de Outobro* 1826.

Strickland, George

Appointed as Master's Mate. *Bahia* 1823–24. Sublieut 18 Sept 1824. *Pirajá* 1824–25. In service 1829.

Taylor, James

Appointed as Midshipman. *Bahia* off Pernambuco 1823–24. *Paraguassú* at Confederation of the Equator 1824–5. Sublieut 1825. Battle of Lara Quilmes July 1826. Wounded. Lieut 1829. *Imperatriz* 1832.

Taylor, John (1796–1855)

Ex-RN midshipman and Lieut. Lieut on HMS *Blossom*, British S America Squadron 1820–22. Appointed as Captain-of-Frigate 9 Jan 1823. Commanded *Niterói* at Blockade of Bahia and pursuit of the Portuguese. Blockade of Recife 1824. Dismissed due to British pressure Aug 1824. Reappointed as Commodore Dec 1825. Aide-de-camp to Naval Headquarters 1831. Suppression of the mutiny of Marine Artillery. *Baiana* 1833. *Principe Imperial* 1834. Officer commanding *Campista* and naval forces against the 'Cabanos' in Pará 1835–36. Rear Admiral 1837. Served on various administrative commissions including the inspection of armaments. Vice Admiral 1851.

Thompson, James

Ex-RN Midshipman and Lieut with experience of the merchant service. Assisted General Brant with the London recruitment. Sailed in the *Lindsays* Jan 1823. Appointed as Captain-of-Frigate 9 April 1823. *Real Carolina* during Blockade of Bahia. Captain Oct 1823. *Paraguassú* 1824. To USA to fit out the *Principe Imperial* 1826. *Principe Imperial* 1827. Discharged Jan 1828.

Thompson, Thomas

Appointed as Volunteer. Sublieut 31 Aug 1824. Commanded schooner *Conceição* at the Plate 1825–26. Battle of Corales and attacks on Colonia and Montevideo 1826. Recommended for an honour. Lieut 1829. Still in service 1835.

Wallace, James

Appointed as Volunteer. Sublieut 12 Oct 1823. *Niterói* during Blockade of Bahia, pursuit of the Portuguese and Blockade of Recife 1823–24. Lieut 30 Oct 1824. *Piranga* during Confederation of the Equator. 1824–5. *Itaparica* 1825. *Paraguassú* 1826. Commanded schooner *Conceição* 1828. In service 1835.

Watson, Charles

Appointed as Sublieut 9 April 1823. *Real Carolina* during Blockade of Bahia. Prize master of *Triunfo da Inveja*. *Paraguassú* at Blockade of Recife

APPENDIX 197

1824. Lieut 9 Aug 1824. *Piranga* 1824–25. Commanded brig *Duquesa do Goias* 1826. Captured during attack on Patagonia Feb/Mar 1827. Commander 1828. *Duquesa do Goias* as part of the (Anti-slavery) Squadron of the East 1828–29.

WATSON, JAMES

Appointed as Acting Sublieut 13 April 1823. *Pedro I* during pursuit of the Portuguese and capture of Maranhão and Pará 1823. Officer commanding *Gentil Americana* acting as mail packet to the north during Confederation of the Equator 1824. Lieut 10 Feb 1824. Deserted from Pará Dec 1824 to avoid court martial.

WELCH, MATEUS

Ex-officer Portuguese Navy. Appointed as Captain of Frigate 12 Oct 1823. *Pedro I* as second-in-command Feb–June 1824. Commanded *Paraguassú* during Blockade of Recife 1824–25. Thesis 1825. *Paraguassú* during the Emperor's visit to Bahia 1826. Thesis 1827. Captain 12 Oct 1829. In service 1835.

WHITE, J.H.B.

Appointed as Midshipman. Sublieut Sept 1824. *Piranga* off Pernambuco 1824. *Maceió* and *Niterói* 1827 at the Plate. Still in service 1835.

WILLIAMS, JOHN

Appointed as Volunteer 26 May 1823. *Pedro I* at Blockade of Bahia and capture of Maranhão 1823. Prize master of the *Ventura Feliz*. Sublieut 22 Jan 1824. *Paraguassú* 1824. *Niterói* and *Pedro I* 1825. Commander 12 Oct 1827. Commanded schooner *Constança* at the Plate 1828. Assisted in the capture of the *General Branzden*.

WILSON, BOURWILL JAMES

Appointed as Acting Sublieut 26 April 1823. *Real Carolina* 1823–24. Sublieut 9 Aug 1824. *Maranhão* 1824–25. Officer commanding *Conceição* 1826–27. Battle of Monte Santiago April 1827, the capture of the *Congresso* and destruction of blockade runners at Salado 1828.

WRIGHT, RAPHAEL

Ex-RN Midshipman and Lieut. Sailed to Brazil in the *Alice*. Appointed as Lieut 29 Mar 1823. *Bahia* off Pernambuco 1823. *Piranga* at capture of Recife 1824. Commanded *Caboclo* at the Plate 1825. Commander 1826. Present at unsuccessful attack on Patagonia Feb/Mar 1827.

YELL, CHARLES F.
Appointed as Volunteer May 1823. *Guarani* off Montevideo 1823. *Carioca* and *Maranhao* of Pernambuco mid–1824. Sublieut 9 Aug 1824. *Guarani* at the Plate 1826. Second-in-command of *Cacique* when captured by the *General Branzden* Sept 1827. Mortally wounded.

NOTES

AN   Arquivo Nacional, Rio de Janeiro
Bib Nac   Bibliotéca Nacional, Rio de Janeiro
PRO   Public Record Office, London
SDGM   Serviço de Documentação Geral da Marinha, Rio de Janeiro. The microfilm collection is of documents from the Dundonald Muniments in the Scottish Record Office. The first number identifies the reel, the second the Box in the SRO, the third the subject reference.

CHAPTER 2

1. The Portuguese force in Salvador consisted of the 74-gun *Dom João VI*, the frigate *Constituição* (50), the corvettes *Dez de Fevereiro* (24), *Calypso* (22), *Regeneração* (18) and *Principe* (20), the brigs *Audaz* (18) and *Promptidão* (16) and the armed-ships *Activa*, *Gaulter*, *Princeza Real*, *Aneas*, *Restauração* and *Conceição Oliveira*.
2. Brant to José Bonifácio, 5 July 1822, *Publicações do Archivo Publico Nacional*, Rio, 1907, vol VII, p 260.
3. José Bonifácio to Brant, no. 8, 3 November 1822, quoted in *Publicações*, p 306.
4. Note on currency. The smallest unit of Brazilian currency in 1822 was the 'real', plural 'reis':

fifty reis (s50) = 1p = 2½d old money
one thousand reis = 1 milreis (1$000) = 20p = 48d old money
one thousand milreis = 1 conto of reis (1,000$000) = £200.

5. Graham, Maria, *Journal of a Voyage to Brazil and Residence there during part of the years 1821, 1822 and 1823*, London 1824, p 219.
6. Brazilian naval ranks and the equivalents used in this volume are Almirante (Admiral); Vice Almirante (Vice Admiral), Chefe de Esquadra (Rear Admiral), Chefe de Divisão (Commodore), Capitão-de-Mar-e-Guerra (Senior Captain), Capitão-de-Fragata (Junior Captain), Capitão-Tenente (Commander), Primeiro Tenente (Lieutenant), Secundo Tenente (Sublieutenant). The honorary title 'Captain' is sometimes used to describe an officer in command of a ship.

7. José Bonifácio to Corrêa dal Camara, 13 September 1822. *Archivo Diplomático da Independência*, vol 4, Rio 1922.
8. Corrêa de Camara to Cochrane, 4 November 1822, *Annaes do Itamaratí*, Ministério de Relações Exteriores, Rio de Janeiro, 1937, vol 2, p 99.
9. Cochrane to Corrêa de Camara, 30 November 1822, *Annaes*, p 178.
10. Hardy to Croker, no. 15, 6 February 1823 and Admiralty Minute of 1 April 1823, PRO, Adm 1/27 and Adm 50/151.
11. Chamberlain to Canning, no. 79, 11 July 1823; no. 97, 4 August 1823; no. 122, 12 October 1823; no. 68, 18 June 1824; no. 74, 6 July 1824, PRO, FO 63/260-1, 63/277-8.

Chapter 3

1. All Brant's letters between 2 February 1822 and 19 August 1823 are printed in *Publicações do Archivo Publico Nacional*, Rio de Janeiro, 1907, vol VII, pp 239-359.
2. Brant to José Bonifácio, 1, 6 May 1822,*Publicações*, vol VII, pp 240-46.
3. Brant to José Bonifácio, Paris, 20 August 1822, ibid., p 264.
4. Brant to José Bonifácio, 18 September 1822, ibid., p 268.
5. See 2 above.
6. Brant to José Bonifácio, 4 December 1822, ibid., p 287.
7. Brant to José Bonifácio, no. 6, 12 January 1823, ibid., p 298. See also Clare to Cochrane, 13 November 1823, Arquivo SDGM Rio (microfilm), 7/6/244/104-107.
8. Brant to José Bonifácio, no. 11, 1 February 1823, *Publicações*, vol VII, p 305.
9. Alexander W. Anderson, William Blakeley, David Carter, Francis Drummond, William January, William March, Thomas Poynton, Charles Rose, Alexander Reid, Joseph Sewell, James Wallace and James Watson. By July 1825, 49 of the 174 commissioned officers in the Brazilian Navy were British.

Chapter 4

1. Madeira de Melo to Lisbon, 13 December 1822. Printed in Braz do Amaral, *História da Independência na Bahia*, Coleção de Estudos Brasileiros, no. 19, seria marajoara, 2nd edn, Salvador, 1957, pp 295-7.
2. Hardy to Croker, no. 130, 2 December 1822; no. 17, 9 February 1823, PRO, Adm 1/27.
3. Hardy to Croker, no. 21, 9 March 1823, PRO, Adm 1/27. Correspondence between Consul-General Chamberlain and José Bonifácio January to July 1823 in *Archivo Diplomático da Independência*, vol 2.
4. Decrees of 25 January, 25 February, 7 March 1823 in *Leis do Império do Brasil 1823*, Bibliotéca da Marinha, Rio.
5. Correspondence between Cunha Moreira, José Bonifácio and Carneiro de Campos, January to September 1823, AN Rio, XM 289.
6. Chamberlain to Canning, no. 31, 11 March 1823, PRO, FO 63/258.
7. Lord Cochrane, 10th Earl of Dundonald, *Narrative of Services in the*

Liberation of ... Brazil, London, 1859, vol II, pp 12–21 for Cochrane's version of these events.

  8. Decree of 21 March 1823. Meirelles da Silva, *Apontamentos para a História da Marinha de Guerra Brazileira*, Rio de Janeiro, 1882, vol II, p 66, and in numerous other collections. Cochrane's annual pay while in command at sea was thus £3458. A British admiral in the same position would have received monthly pay of £140 x 13 plus allowances = £2936 per annum.
  9. Graham, Maria, *Journal of a Voyage to Brazil and Residence there during part of the years 1821, 1822, and 1823*, p 221.
  10. Report of the Junta da Fazenda da Marinha, 10 April 1823, AN Rio, XM 80.
  11. Portaria of 30 March 1823, AN Rio XM 1232 and Meirelles da Silva, *Apontamentos*, p 203.

Chapter 5

  1. Graham, Maria, *Journal of a Voyage to Brazil and Residence there during part of the years 1821, 1822, and 1823*, p 222.
  2. Cochrane to Cunha Moreira, no 1, 2 April 1823, Arquivo SDGM Rio.
  3. Sir T. Hardy's Journal, entries for April 1823, PRO, Adm 50/151. Vice-Consul Follet to Canning, 29 April 1823, PRO, FO 63/263.
  4. 'Diary of Chaplain Manoel Moreira de Paixão e Dores', printed in *Anais da Bibliotéca Nacional do Rio de Janeiro*, 1938, vol LX, p 204.
  5. Cochrane's *Narrative*, pp 27–8 says that the *Pedro I* attacked the Portuguese line alone. This is untrue. For the part played by the *Piranga* and *Niterói*, see: 'Diary of Chaplain Manoel Moreira', p 204; Pereira de Sá to Félix de Campos (see Note 6 below); Pio dos Santos to Minister of Marine, 5 May 1823, printed in Meirelles da Silva, *Apontamentos para a História da Marinha de Guerra Brazileira*, pp 207–8.
  6. Captain Pereira de Sá to Félix de Campos, 5 May 1823, printed in *A Marinha da Guerra do Brasil na Lucta da Independência*, Anonymous, Rio de Janeiro, 1880, p 72.
  7. Félix de Campos to Madeira de Melo, 6 May 1823, printed in Braz do Amaral, *História da Independência na Bahia*, Coleção de Estudios Brasileiros, no. 19, 2nd edition, Salvador, 1957, p 349.
  8. Cochrane to José Bonifácio (Secret), 5 May 1823, Arquivo SDGM Rio (microfilm), 8/6/245/177–180; Cochrane, *Narrative*, pp 29–32.
  9. Correspondence from Ministry of Marine to Cochrane, March to July 1823, AN Rio, XM 1282.
  10. Madeira de Melo to Félix de Campos, 19 May 1823, in Braz do Amaral, *História*, p 363.
  11. Madeira de Melo to Dom João VI, 10 June 1823, ibid., p 365.

Chapter 6

  1. Cochrane to Cunha Moreira, 2 July 1823, Arquivo SDGM Rio (microfilm), 8/6/245/226–7.
  2. Cochrane, *Narrative*, p 55.

3. Sir T. Hardy's Journal: letters dated 22 August 1823, PRO, Adm 50/151. Chamberlain to Canning, no. 112, 18 September 1823, PRO, FO 63/260.
4. 8 prizes were taken by the *Pedro I*, 1 by the *Bahia*, 3 by the *Real Carolina* and 1 by the *Niterói*. AN Rio, XM 1257. 'Diary of Chaplain Manoel Moreira da Paixão e Dores' gives the daily catch.
5. 'Diary of Chaplain Manuel Moreira', p 240.
6. Meirelles da Silva, *Apontamentos para a História da Marinha de Guerra Brasileira*, pp 242-3.
7. The story of the voyage can be found in *Relação Nautica Militar da viagem da fragata do Império 'Niterói'*, attributed to Commander Luis Barroso Pereira, printed in Meirelles da Silva, *Apontamentos*, pp 234-64.
8. Meirelles da Silva, *Apontamentos*, p 227.
9. Ibid., pp 229-32; Order of 3 October 1823 printed in 'Avisos do Governo Portuguese', *Revista do Instituto Histórico e Geographico Brasileiro*, Rio, Imprensa Nacional, 1922.

Chapter 7

1. Junta Provisoria de Itapicurú-mirim to Dom Pedro, 23 July 1823, Arquivo SDGM Rio (microfilm), 5/5/463/32-7.
2. Dom Joaquim de Nazareth to Dom João VI, 22 July 1823, printed in Viera da Silva, *História da Independência da Maranhão*, S. Luis, 1862, p 162.
3. Cochrane to Portuguese military commander, 26 July 1823, Arquivo SDGM Rio (microfilm), 5/5/436/37-8. Lord Cochrane states that the *Pedro I* approached S. Luis flying Portuguese colours, and his various biographers have repeated the story. All contemporary observers (including the chaplain of the flagship and Maria Graham, repeating the description given her by officers who were present) say that the ship arrived wearing the British flag.
4. Agostinho de Faria to Cochrane, 31 July 1823, Arquivo SDGM Rio (microfilm), 3/5/458/170. Cochrane to Cunha Moreira, 13 August 1823, AN Rio, XM 254.
5. Cochrane, *Narrative*, p 81.
6. Cochrane to Junta, 28 July 1823, Arquivo SDGM Rio (microfilm), 5/5/463/42-44. All the financial reports are in ibid., 2/5/454.
7. Junta to Cochrane, no. 27, 14 August 1823, Arquivo SDGM Rio (microfilm), 5/5/462/169-70.
8. Junta to Cochrane, no. 55, 27 August 1823, ibid., 5/5/463/10-11.
9. Cochrane, *Narrative*, pp 82 and 222.
10. Cochrane to Vilela Barbosa (Secret), 18 November 1823, Arquivo SDGM Rio (microfilm), 8/6/245/182.

Chapter 8

1. Cochrane to Grenfell, 5 August 1823, Arquivo SDGM Rio (microfilm), 2/5/456/163-4.
2. Act of 11 August 1823, printed in Levy Scavarda, 'O Almirante Grenfell na Marinha e na História do Brasil', *Navigator*, June 1970, no. 1, SDGM Rio, pp 56-7.

NOTES 203

3. Grenfell to Cochrane, 11 September 1823, Arquivo SDGM Rio (microfilm), 5/5/465/51-54.
4. Grenfell to Cochrane, 4 November 1823, ibid., 5/5/465/48-50.
5. Grenfell to Cochrane, 27 August 1823, ibid., 5/5/465/45-7.
6. Grenfell to Cochrane, 11 September 1823, ibid., 5/5/465/51-4 (Postscript dated 13 September).
7. Junta to Grenfell, 18 October 1823, printed in Henrique Boiteux, *Os Nossos Almirantes*, Imprensa Naval, Rio, 1915, vol I, p 202.
8. Domingos Antônio Raiol's classic and comprehensive work *Motins Políticos do Pará*, vol I, pp 83-8, takes a strong pro-patriot line, and repeats many of the horrific and prejudiced stories that were current at the time – for example, that the captors poured lime over the prisoners, laughed and mocked at their struggles, etc. Raiol sees Grenfell unjustly as the evil genius behind this and other persecutions of the patriots.
9. Proclamation printed in *Os Nossos Almirantes*, vol I, p 202.
10. Judgement on Baptista Campos in Arquivo SDGM Rio (microfilm), 2/5/452/83-4.
11. Grenfell to Junta, 23 February 1824, printed in *Os Nossos Almirantes*, p 208.
12. Junta to Grenfell, 28 February 1824, ibid., pp 209-10.

CHAPTER 10

1. Of the 159 officers in the Brazilian Navy in July 1824, 45 were British: Lord Cochrane himself, 3 of 9 captains, 2 of 24 captains-of-frigate, 5 of 19 commanders, 11 of 36 lieutenants, and 23 out of 56 substantive or acting sublieutenants.
2. By the time Cochrane wrote his *Narrative* in 1859, these figures had risen to 120 ships worth 2000 contos of reis (vol II, p 105). The claims submitted by Cochrane in 1824 were:

Public and private property in Maranhão and Pará	619,986 milreis
Value of warships	140,000 milreis
Ships and cargoes	499,986 milreis
Total	1,259,972 milreis (= £252,000)

Cochrane to Vilela Barbosa, 31 January 1824, AN Rio, XM 254.
3. Brazilian rules for the distribution of prize money were almost identical to British practice before 1808:

Commander-in-Chief	one-eighth
Captain	two-eighths
Commissioned and Warrant Officers	two-eighths
Petty Officers	one-eighth
Others	two-eighths

4. Vilela Barbosa to Auditoria da Marinha, 17 December 1823, AN Rio, XM 678.
5. Cochrane to Vilela Barbosa, 31 December 1823 and his replies dated

3 and 12 January 1824, AN Rio, XM 1232. Arquivo SDGM Rio (microfilm), 7/6/243/66.
 6. Chamberlain to Canning, no 18, 10 February 1824, PRO, FO 63/276. Admiral Sir George Eyre to Croker, 17 February 1824, PRO, FO Adm 1/29.
 7. Minutes of the Council of State, 12 February 1824, printed in *Documentos da Independência*, Bib Nac Rio, 1923, p 457.
 8. Taylor's instructions dated 29 February 1824, Arquivo SDGM Rio (microfilm), 7/6/243/146–9.
 9. Cunningham, John RN, *Remarks during a Voyage to the Pacific 1823–5*, National Maritime Museum, Greenwich, JOL /21.
 10. Vilela Barbosa to Auditoria da Marinha, 17 December 1823, AN Rio, XM 678.
 11. Vilela Barbosa to Supreme Military Council, 3 January 1824, AN Rio, ibid.
 12. *Exposição do Estado da Fazenda Publica*, September 1823, AN Rio.
 13. Vilela Barbosa to Intendência, 12 December 1823, AN Rio, XM 678. Intendência to Cunha Moreira, 22 July 1823, AN Rio, XM 101.
 14. J.S. Maciel da Costa to Cochrane, 20 April 1824, Arquivo SDGM Rio (microfilm), 1/5/445.
 15. Judgement of 4 March 1824, printed in *Os Nossos Almirantes*, vol II, p 189.
 16. Vilela Barbosa to Cochrane, 24, 25 May 1824, AN Rio, XM 1232.
 17. *Archivo Diplomático da Independência*, vol 1. Chamberlain to Canning, no. 69, 18 June 1824, PRO, FO 63/277.
 18. Carvalho e Melo to Brant and Gameiro, 16 and 17 July 1824. Brant and Gameiro to Carvalho e Melo, no. 13 and 10 August 1824, *Archivo Diplomático*, vol 2.
 19. Cochrane, *Narrative*, II, p 150. Arquivo SDGM Rio (microfilm), 2/5/453/20–21.
 20. Vilela Barbosa to Cochrane, 11 June 1824, Arquivo SDGM Rio (microfilm), 7/6/243/253.

CHAPTER 11

 1. Hayden to Cochrane, 22 July 1823, Arquivo SDGM Rio (microfilm), 5/5/465/2–3.
 2. Hayden to Cochrane, 14 December 1823, AN Rio, XM 254.
 3. Hayden to Cochrane, 25 December 1823, Arquivo SDGM Rio (microfilm), 5/5/465/12–13.

CHAPTER 12

 1. Correspondence between 31 March and 7 April 1823 printed in *Os Nossos Almirantes*, vol II, pp 170–77.
 2. Taylor to Cochrane, 8 April 1824 printed in L. Boiteux, 'A Armada Imperial Contraposta a Confederação do Equador', vol II, pp 55–6.
 3. *Os Nossos Almirantes*, pp 178–9.
 4. Taylor to Cochrane, 30 April 1824, in 'A Armada Imperial Contraposta', pp 58–9.

5. Taylor to Cochrane, 16 May 1824, Arquivo SDGM Rio (microfilm), 1/5/449/25-7.
6. Taylor to Cochrane. 29 May 1824, *Os Nossos Almirantes*, vol II, pp 180-82.
7. Midshipman de Oliveira Figueiredo to Taylor, 27 May 1824, Arquivo SDGM Rio (microfilm), 7/6/244/58-9.
8. Taylor to Cochrane, 11 June 1824, Arquivo SDGM Rio (microfilm), 7/6/244/50-7.

CHAPTER 13

1. Boiteux, 'A Armada Imperial Contraposta a Confederação do Equador', pp 93-4.
2. Gameiro to Carvalho e Melo, 7 April 1824, *Archivo Diplomático*, vol 2.
3. Silvestre Rebello to Carvalho e Melo, 26 July 1824, *Archivo Diplomático*, vol 5.
4. Vilela Barbosa to Cochrane, 6 July 1824, Arquivo SDGM Rio (microfilm), 7/6/243/308-9. The *Real Carolina* had been renamed *Paraguassú* on 19 May 1824.
5. Chamberlain to Canning, no. 95, 22 August 1824, PRO, FO 63/278. British-Brazilian correspondence between March 1823 and August 1824 is printed in *Archivo Diplomático*, vol 2.
6. Correspondence between Cochrane and Consuls Bennett and Parkinson, 18 and 19 August 1824, Arquivo SDGM Rio (microfilm), 1/5/448/5-6; 1/5/449/23-9.
7. Hunn to Cochrane, 27 August 1824, ibid. 1/5/449/19-20.
8. Manuel de Carvalho to Cochrane, 25 August 1824, ibid., 2/5/445/2.
9. Cochrane to Vilela Barbosa, no. 252, 29 August 1824, AN Rio, XM 254.
10. Cochrane to Lima e Silva, 4 September 1824 and reply dated 5 September 1824, AN Rio, XM 254.
11. Jewitt to Vilela Barbosa, 19 September 1824, printed in Meirelles da Silva, *Apontamentos, para a Historia da Marinha de Guerra Brazileira*, pp 335-42.
12. Jewitt to Lima e Silva, 14 September 1824, Arquivo SDGM Rio (microfilm), 6/6/237/4. Lima e Silva to Jewitt, 14 September 1824, ibid., 5/5/462/20.
13. Norton to Jewitt, 18 September 1824, ibid., 6/6/237/7.
14. Lima e Silva to Vilela Barbosa (Secret) 18 September 1824, Meirelles da Silva, *Apontamentos*, pp 352-3.
15. Jewitt to Vilela Barbosa, 19 September 1824, *Apontamentos*, pp 340-43.
16. Cochrane, *Narrative*, p 169.
17. Chamberlain to Canning, no. 108, 4 October 1824, PRO, FO 63/279.
18. Jewitt to Cochrane, 2 October 1824, AN Rio, XM 1063.
19. Welch to Jewitt, 22 September 1824, Arquivo SDGM Rio (microfilm), 6/6/237/9-10.
20. Norton to Jewitt, 23 September 1824, ibid., 6/6/237/14-15.
21. Lima e Silva – Cochrane correspondence 26 September to 4 October 1824, ibid., 1/5/448/14-36.

22. Cochrane to Vilela Barbosa, no. 264, 3 October 1824, Instituto Histórico e Geographico Rio, Latta 221.
23. Cochrane to Hayden, 10 October 1824, *Os Nossos Almirantes*, vol IV, p 246.

Chapter 14

1. Azevedo e Sá to Cochrane, 18 October 1824, Arquivo SDGM Rio (microfilm), 3/5/458/96.
2. Proclamation of 20 October 1824, ibid., 3/5/458/96-7.
3. Jewitt to Cochrane, 21 October 1824, ibid., 2/5/456/128-9.
4. Cochrane to Vilela Barbosa, no. 274, 28 October 1824, ibid., 2/5/451/82-3.
5. Decree by Azevedo e Sá, 14 November 1824, ibid., 3/5/458/48.
6. Cochrane to Vilela Barbosa, 9 December 1824, ibid., 2/5/451/69.
7. Jewitt to Cochrane, 10 December 1824, ibid., 2/5/456/68.
8. Vilela Barbosa to Cochrane, 5 December 1824, AN Rio, XM 1232.
9. Cochrane to Teles Lobo, 20 January 1825, printed in Viera da Silva, *História da Independência do Maranhão*, S. Luis, 1862, p 320; *Narrative*, p 222. Cochrane's original grounds for claiming all captured property in S. Luis were that it had been 'awarded to the captors by the Imperial Decree of 11 Dec 1822 issued to induce foreign seamen to enter the service'. Alas, only in Cochrane's mind was there a link between general property confiscated under this decree and the recruitment of sailors. On his return in 1825 he elaborated this argument, claiming further that the Emperor's agreement of 12 February 1824 accorded 'the value of seizures to the officers and men as a reward for their exertions and services', and that it applied not only to ships and cargoes (which was clearly its intention) but to confiscated property as well.
10. Lobo to Cochrane, no. 47, 4 February 1825, Arquivo SDGM Rio (microfilm), 5/5/463/99.
11. Cochrane to Vilela Barbosa, no. 291, 17 March 1825, *Os Nossos Almirantes*, vol I, pp 92-3.
12. Viera da Silva *História da Independência*, pp 329-36.
13. Jackson's Diary, Arquivo SDGM Rio (microfilm), 6/6/237.
14. Graham, Maria, 'Escorço Biográphico de Dom Pedro I', printed in *Anais da Bibliotéca Nacional*, Rio, 1938, vol LX, pp 143-8.
15. Brant to Carvalho e Melo (Secret), 26 January 1825, *Archivo Diplomático*, vol 2.
16. Cochrane to Carvalho e Melo, 22 March 1825, *Os Nossos Almirantes*, vol I, pp 94-5.
17. Tobias Monteiro, *Historia do Imperio*, Rio, 1939, vol I, pp 285-6.
18. Cochrane to Vilela Barbosa, 20 March 1825, Instituto Histórico e Geographico, Rio, Latta 221.
19. Cochrane to Chamberlain, 31 March 1825, Arquivo SDGM Rio (microfilm), 1/5/450/66-8.

Chapter 15

1. Chamberlain to Canning, no. 73, 20 July 1825, PRO, FO 13/9.

NOTES 207

2. Gameiro to Carvalho e Melo, no. 3 (Secret), 13 July 1825, *Archivo Diplomático*, vol 2.
3. Chamberlain to Canning, no. 18, 31 January 1825, PRO, FO 63/276.
4. Gameiro to Vilela Barbosa, 9 July 1825, in Meirelles da Silva, *Apontamentos*, p 129.
5. Gameiro to Carvalho e Melo, no. 3 (Secret), 13 July 1825, *Archivo Diplomático*, vol 2.
6. Gameiro to Carvalho e Melo, no. 49, 26 August 1825, ibid.
7. Cochrane to Gameiro, 6 September 1825, in *Narrative*, p 254.
8. Gameiro to Vilela Barbosa, 5 December 1825, in Meirelles da Silva, *Apontamentos*, pp 133–7.
9. Cochrane, *Narrative*, p 260–61.
10. Gameiro to Shepherd, 7 November 1825, *Archivo Diplomático*, and *Os Nossos Almirantes*, vol I, p 102.
11. Cochrane to Vilela Barbosa (Paranaguá), 5 November 1825, Arquivo SDGM Rio (microfilm), 2/5/451.
12. Cochrane to Vilela Barbosa (Paranaguá), 10 February and 16 March 1826, Arquivo SDGM Rio (microfilm), 7/6/241/205–15.
13. Ibid.
14. Meirelles da Silva, *Apontamentos*, p 404.

CHAPTER 16

1. Stuart to Canning (Private), no. 8, 20 August 1825, PRO, FO 13/20.
2. Canning to Chamberlain, no. 4, 8 March 1824, PRO, FO 63/275.
3. Chamberlain to Canning, no. 118, 28 October 1824, PRO, FO 63/279.
4. Chamberlain to Canning, no. 18, 31 January 1825, PRO, FO 13/8.
5. José Bonifácio to Vasconcellos Drummond, quoted in John Armitage, *História do Brasil* (translation), Edições de Ouro, Rio, 1943, p 171.
6. Chamberlain to Canning, no. 7, 9 January 1825, PRO, FO 63/276.
7. Brant and Gameiro to Carvalho e Melo, no. 18, 29 September 1824, *Archivo Diplomático*, vol 2.
8. Gameiro to Vilela Barbosa, nos 16 and 34, 6 August and 19 November 1825, AN Rio, XM 453.
9. Brant and Gameiro to Carvalho e Melo, no. 24, 5 November 1824, *Archivo Diplomático*, vol 2; Pereira da Cunha to Paranaguá, no. 72, 3 January 1827, AN Rio, XM 453.
10. Gameiro to Vilela Barbosa, no. 15, 9 July 1825, AN Rio, XM 453.
11. Gameiro to Vilela Barbosa, no. 4, 7 May 1825, ibid.
12. Gameiro to Vilela Barbosa, no. 41, 19 December 1825, ibid.
13. Carvalho e Melo to Silvestre Rebello, 21 January 1824, *Archivo Diplomático*, vol 5.
14. Silvestre Rebello to Carvalho e Melo, no. 19, 26 March 1825, ibid.
15. Faustino to Vilela Barbosa, 25 April 1825, AN Rio, XM 210.
16. The warships comprised *Pedro I*, the frigates *Niterói, Paraguassú, Piranga, Thetis, Imperatriz, Dona Paula, Isabela* and *Príncipe Imperial*; the corvettes *Maceió, Maria da Glória, Liberal, Carioca* and *Itaparica*; the brigs *Cacique, Bahia, Beaurepaire, Maranhão, Pirajá, Real Pedro, Guarani, Caboclo* and *29 de Agosto*; and the brigantines

208   INDEPENDENCE OR DEATH!

Rio da Plata, Atlanta, Pará, Andorinha, Leopoldina, Independência ou Morte, Empreendador and *Dona Januária.*
  17. See Chapter 2, Note 11.
  18. Brant to Carvalho e Melo, no. 19, 2 October 1824, *Archivo Diplomático,* vol 2.
  19. Gameiro to Vilela Barbosa, 27 June 1825, 11 November 1826, AN 453.

Chapter 17

  1. *Os Nossos Almirantes,* vol III, pp 1–28.
  2. Relatório da Repartição dos Negócios da Marinha, Rio, 1828, Bib Nac Rio.
  3. Relatório da Repartição dos Negócios da Marinha, Rio, 1832, Bib Nac Rio.
  4. These officers were: Commodores John Taylor and James Norton; Captains Mateus Welch and John Pascoe Grenfell; Captains-of-Frigate George Manson, Bartholomew Hayden, William Eyre, Stephen Clewley and William James Inglis; Commanders George Broom, William January and William Parker; Lieutenants James Wallace, David Carter, C. J. Appleton, R. N. Murphy, Richard Hayden, William MacErwing, Thomas Thompson and Charles Rose; and Sublieutenants J. H. White and Edward Newton. See *Almanack da Marinha 1835,* Bibliotéca da Marinha, Rio.
  5. London Correspondence (May 1836) PRO, FO 13/131; Reports from Rio (April 1837) PRO, FO 13/134.
  6. *Os Nossos Almirantes,* vol II, pp 159–205.
  7. Ibid., vol IV, pp 243–64.
  8. Ibid., vol III, pp 210–226.
  9. Ibid., vol IV, pp 135–153.
  10. Ibid., vol I, pp 193–265.
  11. Foreign Office to Cochrane, 11 October 1847. Arquivo SDGM Rio (microfilm), 3/5/460.
  12. Foreign Office to Cochrane, 24 July 1855, ibid., 1/5/445.
  13. James Moore & Co. to Cochrane, 11 August 1855, ibid., 1/5/443.
  14. James Moore & Co. to Cochrane, 12 June 1857, ibid., 1/5/447.
  15. James Moore & Co. to Cochrane, 15 December 1856, ibid., 1/5/443.
  16. See *The Times,* 26 February 1856.
  17. For Jackson's Journal, see Arquivo SDGM Rio (microfilm), 6/6/237.
  18. Arbitration Award, ibid., 1/5/444. For lists of prizes, see Minister of Marine to Procurador da Coroa, 12 February 1849, AN Rio, XM 521.
  19. Buckley Mathew to Dundonald, 23 December 1874. Arquivo SDGM Rio (microfilm), 1/5/444.

BIBLIOGRAPHY

Amaral, Braz do, *História da Independência na Bahia*, 2nd edn, Salvador, 1957. A comprehensive account with a large appendix of documents, many from the Arquivo Historico Militar, Lisbon.

Anais do Bibliotéca Nacional, Rio, 1938, vol LX. Contains both the detailed diary of the Chaplain of the *Pedro I*, March to December 1823, and Maria Graham's 'Escorço Biographico de Dom Pedro I', with private correspondence with the Empress Leopoldina.

Armitage, John, *History of Brazil from the arrival of the Braganza family in 1808 to the abdication of D Pedro I in 1831*, 2 vols, London, 1836. An indispensable contemporary account.

Archivo Diplomático da Independência. Ministério de Relações Exteriores, Rio de Janeiro, 1922, vols 2, 4 and 5. Correspondence with Brazilian missions in, respectively, London, Buenos Aires and Washington.

Bethell, Leslie, *The Abolition of the Brazilian Slave Trade*, Cambridge University Press, Cambridge, 1970, Chapters 1 and 2 for the independence period.

Bethell, Leslie (ed.), *Brazil, Empire and Republic 1822–1930*, Cambridge University Press, Cambridge, 1989. The best brief modern account in English.

Boiteux, Henrique, *Os Nossos Almirantes*, Imprensa Naval, Rio de Janeiro, 1915, vols I to V. Potted biographies of the participants who reached flag rank, containing many reprinted documents.

Boiteux, Lucas, *A Marinha Imperial*, Imprensa Naval, Rio de Janeiro, 1954.

Boiteux, Lucas, 'A Armada Brasileira Contraposta a Confederação do Equador', in *Subsídios para a História Marítima do Brasil*, Rio de Janeiro, 1957, vol 13. An excellent account of the campaign.

Caio Prado Junior, *The Colonial Background to Modern Brazil*, Berkeley, CA, 1967. An analysis of the economic and political tensions underlying independence.

Cavaliero, Roderick, *The Independence of Brazil*, British Academic Press, London, 1993. The most vivid and detailed account of Brazil during the early nineteenth century, and of the astonishing personalities which determined its destiny.

Cochrane, Lord, 10th Earl of Dundonald, *Narrative of Services in the Liberation of Chile, Peru and Brazil*, London, Ridgeway, 1859, vol II. The Cochrane–Earp–Jackson version of events.

Graham, Maria, *Journal of a Voyage to Brazil and Residence there during part of the years 1821, 1822 and 1823*, London, 1824. Delightful contemporary account in extended diary form by a friend and confidante of Cochrane and his officers.

Grimble, Ian, *The Sea Wolf: The Life of Admiral Lord Cochrane*, Brand & Briggs, London, 1978. Interesting personal details and illuminated by reference to Maria Graham's Journals, but still Cochrane's version.

Lloyd, Christopher, *Lord Cochrane*, Longmans Green, 1947. The first biography which tries to be objective.

Manchester, Alan K., *British Preeminence in Brazil: Its Rise and Decline*, Durham, NC, 1933. A classic. Still relevant.

Mattison, Gilbert Farquahar, *Narrative of a visit to Brazil, Chile, Peru and the Sandwich Islands 1821-22*, London, 1825. A critical contemporary description of life in Brazil on the brink of independence.

Meirelles da Silva, *Apontamentos para a História da Marinha de Guerra Brazileira*, Rio de Janeiro, 1882, vol II. A collection of basic documents.

Monteiro, Tobias, *História do Imperio: A Elaboração da Independência*, Rio de Janeiro, 1927.

Monteiro, Tobias, *História do Imperio: O Primeiro Reinado*, Rio de Janeiro, 1939. Like its predecessor, a classic and detailed account of political events.

Navigator (Revista do Serviço de Documentação Geral da Marinha), 'Cartas do Comodoro Sir Thomas Masterman Hardy', no. 5, June 1972. A collection of Hardy's correspondence with the Admiralty in 1822 and 1823, in English with Portuguese summaries.

Navigator, 'A Marinha nas Lutas da Independência', no. 4, December, 1971. A collection of papers presented in a cycle of conferences organized to commemorate the 150th Anniversary of Brazilian Independence.

Purdy, John, *Sailing Directions for the Eastern Coast of Brazil* ... , Whittle, Holmes, Laurie, London, 1818.

Publicações do Archivo Publico Nacional, Rio de Janeiro, 1907, vol 7. A complete set of the despatches of Felisberto Brant Pontes from London 1822-23.

Raiol, Antônio Domingos, *Motins Políticos do Pará*, Belém, 1970, vol I. A polemical account of rebellion and repression in Pará during the period.

Thomas, David, *Cochrane: The Last Sea King*. André Deutsch, 1978. Racy and readable life of Cochrane. The chapter on Brazil to be avoided, as it is based entirely on the Cochrane-Earp-Jackson narrative.

Varnhagen, Francisco Adolfo de, *História da Independência do Brasil*, Rio de Janeiro, 1917. One of the classic Brazilian histories of political events.

Viera da Silva, *História da Independência do Maranhão*, S. Luis, 1862.

Webster, C.K., *Britain and the Independence of Latin America 1812-30* (reprint), Oxford University Press and the British Council, 1944.

INDEX

Aberdeen, Slave Trade (Brazil), Act of 1845, 178
Abreu, Geraldo de, President of Pará 1823, 84–5, 117
Activo Portuguese armed ship, 46, 199
Alagoas, 9, 116, 118, 122, 126, 133
Alençar Araripe, Tristão de, rebel President of Ceará 1824–5, 117, 123, 144–5
Alexander merchantman, 32
Alexandre Brazilian merchantman, 114
Alice merchantman, 32, 57
Alvaras (Royal Ordinances) on Prizes, 77, 99, 104, 107
Álvaro da Costa General, Portuguese commander in Montevideo 1822–23, 9, 34, 93
Amherst, Lord, 90, 161
Anderson, William George, 92, 173, 188
Andrada e Silva, Antônio Carlos, 28, 91
Andrada e Silva, José Bonifácio, becomes chief minister, 7, 13; 17–18, 21, 24, 40, 42; fall and deportation, 90–2; 164, 174
Animo Grande trans, 122, 133, 148
Appleton, C.J., 188
Atlanta brigtn, 16, 38, 57, 98, 102; blockade of Pernambuco, 118, 121–2; 142, 144, 146–7
Audaz Portuguese brig, 11, 50, 113, 199
Aurora Danish merchantman, 16
Avilez de Souza Tavares, General Jorge, 6
Azevedo e Sá, José Félix, Acting President of Ceará 1825, 144–6, 153

Bahia, 6; beginnings of patriot resistance, 9–10; siege begins, 34; Portuguese defensive strategy, 35; effects of the blockade, 58–60; evacuation, 61; 92, 113–4, 140–1, 154
Bahia (ex-*Colonel Allen*) brig, 57, 61; 64, 102; off Pernambuco, 113–5; blockade of Pernambuco, 118, 121–2, 126
Banda Oriental (*see also* Montevideo), 9, 166, 171
Barra Grande, 116, 119, 120–2, 126, 130, 133, 153
Barão de Bagé Admiral, 42
Barroso Pereira, Cdr Luis, 66, 119–20
Battle of 4 May 1823, 46; 51–3
battles in Buenos Aires War 1825–8
  Corales, 190–2
  Lara-Quilmes, 172, 190–7
  Los Pozes, 172, 188, 194
  Patagonia, 172, 190, 194, 196
  Monte Santiago, 172, 190, 192, 197
Beaurepaire, Capt Teodoro de, 45, 122, 169
Belém (*see also* Pará), 81, 83, 85–9
Berefim (Empreendador), 166
Bibiano de Castro, Cdr F., 122, 133
Blakeley, William, 58, 170, 188
Bompland, Madam, 108
Bramley Moore & Co, 178
Brandywine USS, 169

INDEPENDENCE OR DEATH!

Brant Pontes, General Felisberto, 12, 15–6; in London, 24–33; career, 24; his instructions, 27; political contacts, 26, 28; recruitment, 29–32, 171, 175; purchases stores, 31–2, 110, 167–8; independence negotiations, 162–3; 150, 165
Brazil, coequal with Portugal, 1; arrival of the Court, 2; consequent development, 2–3; population and geography, 8–9; financial problems, 15, 105; political divisions 97; *de facto* independence 1825, 160; separatist tendencies, 160; independence negotiations, 160–2; recognition, 162–4; finances, 165; indigenous nobility, 164; war with Buenos Aires, 166, 169, 171–2; political revolution 1830–1, 174; regional rebellions, 175
Brazilian Constituent Assembly, 7, 55–6, 90–1; effects of dissolution, 114–7
Brazilian naval policy, 13, 165–6, 169, 174
Brazilian Navy, state of in 1821, 14–15; acquisition of ships, 15–16, 116; shortage of officers, 16–17; pay and contracts, 29–30, 171; administration, 36–7; state of in 1823, 37–8; expenditure, 106, 173; fall in morale, 98–100; need for, 101; concentration on Rio, 111; Confederation of the Equator, 131–9; bargaining counter in negotiations, 163–4; purchases in England and USA, 167–9; state of in 1828, 173; cuts and new role, 174–5; mobilization against Buenos Aires, 171; 1836 expansion, 175
British seamen, recruitment of, 26, 28–32, 64, arrival and distribution, 43, 57–8, 61; British concern at desertion, 63; contracts and desertion in Rio, 100–101; pay rise, 110; transferred to *Pedro I* off Recife, 135, 141; desertions from *Piranga*, 157; 141; 1825 recruitment, 171; 1836 recruitment in Orkney and Shetland, 175

British trade and commerce, 1808–20, 3, 25, 151, 161–2, 172
Broom, George, 32, 172, 177, 188
Brown, Louis, 171, 189
Brown, William, Admiral of Buenos Aires 1826–8, 170, 172
Bruce, Miguel Freire President of Maranhão 1823–5, 76–7, 80, 129, 146
Buenos Aires, tension over Banda Oriental, 171; war and British mediation, 172; prize claims, 179, 181
Burgos, José Félix Pereira, Brazilian Commander in Maranhão 1823, 72, 80, 129

Caboclo (ex-*Maipú*) brig, 16, 20, 38
Cacique (ex-*Reino Unido*) brig, 38, 57–8, 92–3; blockade of Pernambuco, 122, 124, 126, 133, 139, 146–8, 152
Calypso Portuguese corv, 11, 46, 199
Cametá, 87–8
Campos, Commodore Félix Pereira de, Portuguese naval commander in Bahia 1822–3, 11, 36, 50–1, 53, 58–9
Campos, Fr João Baptista, 81, 84, 87
Caneca, Fr (Joaquim do Amor Divino Rebelo), 114, 120, 127, 146, 153
Canning, George, 26, 28, 155, 161–2, 172
Carioca (ex-*Leal Portuguêz* prize) corv, 110; Confederation of the Equator, 132–3, 136–7, 142
Carlotta, Queen of Portugal, 5, 131
Carolina sch, 14, 39, 111, 126
Carter, David, 92, 173, 189
Carvalho, Cdr José A. de, 131, 137, 140
Carvalho e Melo, Luis, Minister for Foreign Affairs, 56, 91, 150
Carvalho VI, prize brig (became *Pirajá*) 100, 115
Castlereagh, Lord, 25–6, 28, 161
Castro, Sub-lieut Justino de, 45, 66
Catarina sch, 14, 39, 47
Caxias, 71, 79
Ceará, 9, 55, 65, 71, 117, 123, 127; Confederation of the Equator, 143–6; trials of rebels, 153

INDEX

Cerqueira prize (became *29 de Agosto*), 166
Challes, Ambrose, 30, 58, 170, 189
Chamberlain, Consul-General Henry, 21, 40, 64, 150, 186
Chester, Samuel, 30, 43, 66, 170, 189
Chichester Packet, 95
Clare, Francis, 30, 43, 189
Clarence, George, 32, 147, 189
Clewley, Steven, 41, 189
Cochrane, Lord Thomas, career, 18–20; recruitment, 18, 27; arrival and appointment 40–2; pay, 42; ordered to Bahia, 44; blockade of Bahia, 45–9, 51–5, 57–61; battle of 4 May 1823, 51–4; pursuit of the Portuguese 62–5; liberation of Maranhão, 73–4; prize seizures and claims, 76–8, 98, 100, 104, 106; orders Grenfell to liberate Para, 82; hero's welcome in Rio, made Marquis of Maranhão etc., 95–6; commander-in-chief 98; for life 118; disputes with the government, 98, 100–1, 105, 107–8, Brazilian attempts to satisfy his claims, 101–2, 106, 110; Confederation of the Equator, 132–42; at Recife; 134–7, negotiations and bombardment, 134–5; 140–1; in Ceará, 143–6; returns to Maranhão, 146–151; sails to England, 152; hero's return, 154–5; Greek invitation, 156; leaves Brazilian service, 157–8; dismissed, 159; 163, 170–1; rehabilitated in England and reinstated in the RN, 177–8; claims against Brazil for backpay and prize money, memorials and petitions, 178–9; settlement offered, 180–1; prize issue, 180–1; produces *Narrative of Services in the Liberation of Chile, Peru and Brazil*, 182–3; subsequent claims of 11th Earl of Dundonald, 183–4; arbitration and the final settlement, 184–5
Colonel Allen merchant brig, 40, 57, 62, 151 (see Bahia)
Conde dos Archos armed ship, 93

Confederation of the Equator, 127–139
Constituição (new) Portuguese frig, 46, 199
Constituição ou Morte rebel brig, 123, 130–1; *Beaurepaire* after capture, 166 constitution and flag, 127–8; arms purchases in Britain and the USA, 129–130; aggressive moves by, 130–1; expedition against, 131–2; campaign in Pernambuco, 132–9; suppression of, 139; in Ceará, 143–6
Constitutional Army of the Confederation of the Equator, 130, 134, 136, 146
Cooperative Army of Good Order, 133, advance on Recife, 136; capture of, 137–9; pursuit of the rebels, 146
Corrêa da Camera, Antônio, Brazilian Agent in Buenos Aires, 18, 20
Côrtes Portuguese, anti-Brazilian mood and legislation, 5; reaction to Brazilian defiance, 8, 11; reinforces garrisons, 27–8, 31; threats by Holy Alliance, 31; overthrow of, 55; news of, 60, 72, 82, 93, 113
Cossaka sch, 14, 39, 93
Costa, Hipólito José da, editor of the London-based *Correio Brasiliense*, 25
Costa Barros, Pedro, nominated President of Ceará, 123; and Maranhão, 147–8, 153
Confederation of the Equator, 132, 136
Couto, Cdr A. Joaquim de, 45, 92;
Cowan, George, 32, 53, 115, 190
Craig, Thomas, 169, 190
Crofton, Vincent, 30, 43, 173, 190
Crosbie, Thomas Sackville, 40–1, 45, 75, 132, 151, 157, 170, 190
Cunha Moreira, Capt Luis, Minister of Marine 1822–3, 13–16, 36, 41; supplies Cochrane, 56–7; 181
Cunningham, John Surgeon RN, 102–3
Cygnet packet, 109

Dean, Henry, 61, 77–8, 140, 154, 158
Delamare, Commodore Rodrigo, (sortie against Bahia), 10–11
Desengano Brasileiro, 127
Dez de Fevereiro Portuguese corv, 46, 113, 199
Diário Fluminense, 133, 140
Diário do Governo, 37, 57
Dickson, Dr John, 94, 150–1
Diligente prison ship, 86–7
Dom João VI, Portuguese 74-gun ship, 7, 11, 27, 50; 4 May 1823, 51–3; 67
Dona Januária brigtn, 147, 166
Drummond, Francis, 66, 108, 190
Dundonald, 11th Earl of; continues with Cochrane's claims, 183–5

Earp, G.P., ghost writer of Cochrane's *Narrative of Services*, 182, 187
Eckford, Henry, US Shipbuilder, 169
Elrick merchantman, 31
Emilia Portuguese sch, 72, 76, 80, (*see* Pará)
Esmeralda, Spanish frigate, 20, 30
Expeditionary Force (to Maranhão), 71–2, 79
Eyre, William, 20, 131, 149, 176, 190

Falcão de Lacerda, Colonel Barros, military commander in Pernambuco and Confederation of the Equator 1823–4, 114, 119, 121, 123, 134, 136, 138, 153
Faria, General Agostino de, Portuguese commander in Maranhão 1822–3, 72, 75
Fidié, Major João da Cunha, Portuguese commander in Piauí 1822–3, 70–1, 79, 116, 153
Filguieras, José Pereira, Brazilian commander in Ceará 1822–5, 71, 79, 117, 119, 123, 143–6, 153
Fitzcosten, Joseph (José), 32, 191
Foreign Enlistment Act 1819, 30, 155, 158
Fortaleza, 144–5, 153
França, General Luis Paulino de, 93
Freitas, Lieut Rodrigo T. de, 122, 131
Fubbs, Daniel, 169, 191

Gameiro Pessoa, Manuel, Brazilian agent in London 22, 109, 155–9, 164, 167
Garção, Cdr A. Salema Freire, 40, 45, 92
Gaulter Portuguese armed ship, 46, 65, 199
Gazeta de Bahia, 51
Gentil Americana armed transport 84, 87, 102, 118, 123, 129
George IV merchantman, 31
Gillett, Samuel, 32, 79, 108, 118, 121, 170, 191
Gleddon, John Rogers, 32, 58, 178, 191
Goiana (*Maria da Glória*) sch, 130–1
Graham, Mrs Maria, 3; arrives in Rio 45, 56; 62; returns to England 94–5; at Recife 1824, 134–5; second visit to Rio 149–51; 158
Greek Committee in London, 156
Grenfell, John Pascoe, 41, 47, 53, 76; liberates Pará, 82–91; his orders, 82; prizes, 84–5; restores order, 86; departs 88–9; arrested, 108; 120; Buenos Aires war, 172; 177, 191
Guadiana, 130
Guarani (ex-*Nightingale*) brig, 16, 38; at blockade of Bahia, 45–7, 49, 53–5; 92–3; blockade of Pernambuco, 122; Confederation of the Equator, 131, 134

Hayden, Bartholomew, 40, 58, 61, 64, 102–3; off Pernambuco, 113–5; 118, 141–2, 176, 192
Haydon, Thomas, 171, 192
Hardy, Commodore Sir Thomas, commander of the S. America Squadron 21, 35–6, 51, 64, 94–5, 186
HM ships
Beaver, 36, 51
Blossom, 21
Brazen, 137
Cambridge, 102–3
Conway, 32
Cormorant, 179
Creole, 62
Doris, 21, 51, 62, 132, 154
Fly, 51
Sparrowhawk, 165

INDEX

Tartar, 44, 50–1
Tweed, 134–5, 137–8, 186
Warspite, 162
Windsor Castle, 131
Holy Alliance, 25, 31, 154–5, 161
Hunn, Captain of HMS Tweed, 137–8, 186
Hunt, Lennon, 184–5

Imperatriz frig, 84, 88–9, 102, 108, 166, 183–4
Independência rebel sch, 130
Independência ou Morte brigtn, 14, 38, 115, 130, 137, 166
Infante Dom Miguel Portuguese brig, 70, 73, 76 (see Maranhão)
Inglis, William James, 32, 172, 175, 192
Isabela frig, US-built, 170
Isabela Maria sch, 39
Itaparica (ex-Portuguese Voador) corv, 93, 173
Itaparica Island, Bahia, 35–6
Itipicurú-mirim Junta, 72, 80

Jackson, William, 40, 63, 110, 149, 158, 178, 182
James Moore & Co, 178–181
January, William, 192
Jewitt, David, 20, 34, 36; commands Piranga at Blockade of Bahia, 45, 52, 60; during Confederation of the Equator, 133, 137, 139–140; at Ceará, 144–5; at Maranhão, 146–7, 150; transferred to Pedro I and departs 151
João Dom, Prince Regent and King of Portugal, arrives in Brazil, 1; opens Brazil to international trade, 2; returns to Lisbon, 4; 66, 72, 77; Miguelite coup, 131, 160–1, 165; death, 174

Kelmare, Benjamin, 30, 140, 171, 193

Labatut, General Pierre, Brazilian commander in Bahia 1822–3, 10–11, 16, 34, 44, 55, 58
Lady Cochrane, 44, 62, 103, 150
Laguna, Barão da, Brazilian commander in the Banda Oriental, 9

Lapwing merchantman, 30, 43
Leal Portuguêz prize (became the Carioca corv), 63, 110
Leghorn merchantman, 31
Leopoldina, Empress, 5, 43, 95, 149, 174
Leopoldina brigtn, 14, 39, 47, 54, 92–3, 122, 126; Confederation of the Equator, 131, 134, 136–7
Liberal corv, 6, 10, 14, 38; at blockade of Bahia, 45–6, 49, 53, 55, 63; 92–3
Liguri armed ship, 93
Lima e Silva, Brigadier Francisco, Imperial commander against the Confederation of the Equator; 132, 133–4, 136–41, 153
Lima e Silva, Colonel José Joaquim, Brazilian army commander in Bahia after Labatut, 36, 58
Lindsays merchantman, 30, 43
Lisboa, João S., 126
Little, Surgeon James, 32
Liverpool, 29–30, 32, 57, 61, 101, 168
Liverpool, Lord, 28, 155
Lobo, Vice-Admiral Rodrigo Brazilian commander at the Plate 1822, 14, 17, 34
London loan, 105, 165
Lord Herbert packet, 109
Luconia, trans, 91–2
Luiza fireship, 43, 48

Maceió corv, 38; Confederation of the Equator, 131, 134–7, 140, 142, 173
MacErwing, William, 193
Maciel da Costa, José Severiano, Minister for the Empire, 91, 106–7
Mackintosh, Robert, 173, 193
Macreights, Duncan, 32, 170, 193
Madeira de Melo, Brigadier Ignacio, Portuguese military commander in Bahia 1822–3, 10, 34–5, 50–1, 53, 58–61
Manson, George, 20, 80, 132, 136, 148, 152, 176, 193
Manuel de Carvalho Paes de Andrade, rebel President of Pernambuco 1824, 114–6, 118–20, 123–6; declares the Confederation of the Equator, 127; military

activity, 129–30; negotiates with
  Cochrane, 134–5; flees, 137–8, 140,
  153
Maranhão, 9, 70; under Portuguese
  control, 72–3, arrival of Cochrane,
  73–4; adheres to Empire, 75;
  seizure of prizes, 76–8; value, 78;
  conflicts in, 79, 127, 129; 92, 95;
  repression by Bruce, 146–8;
  Cochrane's prize demands, 147–92;
  154
Maranhão (ex-*Infante Dom Miguel*) brig,
  76, 82–3, 85–6; Confederation of
  the Equator, 132–3, 136
March, William, 146, 155, 193
Marchioness of Salisbury packet, 103
Maria da Glória (*Goiana*) sch, 14, 39,
  121, 130, 142, 144, 146, 166
Maria da Glória corv, 10, 14, 38, 40, 42;
  at blockade of Bahia 45–6, 49,
  54–5, 59–60, 63–5; 122;
  Confederation of the Equator,
  131–2, 134
Maria Francisca sch, 14, 39
Maria Isabela sch, 39, 153
Maria Teresa sch, 14, 17, 93
Maria Zeferina sch, 14, 39
Mary merchantman, 32, 58
Mathew, George Buckley, 184–5
Maximiliano de Souza, Commodore
  Francisco, 7
May & Ludkin, 94, 110
Mayrinck da Silva Ferrão, José, 109,
  124–5
Meirelles Sobrinho, Antônio,
  Brazilian Vice-Consul in
  Liverpool, 29–32, 100
Meruí, trans, 122
Metrowich, João, 130, 153
Miguel, Dom, 5, 131, 174
Minas Gerais, 6, 9–10, 124
Molloy, John R., 141
Montague packet, 32
Montevideo, 10; Portuguese besieged
  in, 17, 34; naval battle off, 92–3;
  Portuguese surrender, 93, 95, 105
Morro de S. Paulo, 53–4, 59–61
Mosselyn, Charles, 32, 170, 193
Moura, Brig José Maria de,
  Portuguese commander in Pará
  1822–3, 81–3

Murphy, R.N., 168, 193

Nancy merchantman, 31, 57
National Subscription for the Navy,
  15–16, 37, 110
Natividade Saldanha, José de, rebel
  Provincial Secretary in
  Pernambuco 1824, 126–7, 153
naval stores, order and purchase, 16,
  30, 32–3, 110, 167; arrival, 57, 167
Nazareth, Bishop Dom Joaquim,
  Portuguese President of Maranhão
  1822–3, 70, 73
Newton, Edward, 169, 194
Nichol, James, 43, 92, 122, 131, 194
Niemeyer, Colonel Conrado de, 153
Niterói (ex-*Sucesso*) frig, 15, 22, 38; at
  blockade of Bahia and Battle of 4
  May 1823, 46–7, 49, 51–2, 55, 61,
  63; chase of the Portuguese to
  Europe, 65–9; 102, 107; blockade
  of Pernambuco, 118, 121–2, 124–6;
  Confederation of the Equator, 130,
  133, 138, 141, 155
Norton, James, 32, 58, 102; blockade
  of Pernambuco, 118, 133; capture
  of Recife, 138–9; 141; against
  Buenos Ayres, 170, 172, 176; 194
Nunes, Capt Antônio Pedro, Brazilian
  commander at the Plate 1823–4,
  34, 92–3

O Paraense, 81
officers, shortages in Brazil, 17; tests
  of loyalty, 16; recruitment in Rio,
  20–1; recruitment in England,
  28–30, 32–6; pay and contracts 30,
  101; 1825 recruitment, 171;
  numbers in service in 1828, 173; in
  1836, 175; biographies of British,
  188–198
Old Bride merchantman, 167
Olinda, 112, 115–6, 138–9, 140
Oliveira Bottas, Sub-lieut João de, 34
Oriental sch, 39
Oudsley, Gore W., 141, 173, 194

Paes Barreto, Francisco President of
  Pernambuco, 115, 118, 124, 126,
  130, 133, 153
Paixão e Dores, Fr Manoel M. da,

INDEX

chaplain of *Pedro I*, 51
Pará, 9; under Portuguese control, 81–2; adheres to Empire 83; revolts in, 86, 89, 92, 95; deaths of detainees, 85–6; 100, 111, 117, 120, 123; during Confederation of the Equator, 127, 129, 131–2, 141, 147
Pará (ex-*Emilia*) sch, captured, 80; Confederation of the Equator, 131–2, 134–5, 139
Paraguassú (ex-*Real Carolina*) frig, Confederation of the Equator, 131, 134–7, 140, 155
Paraiba, 9, 116, 123, 126, 129, 134, 143
Parish, Woodbine, Consul-General Buenos Aires, 103, 172, 186
Parker, William, 43, 176, 194
Pedro, Prince Regent (later Emperor) of Brazil, agrees to remain, 6; ejects Portuguese troops, 6–7; the 'cry' of Ypiranga, 8; becomes Emperor, 8; 16; coronation, 17; 40–1; sees off the Squadron of Independence, 45; opens Constituent Assembly, 65–6; dissolves Assembly, 90–1; writes constitution, 97; 101–1, 113, 124; Confederation of the Equator, 132; court atmosphere, 149–50; expands the navy, 163–4; need for recognition, 160; role in negotiations, 3; abdicates and death in Portugal, 174
Pedro I (ex-*Martim de Freitas*) line-of-battle ship, 15, 22, 37, 40, 42–3; at blockade of Bahia and Battle of 4 May 1823, 45–9, 51–5, 59–65; at Maranhão, 73, 75, 80, 95, 110; Confederation of the Equator, 132–3, 135–6, 140–1, Ceará, 144, 146; Cochrane hands over to Jewitt, 151
Pedro II Emperor of Brazil, 174, 178, 180–1
Pernambuco, 9, 35; 1817 revolt, 112; 55, 64, 102–3, 109, 111–4 conflicts, 115–7; blockade of, 118–126; navigational hazards, 121; spread of the revolt, 124–5; compromise rejected, 124–5, 125–6, 131 (*see* Confederation of the Equator)

Pérola Portuguese frig, 31, 50; Battle of 4 May 1823, 46, 51–3, 199
Phibbs, Richard, 30, 43
Piauí, 9, 55, 70–1, 116, 127, 129
Pinto Guedes, Admiral Rodrigo, 42
Pio dos Santos, Capt Tristão, Intendant of Marine Bahia, 35, 47
Pirajá (ex-*Carvalho VI*) brig, 110, 142
Piranga (ex-*União*) frig, 10, 36–7, 40, 42–3; at blockade of Bahia and Battle of 4 May 1823, 45–6, 49, 51–3; blockade of Pernambuco, 102, 118, 122, 126; Confederation of the Equator, 132–3, 137–8, 141–2; Ceará, 144, 146; Cochrane transfers into, 151; to Portsmouth, 152; in England, 155, 157–8; returns,177; 177, 181, 183
Portugal, constitutional revolt, 4; attempts to reimpose colonial status, 5; reinforces garrisons, 27–8, 31; overthrow of the Côrtes, 55; peace overtures, 93; plans for reconquest, 109; Miguelite coup 131; abandonment of the invasion, 131; sues for peace, 161–2; demands for dismissal of British officers, 163; treaty signed, 162; war for the succession, 174
Portuguese Navy, strength in Bahia 1821, 13, 51; Battle of 4 May 1823, 51–3; off Montevideo, 92–3
Poynton, Thomas, 108, 170, 195
Princess Elizabeth packet, 109
Princeza Real Portuguese armed ship, 52–3
Principe Imperial frig, US-built, 169
Principe Portuguese corv, 46, 199
prize ships
Alegre, 67
Alexander I, 114
Amazonas, 55
Andorinha, 85
Astrea, 85
Bizarria, 63, 191
Bon Successo, 67
Borges Carneiro, 92, 189
Caridade, 63, 109
Carvalho VI, 109, 115
Cerqueira, 166
Conceição, 55

Conde de Peniche, 63
Correio de S Miguel, 67
Deus te Guarde, 114
Diana, 64
Diligente, 85
Dos Amigos, 115
Emilia, 68
Esperança, 67
Feliz Ventura, 194
Fragatinha de Macao, 63
Exchange, 142
Grão Pará, 63, 66
Gen Noronha, 85
Gen Rego, 85
Harmonia, 63, 109
Harmonia (2), 68
Holstein, 115
Incomparavel, 115
John Thomas, 55
Leal Portugêz, 63, 109
Lucrecia, 85
Maria, 92
Meteor, 63
Nova Amazonas, 67
Nova Constituição, 55
Nova Iphigenia, 85
Paquete do Setibal, 68
Pombinha, 78, 190
Prazeres e Alegria, 67, 107
Principe Real, 63
Promptidão, 63
Providencia, 67
S. Andre Diligente, 114
S. Antônio Triumpho, 68
S. José, 67
S. José Triunpho, 63
S. Manuel Augusto, 68, 190
Triunpho da Inveja, 64, 196
Ulysses, 63
União, 55
União (2), 65
Ventura Feliz, 197
Vigilante, 67
Vigilante Guerreiro, 55
Visconde de S Lourenço, 60
prizes, during blockade of Bahia,
  55-6, 60; from the Portuguese
  convoy, 63-4; of the Niterói, 66-8;
  Maranhão, 76-8; Pará, 84-5; in
  Rio, 92, 95; 98-9; prize laws and
  legal problems, 199-100; political
problems, 100; the solution, 101;
  infringements, 76, 104, 107;
  payments and purchases, 109-110;
  off Pernambuco, 114; 141;
  Cochrane in Maranhão, 147, 149;
  claims dealt with, 180-2, 185

Ratcliffe, João Guilherme, 130, 153
Real brigtn, 14, 38; at blockade of
  Bahia, 45-7, 49, 53
Real Carolina frig, 7, 14, 38, 43; at
  blockade of Bahia, 56, 59-61;
  pursuit of the Portuguese, 63; 131
  (see Paraguassú)
Real Pedro brig, 14, 38, 92-3
rebellions post-1830
  Balaiada Maranhão, 175
  Cabanos Pará and Pernambuco,
    175, 190, 192, 196
  Farrapos Rio Grande do Sul, 175,
    188, 191, 194
  Sabinada Bahia, 175
Rebello, Silvestre, Brazilian agent in
  USA, 168-9
Recife, (see also Pernambuco) 63-4,
  113, 119-20; British property 134;
  bombardment, 136; capture of,
  137-9; 143, 146. Map, 128
Regeneração Portuguese corv, 46, 199
Reid, Alexander, 147, 173, 195
Reino Unido brig, 10, 15 (see Cacique)
Restauradora armed ship, 92-3
Reynaldo packet, 134, 149
Rio de Janeiro, residence of the
  Court, 2-4; hostility to the Côrtes,
  6, 9, 13; installations and ships at,
  14-5; war preparations, 36-7,
  40-4; blockade of Bahia, 45, 56-7;
  opening of the Assembly, 55-6;
  political crises, 90-2; re Portuguese
  peace feelers, 93; Cochrane's
  return, 95-6; problems with
  Cochrane, 98, 100-1, 105-8;
  blockade of Recife and the
  Confederation of the Equator,
  118-25, 131-2; defence against
  invasion, 109, 131; retribution, 153;
  treaty negotiations and
  consolidation of the Empire, 162-5
Rio Grande do Norte, 9, 116, 123,
  127, 143

INDEX

Rio da Plata brigtn, 16, 38, 57, 126, 132
Rio-Maior, Conde de, 93
Rose, Charles, 195
Royal Navy, post-Napoleonic War slump, 21, 29
Rozo, José de Araujo, President of Pará 1824–5, 129, 147

Sá, Capt Pereira de, of the Portuguese armed ship *Princeza Real*, 51–3
Salvador (*see also* Bahia), 10, 11, 13, 21, 34–5, 44–9, 58, 60, 63, 118, 130, 141
Sandwich packet, 131
São Paulo, 6, 7–10
Scully, Mr, 184, 187
seamen, (*see also* British seamen), shortages of, 22–3, 39, pay and recruitment, 22–3, 39; unreliability of Portuguese, 11, 41, 53–55
Seis de Fevereiro sch, 14, 39, 92–3
Sentinella de Liberdade, 114
Sesostris merchantman, 44, 62, 159
Sewell, Joseph, 58, 108, 170, 195
Shepherd, James, 41, 47, 157–8, 173, 195
ships, purchase and construction, 15–3, 37–9, 109–10, 147, 166, 167–70, 173, 175
Silva Lisboa, Sublieut Wenceslau da, 66, 67
Sir William Curtis cutter, 165
slavery and the slave trade, 9, 23, 26, 39, 94, 112, 146, 161–2, 178–9
Spain, invasion of, 31, 55
Squadron (anti-slave trade) of the East, 173, 176, 192, 196
steam ships, 24, 98; purchased in England
Britannia (*Correio Brasilense*), 167–8
Hibernia (*Correio Imperial*), 167–8
Steel, Robert, 195
Strickland, George, 196
Stuart Sir Charles, 162–3
Subrá, Lieut Victor S., 82
Surat Castle East Indiaman (became *Dona Paula* frig), 167, 171

Tamandaré, Admiral, 66, 186

Taylor, James, 173, 196
Taylor, John, recruitment, 21; British protests, 22; commands the *Niterói*, 22; 40; blockade of Bahia, 47, 61; pursuit of the Portuguese, 65–9; 102, 107, 111; blockade of Recife, 118–20; dismissal, 133; 149; reinstated, 176, 186, 196
Teles Lobo, José de, Provincial Secretary and Acting President of Maranhão, 147–8
Thesis frig, 14, 38
Thompson, James, 15, recruiting in London, 27, 29–30; blockade of Bahia, 43, 61, 63; to USA, 165; 196
Thompson, Thomas, 196
Treaty of Recognition, Brazilian need for, 160; irreconcilable views, 160–1; mediation requested, 161–2; British policy and link with slave trade, 161; signed, unpopularity, 162–3
Treze de Maio Portuguese packet, 93
Typhys Pernambucano, 114, 127

US recognition, 140, 143

Vasconcellas, Capt of the *Pérola*, 50
Verona, Congress of, 26
Vilela Barbosa, Francisco, Minister of Marine 1823–7, 91, 99, 105, 108, 121; Confederation of the Equator, 133, 139, 159
Villa Real, Count of, 161–3
Voador Portuguese corvette (became *Itaparica*), 93

Wallace, James, 66, 196
Watson, Charles, 32, 58, 196
Watson, James, 82, 84, 87, 101, 118, 170, 197
Welch, Mateus, 131, 140–1, 197
White, J.H.B., 197
Wigram-Green, shipbuilders of Blackwall, 167
Williams, John, 197
Wilson, Bourville, J., 197
Wright, Raphael, 32, 61, 197

Yell, Charles F., 175, 197

www.ingramcontent.com/pod-product-compliance
Lightning Source LLC
Chambersburg PA
CBHW072151290426
44111CB00012B/2031